DISCARDED

Running an Effective Help Desk

Barbara Czegel

Running an Effective Help Desk

- Planning - Implementing - Marketing -
- Automating - Improving - Outsourcing -

A Wiley-QED Publication

John Wiley & Sons, Inc.

New York • Chichester • Brisbane • Toronto • Singapore

Associate Publisher: Katherine Schowalter
Editor: Theresa Hudson
Managing Editor: Mark Hayden
Editorial Production & Design: SunCliff Graphic Productions

Designations used by companies to distinguish their products are often claimed as trademarks. In all instances where John Wiley & Sons, Inc. is aware of a claim, the product names appear in initial capital or all capital letters. Readers, however, should contact the appropriate companies for more complete information regarding trademarks and registration.

This text is printed on acid-free paper.

This publication is designed to provide accurate and authoritative information in regard to the subject matter covered. It is sold with the understanding that the publisher is not engaged in rendering legal, accounting, or other professional service. If legal advice or other expert assistance is required, the services of a competent professional person should be sought.

Library of Congress Cataloging-in-Publication Data

Czegel, Barbara, 1953–
    Running an effective help desk : planning, implementing, marketing, automating, improving, outsourcing / by Barbara Czegel
        p.   cm
    Includes bibliographical references and index.
        ISBN 0-471-02544-5 (pbk.)
        1. Computer industry—Customer services—Management.   2. Electronic office machine industry—Customer services—Management.   I. Title.
    HD9696.C62C96   1995   94-26250
    004'.068'8—dc20   CIP

Printed in the United States of America

10 9 8 7 6 5 4

To Dad. Please get better.

About the Author

Barbara Czegel is a freelance writer and consultant with twenty years of experience in the computer industry. She has worked with both the technical and human facets of the industry, in positions ranging from a computer programmer developing mainframe systems to Manager of Business Support, supporting the PC environment for Canadian Tire Corporation, Ltd. She has been involved in the planning, development, analysis, and support of retail business systems, planning systems, and manufacturing systems. At Canadian Tire Corporation, Ltd., she was responsible for justifying, establishing, and managing a PC Help Desk whose customer base skyrocketed in the first year of Help Desk operation. She is also an experienced communicator, and has worked in and managed areas dealing with strategic planning, written communications, and training. Her current writing is focused on business and technology, and she facilitates training in management.

Ms. Czegel received her Bachelor of Science in Computer Science and Mathematics from University of Toronto in 1975.

Contents

PART TWO   Internal Workings of the Help Desk 35

CHAPTER TWO Structure 35

CHAPTER THREE   Problem and Work Management   67

CHAPTER FOUR Tracking 101

CHAPTER SIX   Help Desk Tools   153

PART FOUR Optimizing Performance 181

CHAPTER SEVEN Measuring Performance 181

CHAPTER EIGHT   Marketing   227

CHAPTER NINE   Cost/Benefit Analysis   269

CHAPTER TEN Outsourcing 305

PART FIVE Case Studies 345

CHAPTER ELEVEN Help Desk Case #1: Setup 345

Preface

Technology continues to change at a fast and furious rate that shows no signs of abating. Support requirements are increasing. Businesses are demanding more support for technology, yet are limiting spending. This puts the Help Desk in an unenviable position, with a difficult assignment: support this changing, increasingly complex environment, but don't spend much money. It's a challenging situation to be in, but there is a solution. Focus on what is important to the business, and achieve an efficiency that allows you to keep costs down while increasing or keeping service levels the same. If you're thinking that this does not sound easy, you're right. It isn't easy, but it is achievable. *Running an Effective Help Desk* can help you achieve it.

Running an Effective Help Desk is divided into five parts: *I. The Basics, II. Internal Workings of the Help Desk, III. Applying Technology, IV. Optimizing Performance*, and *V. Case Studies*.

Part I, The Basics, contains Chapter 1, *Getting Focused*. Being focused means understanding what you have to do and how you're going to do it. For a Help Desk, this means having a clearly defined set of services, clear and measurable objectives, and a strategy for delivering them. Becoming focused involves gathering expectations of senior management and the rest of IS, learning as much as you can about your customers, and ensuring that the needs of the business come before anything else. *Getting Focused* deals with setting your Help Desk up for success.

Part II, Internal Workings of the Help Desk, deals with setting up and managing what goes on inside the Help Desk. The section contains three chapters: Chapter 2, *Structure*, Chapter 3, *Problem and Work Management*, and Chapter 4, *Tracking*.

People within the Help Desk are critical to its success. One unsatisfactory interaction with Help Desk staff can turn customers away from the Help Desk and to other sources of support. *Structure* deals with the issue of staffing, Help Desk roles, and number and location of Help Desks.

As problems and work come into the Help Desk, they need to be managed to prevent the Help Desk from falling into a vicious cycle of never-ending support: staff barely start to resolve one problem before they have to drop it and start on another one. Keys to effective problem and work management are priorities, procedures, ongoing evaluation, and constant improvement. *Problem and Work Management* deals with these in detail.

Another important part of the internal workings of the Help Desk is tracking information. Tracking information gives the Help Desk the ability to identify major problems before they occur, measure performance, and identify trends in hardware and software performance. *Tracking* discusses these and other accomplishments that your Help Desk can realize and suggests what kinds of information to track.

Part III, Applying Technology, deals with the use of technology to improve Help Desk effectiveness. It contains two chapters: Chapter 5, *Toward Automation*, and Chapter 6, *Help Desk Tools*.

Automation on the Help Desk is not about losing jobs or automating what already exists. It's about staying in business and examining the existing processes to see if there might be a better way. Technology is changing too rapidly and becoming too complex to be supported manually. *Toward Automation* talks about what automation can accomplish, success factors for an automation project, and the importance of the human aspect in any automation initiative.

Help Desk Tools is an overview of tools that can make your Help Desk more effective, including those that will allow you to automate various Help Desk functions. It includes descriptions of technology such as computer telephony, remote control software, and automated asset management.

Part IV in *Running an Effective Help Desk* is *Optimizing Performance*. It deals with measuring, improving, and marketing performance, and contains four chapters: Chapter 7, *Measuring Performance*, Chapter 8, *Marketing*, Chapter 9, *Cost/Benefit Analysis*, and Chapter 10, *Outsourcing*.

To get a true picture of Help Desk performance, you need to look at it from four perspectives: customer, Help Desk staff, Help Desk manager, and senior management. *Measuring Performance* discusses how to get these perspectives, what measures to use for performance, how to interpret them, and how to present the interpretation to management.

Complementary to the discussion on measurement is a look at marketing the Help Desk. The Help Desk is a business with products and services to sell, and customers to sell them to. Customers won't buy from the Help Desk just because it's there, nor will management fund or support it just because it's there. The Help Desk needs to show customers and management what it offers, what it can do for them, and what it can do for the business. Chapter 8, *Marketing*, shows how this and more can be accomplished through marketing initiatives. It talks about how to market, what information needs to be communicated, image, communication vehicles, and putting a marketing plan together.

In measuring the performance of your Help Desk, you may have discovered some improvements that you need to make. If you need to cost-justify these, the chapter entitled *Cost/Benefit Analysis* can help. It deals with putting a cost/benefit analysis together and gives three specific examples: justifying a Help Desk, justifying a voice response unit, and justifying outsourcing of the training function.

Optimizing Help Desk performance sometimes involves a process whose name is typically greeted with dread and fear. Outsourcing need not be a dirty word. It is a tool, much as a voice response unit is, and it can bring tangible benefits, such as reduced costs, increased flexibility, and improved performance. As with other kinds of tools, outsourcing needs to be used with an eye toward what is best for the business. *Outsourcing* discusses when to outsource, various outsourcing options, the outsourcing process, and dealing with fear and possible layoffs.

The fifth and final part, *Case Studies*, contains three Help Desk case studies in chapters 11 through 13. The first, in Chapter 11, involves a Help Desk that is going through the initial setting up process. The second, in Chapter 12, involves a Help Desk that is adding automation. The third, in Chapter 13, involves an established, very successful Help Desk.

A Help Desk can be a wildly busy, exhilarating, frustrating, yet lonely place. When you're running a Help Desk, you can use all of the help you can get. Hopefully, you'll get some of that help in *Running an Effective Help Desk*.

Acknowledgments

Thank you Les, for your incredible confidence in me, for your endless and patient proofreading, for checking my sometimes (OK, often) questionable math, and for keying in references when I ran completely out of steam. I think I'll keep you.

Thank you Chris and Carolyn for not bugging me too much while I was working. Thank you Carolyn for helping me key in some of the case studies, and thank you Chris for keeping me entertained with your SYSOP adventures.

Thank you Mom, for taking care of Dad.

Thank you Shelley and Megan for keeping me company when everyone else was in bed, for keeping my feet warm as I worked, and for not chewing up my notes more than once.

Thank you Albert for not driving me completely crazy with your squawking, dive bombing, and attempts to chew through my mouse cord. Thank you Fanny for being such a quiet, nondescript bird.

Thank you Reggie for providing a much-needed diversion and for not throwing me off and trampling me to death.

Thank you Arnold Farber and Rosemary LaChance for many things. For that first phone call: it inspired me to do things. For teaching me so much about automation: it really is better with the lights out! And for recommending me for this project (ours is still there, somewhere!).

Thank you to Russ Williams, June Holland, and Diane Miller for spending so much time talking to me about Help Desks.

Thank you Joyce Richardson for your occasional flashes of brilliance.

Thank you to Howard Board for taking time from doing whatever it is chief financial officers do to critique my analyses.

And thank you Terri Hudson for the opportunity.

CHAPTER ONE

Getting Focused

Developing a focus for your Help Desk is, in essence, creating your formula for success. There is, unfortunately, no one magic formula for success in the Help Desk world—the parameters vary too much from one Help Desk to another. Each Help Desk is unique and therefore so is its focus. Your focus will be determined by management, the rest of IS, your customers, and your budget, and will reflect the needs of the business. Your focus will ensure that you concentrate on what is important to the business.

How important is focus? Going about your Help Desk business unfocused, handling whatever happens to come up, will lead only to confusion, lack of control, and unhappy customers. This is not exactly a formula for success. As a Help Desk you have a limited budget, a limited head count, and only 24 hours in each day. You can try to do it all and end up doing many things poorly, or you can focus on providing a specific set of services that add value to the business, and doing a quality job in each. This kind of focus will give you your formula for success. Those services that you can't provide yourself can be dropped (if they are not important to the business), provided by another department, or outsourced.

Getting focused involves developing a set of objectives for your Help Desk and a list of services that you provide. This is just as important for an existing Help Desk that wants to improve as it is for a new one. When you don't have your services clearly defined, every new request becomes a "should I or shouldn't I?" decision, and whether it gets accepted depends on who answers the phone.

For example, suppose someone calls the Help Desk with a request to borrow a laptop computer. No one has made that request before. As a Help Desk employee, wanting to please, you say yes and dig up one of the laptops that the team isn't using at the moment. The customer comes

1

to get the laptop and is annoyed to find that it isn't loaded with the software required. You spend an hour loading the correct software (because the customer needs it that evening), while other more important problems sit waiting and calls accumulate. When the customer leaves, you scramble to get to the other calls, but a lot of customers are annoyed at having had to wait. The next morning the laptop isn't returned ("Oh, I thought I'd keep it for a couple of days—it's really coming in handy"), which is a real inconvenience for you—it was the only one free and your manager wanted to use it for a presentation at a senior management meeting that afternoon.

Later on in the day another customer calls and says, "I hear you loan out laptops—I need one for tonight." You have no time for this call, and you are annoyed at the fact that the first laptop was not returned. "We don't lend laptops out" is what you tell the customer, rather curtly. The customer argues that someone else got a laptop just yesterday, which wasn't fair. You persist with a "no," and end up with an irate and unhappy customer.

By accepting that first request you created a work backlog, a lot of unhappy customers who had to wait to get their calls answered, unrealistic expectations, and some real inconvenience for yourself and your team. You set an expectation and then could not meet it. By trying to do something that you couldn't handle and that you hadn't planned for, you alienated several customers and wasted a lot of time. There wasn't much business value in what you did.

Now let's turn that scenario around. The customer calls asking to borrow a laptop. You know what your services are and lending out computer equipment is not one of them. "No," you reply, "we don't have any equipment for loan, but I can give you the name of a company that does rent out hardware." In 30 seconds you've handled a request that took you hours previously. You've satisfied your customer and have not kept any others waiting. If you didn't know the names of companies that provided the rental service, you could look the information up and get back to the customer, and then save that information in a Help Desk reference library for quick access the next time you received that same request. You could even work with the rental company to set up some kind of service-level agreement to make sure that any of your customers who called got the quick service they needed.

If you have focus, you're set up for success. You have a clear picture of your goals, which is a good start toward attaining them. Both you and your customers understand what your responsibilities are, which makes it easier for you to keep them satisfied. You have the support of senior management because you are adding value to the business.

The process of getting focused, of developing objectives and a list of services, requires several input parameters: expectations of senior management, expectations of other IS departments, your customer profile, and your Help Desk budget. The more of this information you have, the better your chance of success. If you can't get it all, you'll have use what you can get, and then get feedback and adjust your focus if necessary as you progress.

Expectations of Senior Management

The Help Desk is not normally a revenue-generating function, and will be showing up on the ledgers as a cost. This makes it more important than ever to ensure that you know what senior management expects of you. You don't want to be caught in a situation where you are providing what management regards as an unnecessary service, especially when costs are being cut.

The simplest way to get expectations is to ask. Some senior managers will appreciate your asking and will take the time to formulate realistic answers; others may think you're a nuisance and will either ignore you or give you a reply without thinking about it ("just keep the computers up and running"), while still others may have completely unreasonable expectations. Whatever the case, get as much information as you can and use it as input to developing your list of services and your objectives. Send these back to management for review. If you don't get a response, call for feedback. If you still get no response, send out a list of your final objectives and services indicating where input came from. Those who chose not to give input will at least be informed of the decisions that were made without them.

An alternate approach to going to senior management for input is to run as fast and far as you can in the direction you believe the Help Desk should be going, before anyone tries to stop you. This might work for a distance, but that distance is getting shorter as budgets get cut. It's also a lot less strenuous to go at a slower pace and know that you don't have to be looking over your shoulder all of the time, expecting to get caught at any moment.

What does senior management typically look for in a Help Desk? Value. Never assume that you will be funded forever. Getting input up front—whether you're starting or improving—will help ensure that management definition of value is in line with yours.

Some management expectations you might encounter:

- Keep costs low.
- Provide good customer support—"We don't want to hear any complaints."
- Fix problems quickly—no computer or user down time is acceptable. Don't let technology failure negatively impact any critical business functions.
- Automate wherever possible—cut costs to the absolute minimum.
- Monitor and report on technology use and performance (justify the capital expenditure).
- Provide personal service ("I don't want to talk to a machine when I call you for help—I want to talk to a person every time"). Not all senior management is embracing automation.

Expectations of Other IS Departments

Your IS partners can be your best friends and your worst enemies. You share the same customers and some common goals, you're both interested in ensuring that the technology is kept up and running, and you're both responsible for keeping that technology up and running. But just where that responsibility begins and ends for each of you is a potential source of conflict and the cause of many turf wars. In fact, there is potential there for two kinds of turf wars: the taking wars ("this is *our* responsibility, so butt out") and the giving away wars ("this is not *our* responsibility—you should be taking care of it").

If you can eliminate or at least minimize these unproductive situations, you've a much better chance at coming to agreement on division of responsibilities. Working together toward a common goal—meeting the needs of the business—will make everyone more lenient about where the divisions of responsibility are drawn.

Dividing responsibilities will take some time, but you don't have to wait until you're finished to continue on setting your Help Desk focus. If all the groups involved agree not to let anything fall through the cracks while you are in the negotiation phase, whether or not it is their responsibility, you can keep your customers happy while you take the time to find a good solution. In fact, the attitude of not letting anything fall through the cracks regardless of responsibility is one you want to encourage and promote, even after you've decided who does what. Fighting wastes time and energy that could be better spent on providing improved service to your customers.

In getting IS expectations, and in negotiating what your responsibilities will be, don't try for perfect delineation. It just isn't possible. As technology keeps changing and new technology becomes available, lines of responsibility that were clear will become fuzzy. The whole process of delineating responsibilities will have to be ongoing to make sure that all aspects of supporting new technology are covered. Figure 1.1 shows an example of delineation of responsibility.

Before going to the rest of IS, take the time to think about what it makes sense for your responsibilities to be. Use this list as a starting point

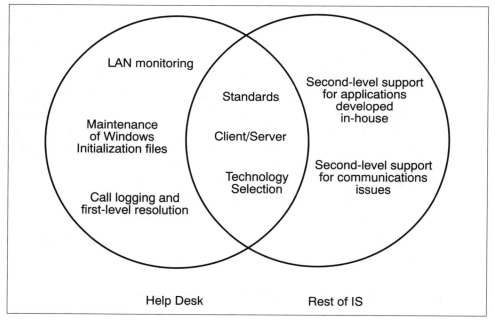

Figure 1.1 Dividing responsibilities between the Help Desk and the rest of IS.

for discussion. It's easier to work with something that you can mark up and cross out than to start from scratch. Be careful to make it clear to your IS partners that this starting point is just that—it is not the world as you say it should be. People will get upset if they think you've made those kinds of decisions on your own.

In areas such as standards, client/server, PC software support, software maintenance, technology selection, and so on, support responsibilities will be foggy and will require some effort to define. Specialty software—software outside the standard PC or mainframe suite—might be a contentious issue. You probably cannot accept first-line support for something that is fairly specialized and time-consuming to learn. You typically have a large customer base to keep happy and can't afford much specialization—but there are solutions that are a good compromise for everyone. In the case of specialty software, you might agree to get the first call but then pass it on directly to the group who knows the software. If you both work toward reaching this decision, it has a better chance of working, because you've both bought in. The Help Desk focus is on receiving and channeling the call; the focus of the other group is resolving it.

You may also have other Help Desks within your IS organization. Getting together with them to clarify roles is a valuable exercise, because you are probably going to be getting each other's calls—people will call the first number that looks like a help line when they run into trouble. It would be helpful to know who has the responsibility for and ability to do what, so that you can get the customer's problem resolved even if the wrong Help Desk was contacted. One of the worst things that could happen to a customer is to be bounced between Help Desks: Help Desk A says, "This is a problem for Help Desk B; I'll transfer your call," while Help Desk B says, "Oh, this is handled by Help Desk A. I'll transfer you." If responsibilities are clear, and if each Help Desk has a "nothing falls through the cracks" attitude, this will never happen.

Some examples of IS responsibility splits:

- Standards: Help Desk participates in setting standards; IS is responsible for setting and enforcing those standards.

- Problems with applications developed in-house: IS is responsible for developing applications and for second-line support; Help Desk will take the first call and pass it on.

- Help Desk is consulted in software selection, but another part of IS actually makes the selection. Help Desk is responsible for notifying everyone of the software installation, for doing the installation, and for getting a pilot out for testing to make sure that it works with all other technology components.

- Help Desk monitors LAN performance and notifies application programmers of any problem applications. Application programmers address the problem applications.

- Help Desk is responsible for maintaining Windows initialization files; the rest of IS is to keep hands off of these files.

- PC/Local Area Network Help Desk and Mainframe/Wide Area Network Help Desk: PC Help Desk handles all things PC and routes mainframe calls (many users access mainframe through the LAN) to the Mainframe Help Desk if it can't help them. PC desk notifies Mainframe desk of any PC/LAN problems, and Mainframe desk notifies PC desk of any mainframe/WAN problems. Desks meet on a regular basis to ensure information exchange and understand each other's processes.

Note: Although this Help Desk split is very common, because PCs were quite separate entities from mainframes when they were first introduced, it is not generally a wise one. A Help Desk that handles both PCs and mainframes is able to deliver better value to the business. (See the section in Chapter 2 entitled *How Many Help Desks?*)

Customer Profile

You want to know your customers because, very simply, you want to know what you have to support. One of your reasons for existence is to keep your customers productive (or to make them more productive). You need to know what they do. Knowing your customers means knowing:

- Who they are, how many of them there are, and where they are.
- What technology they use.
- What they use it for.
- How often and when they use it.
- How technology-literate they are.
- How technology-friendly they are.

- How controlled their environment is.
- Their priorities.
- What they want.

Who They Are, How Many of Them There Are, and Where They Are

You might be surprised by who your customers include. PCs, standalone or on their own small LANs, have a tendency to pop up everywhere. You might uncover small departments with outdated (or even ultra-modern) equipment that have existed on their own, however efficiently or inefficiently, for years. One company Help Desk uncovered an Ethernet LAN in an area using CADD during a routine Help Desk call. It was a total surprise to them. It was also a total surprise to the customers who had made the call—they hadn't realized that they were on a LAN. Before the Help Desk came into existence, they were being supported by an external company that came every once in a while or when there was a problem, did things, and then left. The Help Desk only found out about the LAN when the customers called with some problems that required the PCs to be opened up. The area was eventually converted to a standard configuration, but supporting them in the interim was painful.

You need to flush all these customers out in order to be able to reach them through your marketing, and to help make sure that they at least know what technology is available, what the standards are, what you offer, and where to get support if you can't provide it. If they're on their own and suddenly have a catastrophe and call for your help, it could mean a lot of expense for you—especially if major things must be fixed very quickly. You'll have to call in outside help or ignore a lot of other inside customers. It makes more sense to spend time up front finding out who and where your customers are and then slowly bringing them on board and up to standards—not that this will be easy. At one major newspaper, a group of users producing an entertainment magazine had gone out on their own and purchased an Apple network. Between actual setup and first issue there were a lot of panic calls to PC Support, even though the configuration was nonstandard and there was little in-house expertise on it. A lot of Help Desk time was spent on this support, and the environment was such that the customers could not be cajoled or coerced into using different but equally effective technology. You can't always help groups like this, but it certainly is an advantage to know about them. If they refuse your advice and you aren't able to support them, perhaps contracting for external support could be a solution. They would pay, and senior management would either approve it or not, in which case you could make a case for a standard configuration.

Flushing all of the technology users out can be accomplished by a thorough hardware inventory or a "calling all PCs" campaign, in which you ask that people call in to register their PCs if they have not already done so. This means that PCs must be labeled and recorded in your asset management system.

Knowing numbers of customers is important to give you an idea of how many potential callers to the Help Desk there are—this will help you determine call traffic and staffing requirements.

If your customers are spread out over several remote locations, some aspects of support, such as servicing their hardware, will be more complex than with local customers. You will need to make provisions to ensure that the service is provided and that you are kept abreast of everything done, so that your hardware/software inventory is kept current and your call tracking information is complete. You might outsource the servicing and have the outsourcing company update your hardware/software inventory and your call tracking system directly.

What Technology They Use

Customers are generally not impressed by technology, especially when it isn't working. They're not interested in the differences between expanded memory and extended memory or why they don't have enough of one or the other; they don't care that the bridge from the mainframe to the LAN is down; they don't care about control unit failures or whether hubs are intelligent. They just want the damned computers to work so that they can get their jobs done. You may find it infuriating at times that they don't want to hear your explanation of why the LAN is down (and they don't accept it with a "well, I understand"), but you have to remember: They're trying desperately to get their jobs done, probably under a tight deadline, and *you* (in the guise of an uncooperative PC or terminal or other technology) are preventing them from doing just that. If the technology is not working, then the business is not working, and someone is losing money and perhaps jobs. No down time is acceptable.

Your users might not care about technology, but you must. You need to know what you will be supporting. An environment of completely standard 486s and laser printers with a stable local area network linked to a

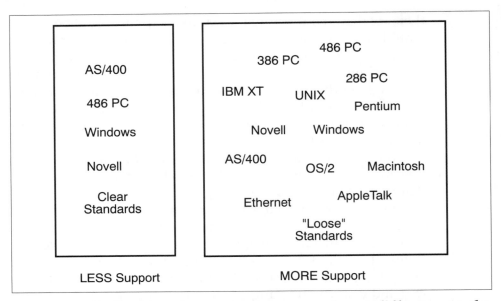

Figure 1.2   Technology that customers use makes a difference to the amount of support they require.

mainframe is a much different support picture than an environment consisting of everything from a low-end 286 to a Pentium machine, with every model of clone imaginable, and a tenuous (read "always going down") mainframe link. Figure 1.2 illustrates differences in environments. In the same way, an environment of completely standard software is very different from an environment in which you have customers using several different brands of products such as word processors and spreadsheets. Knowing what technology is used will give you a better idea of how big the support requirement is. This will help you determine what aspects of support you need to focus on, what problems to expect, what things you need to clean up, how many people you need, and what services you might outsource.

If you have a hardware/software inventory, then you already know what hardware/software you have; if you don't, now is the time to get one. You may be able to outsource this process, or use asset management software that will give you hardware and software configurations of all the nodes on your local area network without your having to go to each one. The software has some limitations, but vendors and customers are working to eliminate them. As well as compiling an initial inventory, you have to make sure you have processes in place that keep this information current. (See *Data Required for Tracking* in Chapter 4 and *Asset Management* in Chapter 6.)

What They Use It For

Help Desk customers call the Help Desk when they can't use the technology to do what they need to do. Unfortunately for you, "using the technology" can mean just about anything from keying in letters to running mission-critical applications such as order processors, and can mean the difference between 2 support staff and 40 support staff. In order to try to determine how much support is needed, you need to know what your customers are doing, not just what software they're using. PC users might use Word for Windows for letters or documents, or they might have developed several macros for production applications using Word. Supporting the former is quite different from supporting the latter.

Knowing what they use the technology for also helps you to be better prepared for when the technology has to change. For example, you might have an accounting department that is using Lotus 1-2-3 macros written by a keen summer student. You are trying to standardize on Excel, another spreadsheet package. Unfortunately for you, the accounting employees don't know how the macros work, they just use them. You want to convert those macros to Excel, but Excel doesn't translate those very complicated macros nicely, and you don't have the time or resources to rewrite them. It's much better to know up front, when you're planning for the Excel conversion, that such macros exist. It would be painful to be hit by them as you go about installing Excel. It would certainly slow down your conversion.

Getting this kind of information is not a trivial matter, but the effort will be worth it. You'll have to talk to your customers, perhaps attend departmental meetings, and watch them at work whenever you get the chance. Do this continuously. You might start up customer focus groups in which the group members do that work for you. They can bring back information on what their areas are doing, and let you know what kind of support they do or will require. If you do decide to go with focus groups, you'll have to make it worthwhile for customers to join. You might consider offering early software releases for testing, free education, or other perks.

How Often and When They Use It

Do your customers use the technology you support 24 hours a day, or only 9 A.M. to 5 P.M.? Do they work extra hours on regular occasions (e.g., at the end of the month)? You need to know this so that you can balance your staff against the support load traffic. Figure 1.3 shows a typical distribution of technology use over a day. You might have staggered working hours in your group, one or more staff members starting as early as 7 A.M. to check out the networks and provide support for any early customers, and one or more staff members finishing as late as 7 P.M. to provide support for the late workers, and perhaps to do some mainte-nance work on the LAN when the traffic is lighter. The peak hours will have the heaviest support coverage, while the fringe hours will have the lightest coverage. Your peak hours might actually be early in the morning or late in the evening, in which case you would stagger your hours differently to accommodate the peaks. You might also be able to offer prearranged support for those times that your customers work extra hours—such as the end of the month or the end of the year. The key to

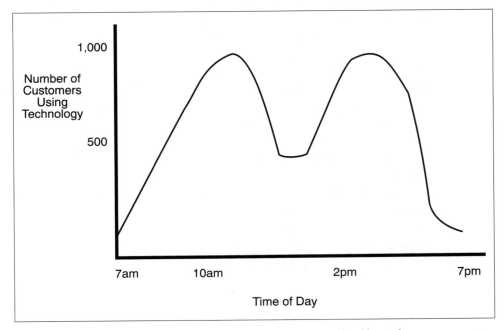

Figure 1.3 When customers use technology will affect the support re-quired for different time periods.

being able to provide all of this support is to know the requirements beforehand so that you can offer suggestions and alternatives. The reality might be that you just don't have enough staff or budget to provide extra occasional support. If that is the case, then one option might be to negotiate with the department in question to have them pay for extra support. You might outsource some standard support so that your staff members who know the systems involved could provide the extra support. Being proactive and finding out which of your customers need extra support and when, and setting up alternatives before the support is actually required, will prevent the panic and possible customer disappointment that result when unexpected support is requested at the last minute.

If you have network monitoring tools, you will be able to get the information you need to determine customer workload patterns just by looking at the network usage statistics over a given period. Looking at the pattern of calls into the Help Desk will also give you some information about when the customer load is the heaviest—if you have call distribution technology, then you will be getting this information automatically. If you don't have any way of getting this information from your system, you'll have to talk to your customers. You can use electronic mail to explain what information you need and why. Your customers will probably respond willingly with the information required, because it is in their best interests to do so. If you have customer focus groups, you can get some of the information you need from them.

How Technology-Literate They Are

How well do your customers understand their technology? Do they just perform the same tasks continuously, panicking if they have to do something new or if they run into problems, or are they reasonably knowledgeable about the systems they use and comfortable with trying new things? More of the former kind of customer will mean a heavier support load for you, and perhaps a need to provide more in-depth training for your customers. They will expect and need a lot more help just doing the basics than the more self-sufficient kind of customer. If training is not one of the services you provide, you will want to at least arrange for external training for these customers. If you are using external training, you will need to make sure that it is appropriate for your environment. It is very frustrating and unproductive for a customer to attend training and then return to the work environment to find that things are set up very differently than they were in the training environment.

On the other side of the coin are power users. Power users can be both a blessing and a big problem. If you can work with them to harness their energy, enthusiasm, and curiosity into pilot projects, software trials focus groups, or help groups, they can be a valuable resource. If, however, you can't or don't work with them, they may cause you grief by doing things on their own: changing configuration files, installing illegal software, and so on, all of which will cost you significant support time.

Knowing what kind of customers you have will give you a better idea of how much of a load they will be, what you will need to do to improve their level of literacy, where potential problem areas lie, and where some potential resources are. Learning what kind of users you have will take time, and will be a matter of monitoring the kinds of calls you get and where they come from. You could ask for volunteers for software piloting—this could flush out some power users. You might not have this information if you're just starting up a Help Desk—you might want to go to various areas and find out how they were getting support, and this might point you to both the power users and those customers needing extra help.

How Technology-Friendly They Are

How technology-friendly your customers are, or are willing to become, will determine how automated you can be, at least initially. It will also determine what tools you will be able to use to greatest advantage with your customers. Will your customers talk to voice mail? Will they use an automated system? In some companies, voice mail is considered the ultimate evil invention and people will not use it. Installing a voice mail system to record support calls that come in while no one is there, or while all the phones are busy, may not be a good idea in an environment that doesn't use voice mail. You'll end up with customers who are irritated, or who may come to where the support desk is physically to find a human being, or complain to senior management. And senior management is not always enamored with voice mail or other automation, either. If you can't automate, if you can't use tools such as voice mail, you will be looking at a more expensive support load—more staff—until you can convince your customers that automation works when used properly (and naturally you will use it properly), and that it is absolutely necessary for the health of the business. Needless to say, this is not an overnight endeavor, but knowing that you need to address this issue will allow you to plan for it and work toward it.

To find out how technology-friendly your customers are, check to see what technology they're currently using. Find out whether other technology has been tried, and try some pilots of your own. Don't be deterred if at first your customers tell you they won't like being talked to by a machine or dealing with other forms of automation. Let them try it. They may just love it, especially if it gets them a quick solution to their problem. They can help you with marketing to the rest of your customers.

Their Priorities

What are your customers' priorities? You can't handle all of the problems that come up at once, so you have to have some mechanism for determining which are the most important. The problems that are most important are those that will have the greatest effect on the business. If a company is dependent on a network for gathering all of its data for nightly processing—be it payments, orders, or whatever—that network had better be high on your list of things that are most important. The same goes for specific applications. If your ordering application is a high priority, and there's a problem with it, you'd better ensure that your staff understand the priority. Otherwise, they might end up spending time on a less important problem while that one is still outstanding.

Aside from talking directly to your customers, there are various other sources of priorities: job scheduling information, IS application analysts (they will most likely know where specific applications fit into the priority hierarchy), company mission statements, and company business plans. These will all give you valuable information about what applications or technologies are most important to a company.

Beware of priorities that reflect what customers want, not what the business needs. Figure 1.4 shows how these can differ. You will want to double-check priorities you get directly from customers against other sources. Once you establish and communicate priorities (see Chapter 3), you might have some disagreement on the part of the customers. Be careful of trying to adjust priorities yourself. If your customers belong to the same company and can't agree on a resolution for conflicting priorities, either you or they will have to go to a higher authority to get the priority resolved. If your customers belong to different companies, they

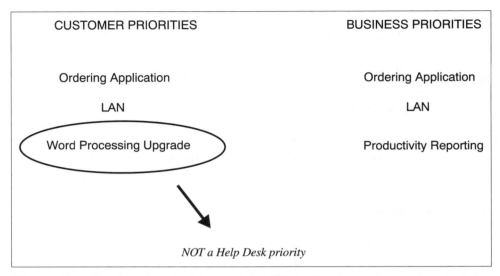

Figure 1.4 Customer priorities won't always be the same as those of the business.

may pay a premium for higher priorities, or may have some kind of agreement stating exact priorities. You need to know what these are. If two problems happen at the same time, and the priority is not resolved, you will lose valuable time trying to resolve the priority rather than solving the problems, or you may work on the wrong problem first. If you are in such a support situation, you might actually have extra staff just to ensure that each company you support gets the agreed-upon priority.

You need to work by priorities that are determined by the business and understood by your customers. If you choose not to do this, working by your own priorities instead—perhaps ignoring a critical customer's problem to install some terrific new technology—you could find yourself out of business.

The Environment: How Controlled Is It?

The reality is that you may work in an environment in which everything the user wants, the user gets. Setting any kind of standards or limitations in this kind of environment is next to impossible. Unless you can change the whole environment, you're stuck with it and have to accept the limitations under which you will work. Your customers have more clout than you, so in any kind of confrontation, you would lose. Accept that you can't change this overnight. Any kind of legislation would mean revolution. You have to convince your customers that what you are offering is better.

This kind of environment would certainly have a strong effect on your services. You would, at least initially, have to support just about anything that came up. You would need to allocate time to selling standards, and you would most likely have to have a base of external contacts to help you out with your hardware and software support.

Alternatively, if the environment you support is highly standardized, life on the Help Desk is going to be a lot easier. You will be able to automate more easily, and you won't need as much breadth of expertise because you will be supporting a limited number of products. You won't have as many technology incompatibility problems as in an nonstandardized environment, so getting things working and keeping them working will be easier.

What They Want

Asking your customers what services they want that they don't currently have could be very dangerous—you could be setting very unrealistic expectations. Don't ask unless you're willing to listen to the responses and address each one. If people ask for things and those things are not delivered, they're going to want to know why they didn't get them.

Honesty is the best approach when trying to get an idea of what customers need without giving them the impression that you're going to deliver everything. Let them know up front that you would like to know what services they need, but that you are constrained by a budget so you will only be able to provide those that deliver most value to the business. Your customers should be able to recognize the legitimacy of what you are trying to do.

Getting to Know Them

How do you find out all these things about your customers without moving in with them? Aside from the suggestions already made, you can attend customer departmental meetings, drop in to talk to your customers informally, call selected customers, constantly check what is happening whenever you happen to be in a customer's area, hold focus groups, send out surveys, and invite customers to participate in the planning or chang-

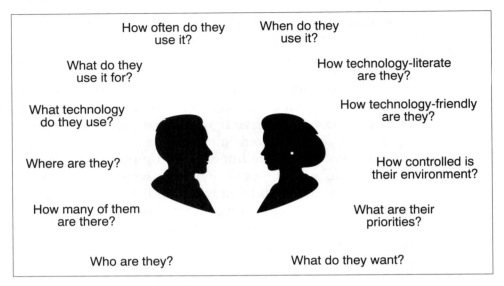

Figure 1.5 Customer Profile.

ing of the Help Desk. But remember, when you ask their opinion, be prepared to listen, and be prepared to hear things that you may not agree with. If you ask and then ignore, you're starting off on the wrong foot and have lessened your chance of success significantly.

You may not be able to get all of the information we talked about here. Time is sometimes an enemy. You'll just have to build or change using the information that you do have, and then adjust your processes as the feedback comes in. Gathering information is really an ongoing process—get information, change, get feedback, change, get more feedback, change, and so on. The more information you do have, the better chance you'll have at success. (See Figure 1.5.)

Sample Customer Profile

- Your customers are everyone in the corporation—not everyone has a PC or a terminal, but everyone has access to one. There are about 2,000 of these customers and they are in four different locations, all within one state.

- They use PCs for both local area network and mainframe access. There are a profusion of IBM clones—about six makes, and within those a profusion of models ranging from 286s to 486s. Memories range from 4 megabytes to 16 megabytes, and hard drives from 30 megabytes to 250 megabytes. Other technology includes a variety of printers, mostly laser printers of one type, a few CD-ROMs, and the mainframe. There is also a super server linking information from several smaller networks and the mainframe together. Software is mostly Windows, with some OS/2, and the network operating system is Novell. There is a standard for software, but it is loose and can be bypassed fairly easily. Some PCs are still running only DOS. You have three word processors, two spreadsheets, four database packages, and two graphics packages. There is also a small department of text editors using Macs. They are hooked together by an AppleTalk network, which is standing on its own.

- The greatest use of PCs is for word processing and spreadsheets. Client/server applications are just starting and will become production in the next six months or so. Word processors are used mostly for correspondence and text editing; spreadsheets make heavy use of macros, and are used for calculation of input into larger (mainframe) systems. You suspect that some of these macros are not quite correct and that there is not a great understanding of what they do. Several mission-critical applications run on the mainframe.

- Customer use of technology takes place from 7:30 A.M. until 6 P.M., with the heaviest use between 10 A.M. and 4 P.M. There is some use after 6 P.M., but this is infrequent and the load is very light—one or two users trying to get some extra work done. When big projects are coming due, about three times a year, some extra support time is required. After 6 P.M., production batch processing starts on the mainframe and finishes early the next morning.

- Most people are not willing to take the time to go to external courses and have not been properly trained in the use of the packages and hardware that they are using. The Help Desk gets a lot of calls for very elementary questions and problems. On the other hand, you have a pocket of Mac users who think they know it all. You wish they did.

- The company implemented voice mail a few years ago, and it has been very well received. There is a fair amount of travel going on in the company, so many people conduct a large proportion of their business via voice mail.

- The priorities are the network (including the mainframe), database access, ordering applications, distribution applications, credit card applications, and links to retail systems.

- The customers want to be able to solve all things instantly with a single phone call. You know you won't be able to give them that for a while yet, and you're kind of sorry you asked.

What This Suggests

Your customer profile is only one of four inputs into developing your list of services and objectives, but taken on its own it can suggest several things that your Help Desk should consider doing to improve service and prevent problems. These, of course, must be tempered by budget, management, and the rest of IS. Using the profile described previously, some suggestions might be as follows:

- Have staggered hours for your staff to cover the Help Desk from 7 A.M. to 7 P.M. Discuss the need for occasional extra support with your customers to ensure that it is there when required.

- Outsource hardware maintenance. You cannot do this as cost-effectively or with as quick response as the maintenance company, which has easy access to all of the parts required and the technical expertise necessary to keep the hardware maintained.

- Work with the IS group that sets standards to encourage making the standards official rather than loose and making compliance mandatory. This means that you will have to do a fair bit of marketing of the advantages of having standards and selling of the chosen standards.

- Use (or purchase) a network monitor and automated asset management software to check network traffic and the configuration of network components to ensure that your network can handle the client/server systems being designed. The asset management software will tell you which machines, if any, need to be upgraded to handle the new system.

- Encourage and promote training of standard software packages. You don't have a training group, so you will outsource the training, but will work closely with the trainers to ensure that your customers are getting the training they need. You will also keep track of call statistics for questions and problems, so that you can show customers the number of calls their lack of training is causing, and demonstrate that they are tying Help Desk resources up for other customers.

- Identify power users and get them on your side before they cause too much trouble. Get them involved in testing new software and upgrades and making recommendations.

- Check out customer priorities with other sources, including management, to make sure they are valid; communicate these to the Help Desk staff. Incorporate these priorities into your Help Desk software if possible.

- Thank your customers for their input into what they would like to see on the Help Desk, and get back to them with your list of services, explaining your budget constraints. Ask for their feedback.

Your Help Desk Budget

If you're just starting up your Help Desk, you will most likely first develop a suggested set of objectives and list of services based on the data you have gathered, estimate the cost, then go after the funding. After some negotiation, for better or for worse, you will have your budget. (For cost and benefit analyses, see Chapter 9.)

If you have been given a budget, you know exactly how much money you can spend. You will have varying degrees of leeway as to how you want to allocate this money—what portion you will spend on payroll, what portion on outsourcing, and so on. Generally, your capital expenditures will be a separate amount, not to be mixed in with the expenses. If you feel your budget is too low, use data gathered from the Help Desk (see Chapter 4) to justify an increase.

If you charge back, things are a bit more complex. You might have to estimate your revenue for a specific length of time (by quarter over a year) and calculate your budget accordingly. You'll have to adjust each quarter (or more often) to ensure that you are not spending more than you are bringing in. If you are a profit center, you'll have to adjust expenditures each quarter (or more often) to ensure that you are making a profit or are meeting profit targets. Things get more complicated if your customers are external to your organization. If this is the case, your budget will most likely be looked after by another department, and you'll get regular feedback as to budget availability and performance.

Your Services

You've gathered all of the information—now what? You know what management expects of your Help Desk, what the rest of IS expects, and your what your customers expect. You also know or have estimated your budget. You have all of the parameters you need to draw up your list of services. This will not be a trivial exercise—you'll have to balance the expectations of management, IS, and your customers against your budget. Your customers might differ substantially from management in their view of the kind of services you should provide. If you go with management's view, then you aren't solving your customer's problems, and they will just learn to live with them or work around them. Neither of these options will do much for customer productivity or business performance. Wise management will listen to the customers and will actually use the Help Desk as a pulse on customer issues—on what is required to become more productive or more profitable. Unfortunately, not all management is wise, but it does pay the bills. Compromise is the answer. You'll have to draft up a starting point of services and then work back and forth between management, IS, and your customers. This will be an iterative process and will be time-consuming, but if you get a list that everyone accepts, the effort will have been worth it.

Management expectations, IS expectations, and customer profile will each determine a portion of your services and objectives. The size of that portion, and how much of the budget is allocated to it, will depend on how much influence each of management, IS, and customers have in your environment. Figure 1.6 illustrates this. For example, you may go into your service negotiations and discover that management expectations are going to carry a lot more weight than customer profile. If management wants a low-staff Help Desk and customers want personal service, you will most likely go with the low cost and automate, or outsource if that option is indeed low cost. Personal service would be overridden by what management wants. Similarly, if customer expectations are more important in your environment, if management is willing to listen to and react to customer requirements, then customer profile would carry more weight. If customers felt they needed more personalized service for whatever reason, you would be able to override the low staff. In both cases, your services would be tempered by your budget—in the first case, you would put in as much automation as your budget allowed, and in the second case, the number of

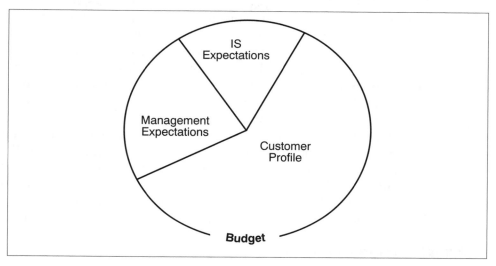

Figure 1.6 Dividing up the services and objectives budget.

staff you had would be tempered by your budget. In these considerations, IS tends to be neutral; its expectations as IS are usually quite different in nature from those of the other two and are not in conflict; its expectations as customers would be part of customer profile.

A pitfall to watch out for is promising too much by making your list of services too long. Your budget should be your watchdog. Don't promise more than you think you can safely deliver. You can always add services once you have set up your Help Desk, but taking them away is a lot more difficult. When negotiating, be creative. If one customer area is demanding extra support that you can't afford, find out how much it would cost to outsource it, and then offer them that as a paid service. They pay while you administer. If you can handle it, you've given them the extra support with almost no investment on your part. You'll be surprised at how departments can find money to pay for such services if they really need them. If you come up with a list that you cannot afford, you may be able to petition for a bigger budget, funded by the company or by individual departments.

When your list of services is done, don't go comparing them to lists from other Help Desks expecting them to look the same. They are your focus for your company in your environment. They are catering to your customers and your management, and conforming to your budget, some or all of which will be different from those of the Help Desks you're comparing yourself to. That is not to say that you shouldn't look at other Help Desks for ideas—just the opposite! Doing so will give you ideas for your own Help Desk and will allow you to see how various ideas have been implemented and how they are working (or not). You may be able to learn about pitfalls to avoid without the actual pain of experience, and you may be able to save yourself time by seeing a better way of doing something that you wanted to do.

If you're already up and running as a Help Desk but have to change your services, most of what was said above still applies. You'll have to be very conscious of letting your customers know how you are changing, or considering changing, and there might be some degree of negotiation involved. You'll also have to mount an extensive customer campaign to let your customers know that things are changing. (See Chapter 8.)

A Sample List of Services

Boundaries:

- Support provided between 7 A.M. and 7 P.M.
- Customers can use electronic mail, phone, or phone mail to request support.
- Support is provided for all standard (or preaccepted) software and all standard (or preaccepted) hardware. Software or hardware falling outside of this will be a lower priority.

Services:

- Provide a central point of contact for any problems with technology. The Help Desk is responsible for problem recording, tracking, ownership, and resolution. Problems that cannot be resolved immediately are passed on to the appropriate areas but monitored to make sure they get resolved.
- Monitor LAN performance and notify appropriate groups of any potential problems.
- Monitor problem trends and notify appropriate groups of recurring problems so that a permanent solution can be found.
- Maintain hardware/software inventory.
- Provide hardware maintenance (outsourced to an external vendor).
- Training/education—either recommend or, if need dictates, administer as a special information seminar.

- Software testing (only for operability in the technology environment) for upgrades and new software.
- Software sourcing, purchase, licensing, and installation.
- Hardware sourcing, purchase, and installation.
- Consulting: hardware/software recommendations based on user requirements.
- Participation in groups determining standards for hardware and software.
- Performance reporting—system and Help Desk.
- Broadcasting of information about system availability.

Objectives

How are objectives different from services? Services are the things you offer for sale—your product line. Objectives are what you plan to accomplish—your sales targets. Objectives are clear and measurable. Objectives must also be attainable. If you are setting objectives that you don't really think you can achieve, but that you feel management wants you to achieve, you are setting yourself up for failure. It's like agreeing to a project deadline that you know you cannot meet, but that management has legislated. You won't meet it—at least, you won't meet it with the quality of product that is expected. Management will be disappointed, your project will be a failure, and you will be history, or at least not in line for a promotion. If objectives are to be what you are measured on, then they are worth fighting for. If management wants you to have objectives that are unattainable, then you will simply have to show them, clearly and concisely, why those objectives are not attainable. Chances are that management wants you to succeed and will listen to valid and logical arguments. If you are forced to accept objectives that you cannot possibly meet, you will have to either accept the consequences of failure or accept the fact that management does not want you to succeed and start looking elsewhere for employment.

Since objectives play such an important role in your success, they need to be reviewed with management. You have to make sure that they know what to expect from you and are in agreement. You want them to be what management measures you on. Depending on your environment, you may also share your objectives with IS and/or your customers.

Sample objectives for the next quarter:

- Reduce call volume by 30 percent through automation of terminal resets.
- Increase percentage of problems resolved at first call to 70 percent (from 60 percent) through use of remote diagnostic software.
- Reduce application questions by 10 percent through customer training.
- Upgrade all PCs in department A that do not have enough memory to handle the new client/server application.

How You Operate: Strategy

You have your services and your objectives (your products and your sales quotas), now you need a strategy. A strategy is your modus operandi, your principles of operation, how you operate on a day-to-day basis. Your strategy will determine how you approach providing services and meeting objectives. If your strategy is customer service above all else, then the way in which you do everything, from answering the telephone to closing a problem, will be focused on keeping the customer satisfied. If your strategy is automation wherever possible, you will focus on automating as much of what you do as possible. Your strategy might also be a combination of the two: customer service above all else and automation. In this case, you would ensure that everything you automated improved customer service or met a specific standard of customer service.

Your strategy will, again, be determined by the parameters of management, IS, customers, and budget. It needs to be clearly communicated to all Help Desk staff so that every act they perform as part of their jobs will conform to it. It needs to be written down, pasted on the wall, etched in brains. It will be the manner in which you provide all services and attain all objectives.

A Plan

Getting a plan together to implement your services and objectives, as per your strategy, seems an obvious step, but many a Help Desk does not have any kind of a plan—and if it's not written down somewhere, then it's not a plan. If you don't have a plan, the process of getting from where you are now to where your objectives say you want to be falls into the same category as an act of God.

You do need a plan, whether you're starting a Help Desk or running (and improving) an existing one. Your plan is a map showing the path to attaining your objectives and providing your services. Your plan will help keep you on track and will help ensure that you meet your objectives in the time that you need to. A plan will even help you determine whether your objectives are attainable, so you will want to do some preliminary planning before you set your objectives.

Your plan must take reality into account, and unfortunately, reality may mean that you have to support an unstable environment while you get things up and running, or while you improve things. Reality is the business screaming, "My PC is broken, fix it" and senior management nagging, "Will you please just stop this fooling around and fix the network? We've got a business to run here!" In this kind of environment, it is easy to get pulled into the whirlpool of endless support—you never have time to improve things, so they keep breaking and people keep calling you. More and more PCs get installed, and the problem is compounded daily. A plan is more important than ever in this kind of environment. A plan will allow you to make compromises and to show management and customers why they are necessary. A plan will give you ammunition for setting attainable objectives. Perhaps you might have to move a little more slowly in your changes, so that you can still maintain the current environment, or perhaps you cut down on the support you need to provide by outsourcing.

Write your plan down, and review it often. Use it to check on your own progress. Give it to management so that they may check on yours. Figure 1.7 shows the interaction among strategy, services, objectives, and plan.

Time and Reality

You have it all. Services, objectives, a strategy to operate by, and a plan to make it all happen. How long did all of this take you? It didn't happen overnight. It may have taken a year; probably it took about four months. It may have happened completely apart from the support environment

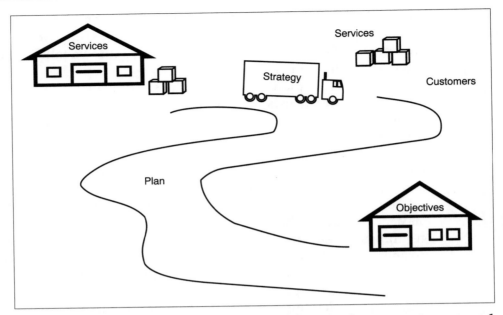

Figure 1.7 Putting it all together: Delivering services to customers and reaching objectives.

and may have been the real beginning of the Help Desk, or it may have taken place in the midst of chaos and confusion as you struggled to support the mess that already existed and that you inherited (or created). Also, some of it may not have happened just as it is laid out in this chapter. Perhaps you couldn't get all of the parameters. Perhaps you couldn't get input from management, or you couldn't get some of your customer information. But you took whatever information you had and used it to develop your services, objectives, strategy, and plan, recognizing that you would probably have to adjust as you got more information and more feedback.

Are You Finished?

Congratulations. You have your focus, your formula for success. But are you finished? No! You need to revisit all components of your focus regularly—every quarter, say—to make sure that they are still valid in your environment, which will probably have changed significantly since your focus was set. If your customers are asking constantly for a service that you don't provide, maybe you should provide that service. If cost cuts have been stepped up, you may have to change your objectives and your strategy. Automating wherever possible might be your new strategy, and your objectives would reflect this—you would be looking at each area of your Help Desk operations and seeing where you could automate. As new technology becomes available, you might have to adjust your services and objectives to be able to support it or to use it. A focus that changes as your environment changes, as the business changes, will ensure that you keep following success, even when success changes direction. Your formula for success won't ever be out of date.

An Example: The ABC Help Desk

Management Expectations

- Fix problems quickly—no computer or user down time is acceptable. Don't let technology failure negatively impact any critical business functions.

- Automate wherever possible—keep costs to the absolute minimum.

- Monitor and report on technology use and performance (justify the capital expenditure).

IS Expectations

- For problems with internally developed applications, the Help Desk will get the initial call, but will pass it on to the applications group for resolution.

- The Help Desk is consulted in software selection, but another part of IS actually makes the selection. The Help Desk is responsible for notifying everyone of the installation, for doing the installation, and for getting a pilot out for testing to make sure that it works with all other technology components.

Customer Profile

- There are 1,500 users in two adjacent buildings (almost everyone in the company).
- Each user has either an IBM-compatible PC (ranging from a 286 to 486) or an Apple, and is hooked to a small mainframe via a local area network. There are about 25 standalone PCs. Laser printers are all Hewlett Packard; impact printers are any of a variety of makes. Software has been standardized to a few Windows applications.
- Applications are being migrated to the local area network from the mainframe. Most customers will be accessing client/server applications from their PCs within the next six months. Currently, most customers use their PCs only for word processing, spreadsheet applications, and host access.
- Customers work mostly from 8 A.M. to 6 P.M., but a few come in early and a few stay late. At year's end, some extra support is required to provide help for customers doing year-end calculations, should they need it.
- Most customers are familiar with how to use the standard software, but have no experience with client/server.
- Electronic mail is used heavily; voice mail is used only by certain departments. Generally, customers have no problem in accepting new technology, but there are a few pockets of resistance.
- Priorities are the network and the applications being migrated to client/server.
- Customers keep asking for client/server training.

Help Desk Budget

- $700,000 for annual capital expenditures—includes only hardware and software tools used by the Help Desk; does not include network hardware and software that is used by customers.
- $800,000 annually for expenses—includes staffing, outsourcing hardware maintenance, and any other outsourcing required.

Services

- Support 7 A.M. to 7 P.M.; extra support available by request, arranged for in advance.

- Customers can use electronic mail, phone mail, or phone to request support.

- Single point of contact for all technology problems: Calls that cannot be resolved within ten minutes will be passed to second-level analysts. All calls are tracked from open to close.

- Management of hardware and software inventory.

- Hardware maintenance—Help Desk has actually outsourced this; a person from the outsourcing company works as part of the Help Desk, maintaining hardware and investigating hardware failures.

- Source and purchase hardware and software.

- Participate in standards setting and change management.

- Monitor LAN performance and notify appropriate groups of any potential problems.

- Monitor problem trends and notify appropriate groups of recurring problems so that a solution can be found.

- Participate in setting of standards.

- Arrange for training for products being supported.

Objectives for Next Six Months

- Increase number of problems resolved at first call to 60 percent from 40 percent.

- Increase accuracy of hardware and software inventory to 90 percent (automating asset management using a tool that has already been selected, installed, and tested) and generate quarterly asset reports for senior management.

- Upgrade PCs to a level that can handle client/server application (using asset management tool to find PCs that need upgrading).

- Find and offer training on client/server package for customers (need to work with IS developers on this).

Strategy

- Improve customer service through automation.

Summary

On a Help Desk, setting yourself up for success means getting focused. Being focused lets you concentrate on doing the things that really count, the things that add value to the business. In order to get focused, you need to determine a list of services that you can provide effectively with the resources you have, and a set of objectives. Having an agreed-upon list of services will help prevent the scenario of trying to do everything and not doing a good job at anything. Your objectives are your targets for a specific period of time; you can measure yourself against them and management can measure you against them. In order to create a list of services and objectives, you must consider four parameters: management expectations, expectations of IS, your customer profile, and your budget. Each of these will have a different weight depending on your environment. If customers have the heaviest weight, then their profile and requirements will have the strongest influence on the Help Desk services and objectives. This is the ideal. If management has a heavier weight, then management expectations will carry the most influence and will override customer expectations that conflict with their own. Setting services and objectives will most likely be an iterative process taking place between the Help Desk, management, customers, and IS. You can be successful only if some level of agreement is reached.

Once you have a set of services and objectives, you need to create a strategy, which determines your day-to-day method of operation. Help Desk staff must have your strategy in mind at all times, in whatever they do during the day. Your strategy is affected by the same parameters as your services and objectives. An example of a strategy is customer service above all else. In this case everything you do, from answering the telephone to selecting a Help Desk tool, will be focused on keeping your customers satisfied.

At this point, you have all of the ingredients necessary to get focused—you now have to put together a plan to make it all happen. A plan will help make sure that you move ahead, even if you are trying to support an unstable environment at the same time that you are trying to improve things. You can use your plan to ensure that there are always some resources dedicated to moving ahead, regardless of how much support there is.

Getting focused doesn't happen overnight. How long it takes depends on your environment and on how fast you can get things done. Typically, it takes a few months. In developing your services and objectives, you might not get all of the information that you want, but you can take whatever information you do get and work with it. You can adjust as you get more information and feedback. You will have to update your services, your objectives, and your strategy as the demands of your customers and your management change, as the business changes, and as technology changes. You must not let your focus, your formula for success, get out of date.

CHAPTER TWO

Structure

The size and shape of a Help Desk are reflections of its customers, its services, and its budget. Just as the concept of "one size and shape fits all" fails to work in the garment industry, it does not work in the Help Desk industry. If your Help Desk is to be successful, its structure must be tailored to the needs of the business it supports and the environment it functions in, and these vary significantly from company to company. Help Desks that support a hodgepodge of technologies will look different from those that support a strictly standardized environment. Help Desks that support on-line, live business functions such as cash registers or banking machines will look very different from those that support an office environment. Help Desks that make extended use of outsourcing and automation will look quite different from those that do not.

If the environment your Help Desk supports has no standards and just about anything goes, you're going to need more support staff, with a wider variety of skills, than if the environment were standardized. If your Help Desk supports an on-line environment, your response times are probably going to be a lot faster than if you were just supporting an office environment, and you will probably have more staff and more tools to make sure that all calls coming in are taken and resolved quickly. If your Help Desk uses automation, you're probably going to have less staff than if you were not automated, and they will probably do much more than take calls. They might be doing research, or analysis into what further automation could be employed. The definition of an efficient Help Desk in your organization will apply to your organization only, and could be quite ineffective in another environment.

When considering Help Desk structure, it is necessary to look at Help Desk roles, staffing, size of the Help Desk (number of staff), how many Help Desks will be needed, and physical location.

Roles

The most important roles in the Help Desk are those of manager (or supervisor, depending on your organization) and front-line staff. Front line staff are the people who answer the phones and try to resolve the problems.

Help Desk Manager

A Help Desk is a bustling, energetic environment. Things happen quickly, and reaction time has to be fast. In the midst of all this, there might be customers who are not satisfied or are angry, Help Desk staff who are not performing well, procedures that are not working or are not followed, and technology that is failing one time too many. In such an environment, it is an advantage to have someone to deal with all of these issues off-line so that the Help Desk staff can get back to work, not having to worry about one specific problem customer or peer. It is also an advantage to have someone with an eye on the future of the Help Desk, planning its direction and making sure that it is moving as planned.

Help Desk managers can oversee the function of the Help Desk, making sure that procedures and priorities are working and changes are made as necessary. They can also look after the performance, training, and career considerations of the staff. Help Desk managers can set objectives and plan for the future to make sure that the Help Desk keeps up with the requirements of the business. Managers can market the Help Desk to customers and management, and make sure that customers get the service that they need.

Having a manager (or supervisor) dedicated to the Help Desk might seem like an obvious idea, but some Help Desks have only part-time managers, in which case the Help Desk is only one of the manager's responsibilities. If you have very few customers, then a dedicated Help Desk manager probably doesn't make sense; by the same token, if you have that few customers, then a dedicated Help Desk probably doesn't make much sense.

Front-Line Staff

Front-line staff are the staff who get the calls. They are closest to the customer, and thus can collect customer feedback and impressions and can influence the customer's perception of the Help Desk, both positively and negatively. Front-line staff can be dispatchers, simply passing problems on to others, or they can be resolvers, trying to resolve problems and only passing on the ones they cannot themselves resolve.

Dispatch Front Line

In a Dispatch front line structure, the people who get the first call on the Help Desk are not the experts with the knowledge to solve the problems. Instead, they act as operators who take the call, log it, and route it to the appropriate area for resolution. They don't take any further responsibility for the call. As an example, if someone calls about a PC that is malfunctioning, the Help Desk operator might log the call then pass it on to a Help Desk analyst. That analyst would then go out and determine what the problem was—hardware, software, and so on—and deal with it accordingly. The analyst would call in whatever technicians or other experts were required.

The staff who receive the routed calls in this structure are the Help Desk analysts—the second line. Help Desk analysts would determine what the problem was and either resolve it or, if it were out of their area of expertise, pass it on to the appropriate expert, such as a hardware maintenance technician or a software support person, for resolution. They would be responsible for picking up logged problems, getting the appropriate people involved to get the problems solved, and closing the problems.

Resolve Front Line

Another option is to staff the front line with people who are more skilled technically and who have analytical skills. These are analysts with experience in the products being supported and, ideally, a broad base of technological knowledge. When someone calls and says, "My PC is down," the Help Desk analyst can, in many cases, determine the cause of the problem and resolve it over the phone with the help of various Help Desk tools. The problem is passed on only if resolving it will take longer than is practical on the Help Desk—calls might be coming in and waiting while the first call is being worked on. In a Resolve front-line environment, automation of routine tasks would ensure that staff are free to handle more complex issues and those most important to the business. Help Desk tools such as expert systems could expand the knowledge of staff so that they could solve a wider variety of problems. Remote diagnostic software would let them diagnose and resolve problems without having to leave the Help Desk.

Dispatch vs. Resolve

The front line is extremely important to the success of the Help Desk. It is the point of first contact with the customer, and therefore careful thought should be given to deciding what kind of front line to set up.

Dispatch...

With a Dispatch structure, the customers might get their Help Desk calls answered quickly, but this says nothing about when the calls get resolved. Help Desk operators can answer and pass on a lot of calls—a lot more than front-line staff who try to resolve the calls can handle—but in doing so they're creating a funnel effect (see Figure 2.1). All those passed-on calls queue up for handling by an analyst. If that queue is too long—a problem that may be caused by not enough analysts, too heavy a workload, or unbalanced priorities—then customers have to wait a long time before their problems get resolved. When calls are resolved by analysts outside the Help Desk, this problem becomes more pronounced. It is difficult to control the priorities of people outside of your own department.

One company that used the Dispatch front line had an average call time of less than 50 seconds, but an average resolution time of greater than eight days! Needless to say, the customers were not impressed. Getting your call answered quickly when you call a Help Desk is nice, but it is certainly not good enough. Customers want their problems solved as quickly as possible, and generally do not consider eight days "as quickly as possible."

Another potential problem with Dispatch front lines is that customers soon learn who actually resolves the problems and start calling these people directly, rather than going through the front line. They don't want to have to describe their problem to more than one person, and they want to talk to the person who will actually be able to help them. Unfortunately,

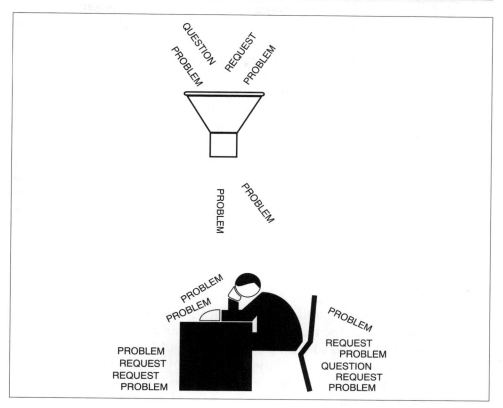

Figure 2.1 The funnel effect.

this kind of activity interferes with the workloads of the analysts and disrupts the balance of priorities.

Another thing to consider with Dispatch front lines is the job itself. Logging calls and passing them on does not take a lot of skill, and can quickly become monotonous. Not many people would be happy in this kind of a job for long. A much more interesting job would be one that involved resolving the problems that came in.

... vs. Resolve

With a Resolve front-line structure, your front-line staff are actually trying to resolve the problems, answer the questions, and service the requests. Each staff member is spending more time on the phone. Other calls are constantly coming in, so you need to put some kind of controls in to make sure that the queues don't become unreasonable in length. You may need to set a time limit. If a call cannot be resolved within a specific amount of time—say, five minutes—then it should be passed on. An automatic call distributor can help control call traffic into the Help Desk and minimize wait time for each caller.

If you have a Resolve front line, you should also be looking at automating routine tasks where possible to free your staff up for more serious calls.

Staff on a Resolve front line need to have technical and analytical skills that are similar to those required by Help Desk staff on the back lines, and by many other IS staff. This common skill base will allow you to rotate staff responsibilities for purposes of cross-training and enhancement of skills and experience. Staff could work on the front line for a few months, then move into other Help Desk areas such as software testing and installation. Your analysts would keep their technology skills sharp by working with new and upgraded products on the back lines of the Help Desk, yet stay close to the customers—know what their problems are, what they use, and what they need—by spending time on the front line. Working on the front line also gives staff an appreciation of the Help Desk workload and a better understanding of the urgency of the problems that might be passed on to them while they are in other roles.

Analysts from areas other than the Help Desk would also benefit by spending some time on the front line. Developers would learn a lot about what kind of problems customers tend to have with systems and what customers want. This could only improve the design of the products they create. The rotation process also creates backups—if someone on the front line is absent, you can rotate another analyst who has spent time on the front line into the position temporarily.

Finally, the Resolve front-line structure, especially when it is combined with automation, makes for an interesting and challenging place to work. Working on the front line offers staff a wonderful opportunity to get an overview of all of the systems in the corporation, talk to customers from all areas of the business, and learn what is most important to the business. Staff also get exposure to all of the technology being used, often before anyone else in the corporation, and their technology knowledge base expands greatly. All of this is valuable training that makes staff more marketable in terms of transferring to other areas.

A summary of the comparison between the Dispatch and Resolve structures is presented in Table 2.1.

Table 2.1 Dispatch vs. Resolve

	Dispatch	*Resolve*
Initial Response Time	Low	Higher. A limit may have to be placed on how long an analyst spends on each call so that other customers are not kept waiting. Tools such as automatic call distributors can be used to handle incoming calls as effectively as possible.
Time Per Call	Low	Higher. The analyst will actually try to resolve the problem. A time limit may be set up so that any problems that cannot be resolved within the time limit are passed on.
Resolve Time	Can get out of control—funnel effect	Low for most problems. Most problems will be resolved immediately by the person answering the phone.
Skill Level Required for Front Line	Low	High. Technical and analytical skills are required.
Job Interest for Front-line Job	Low—like a switchboard operator	High, especially if automation is used to eliminate the repetitive, mundane work.
Customer Response	Frustrated customers may start calling the analysts directly, resulting in lost statistics and interrupted workloads.	Customers need only explain their problems once—to the people who actually resolve the problem.
Other Considerations	Career prospects are not good.	Can rotate analytical staff through the front line; other analytical staff can fill the front-line positions in case of absence. Career prospects for front-line analysts are good—they expand their technical knowledge, customer knowledge, and business knowledge while on the front line.

Help Desk Analysts

Help Desk analysts can exist as part of the Resolve front line and within the Help Desk as a second line of support. Help Desk analysts resolve problems and answer questions that come into the Help Desk. They look for ways to prevent recurring problems, and they analyze trends to see whether they are an indication of a defective piece of technology or a defective program. Analysts within the Help Desk are not the only ones solving the calls coming into the Help Desk. Problems can get passed to experts in other areas such as Communications Support, Technical Support, and Applications Support.

Other Roles

A Help Desk typically does a lot more than respond to calls that come in. Depending on the services it supplies, a Help Desk might contain several other roles. Examples of some other roles that might exist in the Help Desk are:

- Technology selection, sourcing, and purchase.
  If your environment is experiencing a significant amount of growth, you might need one or more dedicated resources to coordinate and/or perform the whole effort of selection, sourcing, and purchase of PCs and software.

- Hardware configuration and installation.
  You need someone to configure and install hardware. This is an area that you might consider outsourcing to the hardware vendors or to the company doing your hardware maintenance. It is time-consuming and monotonous work. Installing specialized hardware often takes specialized skills that the vendors may have, but that you may not.

- Hardware maintenance.
  This is another function you might consider outsourcing. Someone needs to look after all of the hardware: do maintenance when necessary and perform diagnostics and repairs. Keeping spare parts and maintaining the technical expertise necessary to do this is expensive. Outsourcing companies can generally perform this function more cost-effectively than you can internally. They can get parts cheaper and more quickly; they can afford to stock more parts than you can, and they have the necessary expertise.

- Software installation and testing.
  Installing software on the network and testing it out might be a function you want the Help Desk to perform. This would not only

ensure that the Help Desk had the skills necessary to support the software, but would ensure that the package was tested thoroughly and all problems resolved before it was rolled out for general use. Help Desk staff know what kind of problems tend to crop up, so they would check for these. If the software installation is an upgrade, the staff would be familiar with the original software and would check all functions to make sure that they worked as advertised. Help Desk staff know what options to install in any customizations because they know their customers—they talk to them every day and hear their problems and their needs. Automated software distribution tools could be used to make the software roll-out process easier.

- Network monitoring.
  Being able to monitor network activity would be a great advantage for a Help Desk. Help Desk staff would be notified of degradation, unusual activity, or other potential problems on the network, and could have these situations resolved before they became real problems. If calls coming in described situations that could not be explained on their own, the network could be checked quickly to see if the problem were there. The Help Desk would also be notified immediately of any network problems that did occur so that quick action could be taken—the problem could be fixed and customers notified of any anticipated down time. A network management system that included functions to monitor various components of the network would make this kind of proactive activity possible. Help Desk analysts could monitor network activity with very little effort as they worked on Help Desk calls. The network management system would be doing all of the work. Figure 2.2 shows the roles in a sample Help Desk structure.

Staffing

The kind of people you're looking for to work on your Help Desk are the kind of people everyone else is looking for: people who care about their customers, are good communicators, and are willing members of the Help Desk team. Following are desired characteristics and sample job descriptions for the major roles in your Help Desk.

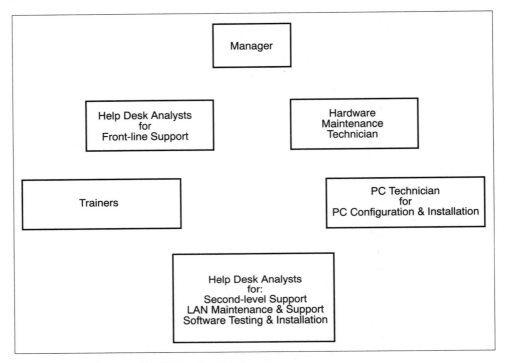

Figure 2.2   A sample Help Desk structure.

Front-Line Staff

The people who answer the phone are critical to your Help Desk, whether you have a Dispatch structure or a Resolve structure. These people have first contact with your customer, and how they handle the call has a lot to do with how the customer will perceive the Help Desk. It can be frustrating to call the Help Desk with a problem, only to be told, "We're pretty busy right now. We'll get to it when we have time." This is quite different from calling and getting the response, "We currently have an emergency on the LAN, so our service staff are tied up. But someone will be sent over to you this afternoon to check out your PC problem. You've been given a priority of 2 and your call number is 143." In the former case, the customer probably does not feel very confident that the problem will be looked at in the near future, if at all; in the latter, the customer has a good idea of what is happening and when the problem will be looked at.

Characteristics that you should look for in a front-line person are:

- Believes in providing the highest quality of service to the customer.
- Is patient, pleasant, and diplomatic even when confronted with rudeness.
- Is a good listener and communicator.
- Reacts quickly to major problems.
- Is a willing and communicative part of the Help Desk team.

Staff who are on a Resolve front line must have these characteristics as well as those of a Help Desk analyst (described farther on). Following are sample job descriptions.

Dispatch Front-Line Help Desk Staff

Goal:

To answer Help Desk calls and pass them on to the appropriate person or department for resolution.

Responsibilities:

- Respond to all Help Desk calls received.
- Ensure that each Help Desk call is immediately logged and passed on to the appropriate person or department for resolution.
- Keep all Help Desk staff informed of any perceived trends, positive or negative, in the calls being received.
- Follow escalation procedures immediately for highest severity problems.
- Keep customers informed of any global problems or scheduled down times.
- Maintain a professional Help Desk image at all times. Be courteous and helpful.

Resolve Front-Line Help Desk Staff

Goal:

To answer Help Desk calls, resolve as many as possible, and pass on those that cannot be resolved to the appropriate person or department.

Responsibilities:

- Respond to all Help Desk calls received.
- Log each call and try to resolve it while the customer is still on the phone. If the call cannot be resolved within five minutes, pass the call on to the appropriate person or department.
- Wherever possible when resolving problems, make whatever modifications necessary to ensure that the problem will not recur—fix causes, not just symptoms.
- Keep up to date on all technology being supported and ensure that you are familiar with it before it is rolled out to customers.
- Keep up to date on new products and methods—apply to attend conferences and training sessions that you feel are relevant.
- Keep all Help Desk staff informed of any perceived trends, positive or negative, in calls being received and/or solutions being employed.
- Follow escalation procedures immediately for highest severity problems.
- Keep customers informed of any global problems or scheduled down times.
- Maintain a professional Help Desk image at all times. Be courteous and helpful.

Help Desk Analysts

Analytical staff still need to have customer service and communication skills, but they also need to have well-developed analytical skills and open, inquisitive minds—this includes the analytical staff who work on a Resolve front line. They aren't afraid of eliminating old ways, of trying new things, of working out new solutions to make the environment better for the customers. Desirable characteristics for analytical staff are:

- Believes in providing the highest quality of service to the customer.
- Good listener and good communicator.
- Good analyst—looks at options and alternatives, digs to find causes and solutions.
- Technically knowledgeable.
- Innovative.

- Patient and diplomatic.
- Self-managing.
- Willing and communicative part of the Help Desk team.

Following is a sample job description.

Help Desk Analyst

Goal:

To analyze and resolve problems that are passed on from the Help Desk.

Responsibilities:

- Resolve and close all problems passed on from the Help Desk in an appropriate time frame and according to priorities assigned to each.
- Get other staff involved, where necessary, to resolve the problem. Keep ownership of the problem even when others are involved. Track calls that have been passed on to ensure that they are resolved correctly and in a timely fashion.
- Wherever possible when resolving problems, make whatever modifications necessary to ensure that the problem will not recur—fix causes, not just symptoms.
- Keep the customer informed of progress on the problem if it will take longer than the agreed-upon time frame, and respond to customer queries about the problem. Ensure that the customer understands what is happening and is cognizant of delays as well as progress.
- Keep up to date on all technology being supported and ensure that you are familiar with it before it is rolled out to customers.
- Keep up to date on new products and methods—apply to attend conferences and training sessions that you feel are relevant.
- Keep all Help Desk staff informed of trends you have noticed, problems that have been resolved, delays that are in effect, and any new processes or technologies that you feel would be of benefit.

Additional Responsibilities (depending on environment):

- Participate in selection of software and setting of standards.
- Install and test software. Ensure that software is tested by a customer pilot group and feedback is received before software is rolled

out to customers on a wide basis. Ensure that customers are informed of all software changes.

- Monitor usage of software and work with appropriate staff to ensure that adequate licensing is in place.
- Monitor network performance and act upon potential problems.
- Recommend software solutions to customer business problems or requirements.

The Help Desk Manager

Help Desk managers need to be focused on both the present and the future. They need to monitor the workings of the Help Desk to ensure that it is functioning effectively, and they need to look to the future of the Help Desk—to set direction and do the planning for the Help Desk function. Help Desk managers need to ensure that the Help Desk is adding business value and that it is meeting the needs of the business and of its customers. Help Desk managers will talk to customers and senior management, get input into directions the Help Desk should be taking, and get feedback on and suggestions for services being provided. Respect will be given to someone who has an honest interest in making things better for the customer and for the business. The Help Desk manager will not be discouraged by the number of calls and problems, but will see them as a challenge and look for ways of reducing them and making things better for both the customers and Help Desk staff. The manager will oversee the workings of the Help Desk team, look after employee issues, check for quality in processes and services, and respond when escalation is required. In short, the Help Desk manager is:

- A businessperson, focused on providing business value.
- A customer service advocate, interested in providing highest quality of customer service.
- A planner, constantly planning for the future.
- A good communicator, collecting ideas and getting ideas across.
- Positive, not brought down easily.
- An innovator, always looking for ways to improve.
- A good manager, monitoring Help Desk functions and managing staff effectively.

Following is a sample job description.

Help Desk Manager

Goal:

To provide customers with support for their use of technology.

Responsibilities:

- Create and maintain a list of services, objectives, a strategy, and a plan for the Help Desk. Ensure that all Help Desk staff are familiar with these, and encourage participation in the creation of these where possible.
- Monitor Help Desk performance. Set quarterly objectives and report to senior management on the objectives and whether they were met.
- Ensure that staff are functioning effectively and are getting the training they require. Make adjustments to staffing as required.
- Keep up to date on Help Desk technology. Ensure that upgrades or additions to tools are made as required.
- Make optimal use of the Help Desk budget—ensure that the most effective combination of staff and technology is being employed. In doing this, explore alternate methods of providing staff and technology.
- Meet with customers on an ongoing basis to get feedback and suggestions for the Help Desk and to inform them of any new developments or changes in the Help Desk service.
- Ensure quality of the Help Desk—check all procedures regularly and ensure that they are in place, correct, and being followed.
- Keep senior management and senior customer management informed of Help Desk performance and issues.

The Cost of Having the Wrong Kind of Staff

Consider the following example: A customer has requested hookup to the LAN with access to a specific, specialized application. The hookup is completed, but refuses to work properly. The Help Desk is called and one of its experts is dispatched. The expert visits the problem configuration, pronounces the problem fixed, and leaves. After the visit, the customer does have access to the application, but it does not appear in full screen format—everything is shrunk down to half size—and the print function does not work. The Help Desk employee's response to this is "The size of screen is small, but it's OK—you can still read the numbers. And the printing should work—I set it up. All the customer has to do is to go into the LAN printer select function, add the printer to the list, and then select it as the default." The customer, in this case, happened to be the definitely nontechnical president of the organization. This response was not beneficial, to say the least, either to the customer or the Help Desk's reputation.

Every interaction between Help Desk staff and customers affects Help Desk image and performance. Taking the time to make sure you have the staff you need will bring instant and ongoing payback.

Where Do You Get Staff?

Traditionally, Help Desk staff have come from IS, but this is certainly not a requirement. Look for power users in the business areas—people who know and use the technology as part of their work in the business. These people will give the Help Desk an incredible advantage: a better understanding of the customers. In order to get these people, you might want to fill some of your Help Desk positions on a rotating basis so that you can offer assignments of several months' duration. A Help Desk assignment would give the business staff wider exposure to technology and to business use of technology. It would also be public acknowledgment of a special status. You'll have to do some selling and work out deals with the various business areas, but the results should be worth the trouble.

Software developers would certainly benefit from a stint on the Help Desk. They would gain a greater understanding of customer requirements and the kinds of problems that come into a Help Desk. They could take these into account, making sure that customer requirements are met and potential problems are minimized, when they go back to developing software. The Help Desk would also benefit in having a resource with a greater understanding of the software and how it works.

Technical support staff and analysts would also benefit the Help Desk and benefit from the Help Desk. Giving these staff an opportunity to work on the Help Desk would let them build their business knowledge and get exposure to the real business world: a dead PC might mean the loss of a significant dollars in a financial trading area, and a problem with a server or mainframe might mean that a distribution center cannot get merchandise in or out. In return, the technical support staff or analysts would give the Help Desk more immediate problem-solving capabilities.

Another place that potential Help Desk employees might be found is in Computer Operations. Computer operators have long had to deal with irate customers and solving serious problems quickly. Some of them might be perfect for the Help Desk.

Trainers would also be good for the Help Desk. The Help Desk would benefit from their product knowledge and their communication skills, and they would benefit from the technical and business knowledge they would gain. Their time on the Help Desk would give them firsthand feedback on the effectiveness of their training and show them ways it could be improved.

So You Don't Have the Perfect Staff . . . What Now?

Often, you don't have the luxury of building a team from scratch, of selecting the individuals you want. You have to take people who were part of a previous support department, or—and this is more common in today's economy—people who have been laid off from their jobs in other parts of the company and have now been assigned to you. You don't always have complete control over who is working for you. Regardless, the Help Desk should not be a dumping ground for undesirable staff. It is IS's closest link with the customers, its ears and eyes into the customer world, and its image in the customer world. The Help Desk can provide IS (and the business) with valuable information about what customers need, the problems they face, what is most important to them and to the business, and what IS could do to help them help the business. You can't afford to staff the Help Desk with less than adequate staff.

Before you start writing off the staff you have, consider their perceived shortcomings carefully. Don't get rid of someone just because that person hasn't had the training they need or hasn't had performance expectations set. Your first step might be an informal skills and training assessment. Find out what training the staff members have had and what skills they lack. If they don't answer the phone professionally, perhaps someone has never told them how they should do it. If they are not self-starters, maybe they don't know that they are allowed to be. Perhaps no one has ever told them that they should be. If they are not patient with customers, perhaps some service quality training and some performance expectation setting may help. Make sure that you—by not giving people a chance, by not setting performance expectations or providing training— are not the block keeping your staff from performing. Give them a chance.

Having said that, if you find that you have staff who just don't measure up, for whatever reason, you may consider a swap. If you see staff you want in other parts of IS or in the business, try to arrange for a swap—on a trial basis, or for a set period of time. Staff who are not appropriate for the Help Desk may work out well somewhere else.

Make use of students wherever possible—they're usually enthusiastic, willing to learn, bright, and inexpensive. Part-time workers might also be able to help you out, especially for staffing peak times. Students and part-time workers can help fill temporary skill gaps.

Help Desk Career Considerations

Boring, repetitive tasks are not meant for humans. They are meant for machines. If you build your Help Desk around this philosophy, you will end up with a stimulating and attractive environment. You will have automated all of the routine tasks. The work remaining will be the kind that people still do better than machines: reasoning and analysis.

Staff on the Help Desk will gain exposure to a wide area of the business, its problems and requirements, and the technology that supports it. If you can offer people this kind of environment, your Help Desk will be regarded as a desirable place to work, although it may take some time and marketing on your part for people to realize this.

Rotating staff from different business and IS areas through some of the Help Desk positions will also help the Help Desk image, especially if you offer opportunities only to those employees who have the qualities necessary to be good Help Desk analysts. Once the Help Desk is perceived as a place where you can learn more about business and technology and gain skills that make you more marketable, you will be able to get staff more easily, and staff from the Help Desk will be able to move into other areas more easily, as well.

If you do not automate or outsource, and you still have clerical or lower-level positions on your Help Desk, you will have a harder time selling them as career moves. Why should skilled people, thinking people, want to spend their time doing simple, repetitive tasks that they know a computer can do better and faster?

Where do you go from the Help Desk? The added business exposure and technology exposure will make you more marketable for just about any job. You have widened your knowledge of the business, its requirements and its problems, and you have widened your understanding of the technology required to support it. You've demonstrated your analytical skills and your communication skills. According to the Help Desk Institute's 1993 Survey of Help Desk Practices, when people leave the Help Desk, but stay with the company, 29 percent go into programming, 22 percent into network management, 19 percent into end-user computing, 19 percent into non-IS departments, and 11 percent into Operations. Figure 2.3 shows career opportunities for Help Desk staff: where they are recruited from and where they go after they leave the Help Desk.

What do you pay your staff? What they're worth to you. If you don't think that they're important, pay them accordingly. You won't have them long because they'll leave, which you shouldn't mind because you didn't think they were important anyway. If you think that's too simplistic, do (or buy) some market research—find out what the market is paying. You might want to adjust that amount depending on your own environment—

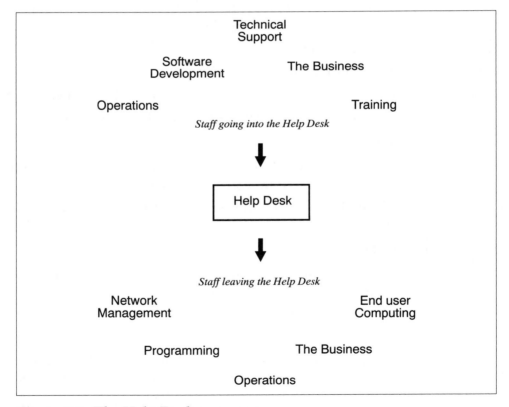

Figure 2.3 The Help Desk as a career.

that is, if your Help Desk employees are doing more than the traditional ones, then pay more. They're worth it. Skimping on salary is false economy and will cost you in the long run. Good people who aren't being paid enough will leave, and you will lose the money and time you have invested in training. Salary should reflect the value of your people.

Training

One of the biggest mistakes Help Desk managers make in trying to save budget is letting people learn on the job. Learning on the job encourages learning other people's mistakes and other people's inefficiencies. It teaches how a certain person or application uses a tool, not what the tool is capable of and what it might be used for in the future. Training is an investment in the present and future of the Help Desk. If you don't spend enough on it, you'll get what you paid for.

The kind of training your Help Desk staff will need might include the following, depending on what their individual roles are:

Technical Training:

- Help Desk tools.
- Foundation products, such as LANs and LAN Operating Systems.
- Products currently being supported by the Help Desk.

Procedural training:

- Help Desk procedures in use at your organization. (This training should be offered by your Help Desk.)
- General procedures and skills for setting up, running, or improving a Help Desk.

Personal training:

- Delivering quality service to customers. (This training should include any organizational initiatives.)
- Communication skills.
- Problem solving.

You can't send everyone out on all the training they need at the same time, so you need to set up a training plan for your staff. Work with your staff to do this. First, find out what skills they have (but remember that saying you have a skill is much different from actually having it), and what skills they need to acquire or enhance. Then find out what training is available. Using schedules of class offerings, plan out a training schedule for each of your employees, ensuring that the Help Desk will have adequate staff at all times, and perhaps planning in students or part-time staff to fill in whatever gaps will occur. Include seminars or conferences in your training plan. These can be a valuable source of new ideas and information exchange for your staff; your Help Desk will benefit. On-site training might be a cost-effective alternative, although it will tie up a lot of your staff at the same time.

Have the procedures you use on your Help Desk documented or incorporated into your tools to ensure that each new person is getting the same training and that it is consistent. Passing on procedures by word of mouth will mean that they will change with each iteration, and important steps might be missed. Reviewing procedures frequently will help weed out processes that no longer make sense.

Help Desk staff should be trained on new products before anyone else—certainly before the products are tested or released to the customers. It is most embarrassing for a Help Desk employee to get a call about a product that was rolled out by the Help Desk but that the Help Desk employee knows nothing about.

What you invest in training will be returned to you in improved Help Desk employee performance, a more professional Help Desk, improved use of Help Desk tools, a better overall understanding of technology in use and technology available, and an innovative Help Desk environment where people are always looking for ways to improve. Your customers will notice the difference.

How Many Staff?

Comparing Help Desk sizes is difficult because of the wide variance in environment—technology, Help Desk customers, and businesses supported—from one company to the next. As an example, consider Help Desks that receive between 1,000 and 1,499 calls per month. According to the Help Desk Institute's 1993 Survey of Help Desk practices, one-third of these support between 500 and 1,499 customers, another third support 1,500 to 4,999 customers, and the remaining third is split evenly between those supporting fewer than 500 customers and those supporting more than 5,000 customers. Of these same Help Desks, roughly 56 percent have

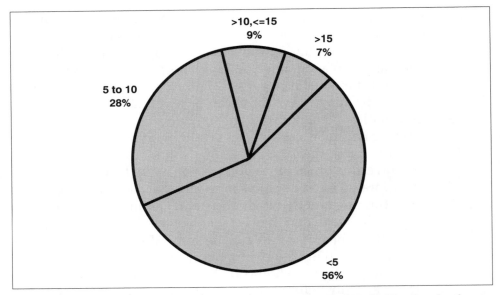

Figure 2.4   Staffing levels, shown by percentage of Help Desks conforming to each level, for Help Desks receiving between 1,000 and 1,499 calls per month.

fewer than 5 employees, 28 percent have 5 to 10 employees, 9 percent have more than 10 and less than or equal to 15 employees, and 7 percent have over 15 employees. That's quite a variance in both customers supported and staff required to support them, as the graph in Figure 2.4 shows.

There are several factors affecting the number of staff that your Help Desk will need. These include:

- The breadth of services you provide (including hours of support).
- The complexity of your technological environment.
- How standardized (or nonstandardized) your environment is.
- How new your environment is.
- The number, sophistication, and knowledge of your customers.
- The automation you employ.

Breadth of Services You Provide

Very simply, if you offer a service, you need to include someone on the Help Desk to provide that service, unless it is automated or outsourced.

The more services you provide, the more such people you will need. The number of staff will also depend on the number of hours of support you need to provide. A Help Desk that operates 24 hours a day, seven days a week will have 118 hours more to cover than one that operates 10 hours a day, five days a week.

Complexity of Your Technological Environment

An environment consisting of several local area networks linked to a wide area network, which in turn crosses several time zones and includes several mainframes and 3,000 PCs, is infinitely more complex than an environment consisting of only a few local area networks supporting those same 3,000 PCs. The former environment involves more complex technology and requires more staff to support.

Standardization

Supporting a completely standardized environment is every Help Desk's dream. An environment in which standards have been established and are being enforced requires less support than one in which there are no standards. There will be fewer problems that are due to software or hardware incompatibility, customers can be trained more easily, Help Desk staff will only be required to know a limited number of software products, and automation can be more easily employed. The Help Desk in the standardized environment will get fewer calls than its counterpart in the nonstandardized environment.

How New Your Environment Is

If the environment you support is just getting into PCs, you will probably require more Help Desk staff during the initial roll-out period. You will be supporting customers who are just getting used to the technology, networks that are just being set up and that might be somewhat unstable, and problems that you have never seen before. Once the environment has matured and settled down somewhat, you will be able to make more extensive use of Help Desk tools and automation, and your processes will be firmly established. Your customers will be more familiar with the technology they are using, and will probably require less training support.

The Sophistication and Knowledge of Your Customers

If your customers are at ease with the technology they use, they are less apt to run into problems than if they are fearful and uncomfortable. The more they know, the less often they will have to call the Help Desk for anything other than a real problem, and the more willing they will be to learn about new technology and to make use of automation.

The Automation You Employ

Eminent automation specialist Rosemary LaChance, a partner in Farber/LaChance Incorporated, estimates that 90 percent of the problems coming into a Help Desk can be eliminated, or their solutions automated. The more automation you can employ on your Help Desk, the fewer Help Desk staff you will need. In a truly automated environment, the only problems those staff should see are problems that have never happened before. Once a problem occurs, its cause should be eliminated or its solution automated. You can realize a significant decrease in Help Desk calls just by taking your most frequently occurring problems (typically, these are terminal resets, printer resets, and server reboots) and automating their resolutions, so that customers can resolve these problems themselves by using a tool such as a voice response unit.

All of these factors will influence the number of people you need to run your Help Desk. When trying to calculate this number, use any data you can get on the number and complexity of Help Desk calls that have been generated in the past by the environment you are supporting. Using this data, and considering the factors mentioned above, you should be able to come up with a number appropriate for your environment. A period of trial and adjustment might be necessary before you get it right.

Staffing for Peaks

If your Help Desk gets 400 calls per day, you can be assured that they aren't going to be spaced out evenly, coming in at a comfortable 40 or so calls per hour. You're going to have peaks, and you'll have to adjust your staffing accordingly—particularly your front-line staffing. If your hours of operation are 7 A.M. to 7 P.M., with the peak Help Desk activity occurring between 10 A.M. and 3 P.M., then you might consider staggering starting times for your staff. You'll want someone there at 7 A.M. and someone to stay until 7 P.M., so you might have staff working from 7 A.M. to 4 P.M. and

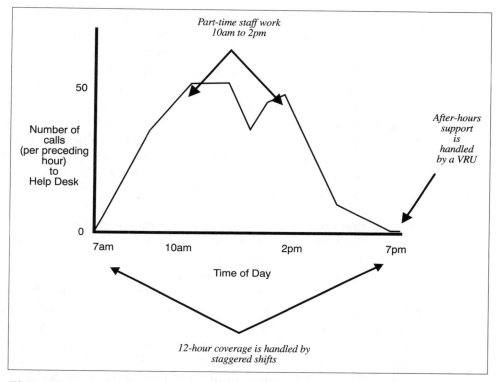

Figure 2.5 Providing required support levels.

10 A.M. to 7 P.M., while the rest work 8 A.M. to 5 P.M. or 9 A.M. to 6 P.M. You may decide to make use of part-time staff or outsourced support to cover your peaks. You could have some of your phone lines going automatically to a third party with which you have a support contract at specific times each day. Figure 2.5 shows some options for providing optimum Help Desk coverage.

How Many Help Desks?

There are a lot of historical reasons for having more than one Help Desk. Most of them are just that—historical. When PCs first started coming in, if support structures were set up, they were usually set up to be completely separate from any mainframe support structures that existed. This may have worked for standalone PCs, but when PCs started accessing mainframes via local area networks, difficulties became apparent. When problems occurred, it was often difficult to tell whether they originated from the local area network or the mainframe. If there were problems with the mainframe, the mainframe support group didn't always bother to tell the PC support group, and vice versa. Both groups could be trying to solve the same problem, which was a waste of time for at least one of them. Customers didn't always know whom they should call for support: was the problem a PC issue or a mainframe issue? Even more basic than that, was the box on their desk a PC or a terminal? In some companies, as specialized applications were created, special groups (with separate phone numbers or electronic mail IDs) were set up to provide support for them. In that kind of environment, a customer could get really confused— when something went wrong, was it a PC problem, a mainframe problem, or an application problem? And if it was an application problem, which application was causing the problem?

In one extreme case, a bank found itself with more than 90 Help Desks, which had sprung up as various applications were developed. When a new application was developed, a hotline support number was established for it. Things got a bit out of control, and support became a real headache for both the IS staff and the 50,000 end users. Communication between Help Desks was a nightmare: when one Help Desk implemented a new technology, other Help Desks might not get to know about it until they started getting calls about it. There was much duplication of effort. Fortunately, the severity of the situation was realized and the 90 Help Desks were consolidated to 3, one for each geographical region that the bank serviced. This resulted in a dramatic improvement in service levels, and thus a much happier customer base.

These kinds of multiple support structures are the legacy that many of us are left with today; in fact, many of us are still creating this kind of legacy for the future. We have to make sure that our Help Desk structures are not confusing our customers, that they are not causing duplication of effort, and that they are as efficient as possible, with no superfluous layers or divisions.

If your customers are confused about whom to call, chances are you have too many Help Desks. If your Help Desks share the same customer base, you probably have too many Help Desks. A PC Help Desk that services the same customers as a mainframe Help Desk and vice versa is one too many Help Desks. Such Help Desks should be consolidated. To leave them separate is to invite confusion, duplication of effort, and general inefficiency.

Some advantages to having consolidated Help Desks are as follows:

- One source for information: if something is wrong with a server, with any network component, or with the mainframe, the Help Desk will know about it. In a multiple Help Desk environment, there is always the danger that one Help Desk does not know when another has detected a problem in its particular piece of the environment. This could result in a wasted effort of trying to resolve a problem that has already been recognized and addressed, and in the dispersal of false information to customers.

- Better use of staff: generally, a consolidated Help Desk requires fewer staff than the sum of the component Help Desks. The higher call load will be easier to balance among staff, and will be less susceptible to dramatic fluctuations. Staff on the consolidated Help Desk will have the opportunity to develop a broader knowledge base. They will have a more complete picture of what is happening, which will make it easier for them to resolve problems. They will gain experience in a broader base of technologies. The Help Desk will become a more interesting place to work.

- Better use of technology: on a consolidated Help Desk, duplication of Help Desk tools will be eliminated, and tools can be more easily integrated so that their functionality and accuracy increases. Tools for one Help Desk generally cost less than the sum of tools for several individual Help Desks.

- More consistent service: a consolidated Help Desk makes it easier to provide consistent service to customers. Putting procedures in place to ensure consistent service is easier to do in a single Help Desk than across multiple Help Desks. Similarly, monitoring and managing these procedures is easier in a single Help Desk environment.

- A consolidated Help Desk will most likely be less expensive to run than several smaller Help Desks. Savings can be realized on tools, on staff, and on office space.

This is not to say that it's always wrong to have more than one Help Desk. If you have separate customer bases with separate requirements and support needs, more than one Help Desk might well be the way to go. In the case of the bank that consolidated 90 Help Desks into 3, each of 3 Help Desks supports a different client base in a different part of the country. A pharmaceutical company with 5,500 PC customers spread among several buildings decided to create several satellite Help Desks to bring support closer to the customers. The Help Desks are administered centrally and draw on the same resources.

Another organization found it advantageous to have a separate Help Desk to service the support requirements for its stores. The stores have their own computer systems and are hooked into the corporate network. The store Help Desk provides help 17 hours a day, across the country, in two languages. The support staff must have detailed knowledge of the store systems—including the cash register systems—and are, in fact, required to have actual store experience.

Communication between Help Desks

If, for whatever reason, you find yourself with more than one Help Desk, there are things you can do to help ensure that communication between Help Desks does take place and customer service does not suffer:

- Have regular meetings between Help Desks. Talk about problem trends, new technology or techniques being employed, and anything unusual that has occurred. Also, review effectiveness of communication between Help Desks.

- Use the same Help Desk software if possible, including a common problem database, so that problems can be passed back and forth easily and workloads can be viewed.

- Ensure that you each understand what your responsibilities are and what the responsibilities of the other Help Desks are. Knowing who does what will help ensure that customers aren't bounced between Help Desks and that there are no cracks for problems to fall through.

- Set up procedures to keep each other informed of problems and new developments. Don't leave this up to the discretion of the staff. Set up clear procedures, ensure that staff understand them and their importance, and ensure they are being followed. If there is a problem on the mainframe, it is important that the PC Help Desk know this, because they will be getting calls about it.

- Set up Help Desk procedures together. Wherever possible, try to make sure that procedures on each Help Desk are the same, to help ensure consistency of service to the customers.

- Share training—try to use the same courses so that training received and skills gained are consistent.

The more consistent the Help Desks are in the service they deliver to their customers, the more successful they will be.

Physical Environment

A pleasant working environment, comfortable furniture, and appropriate technology are all important to the health, well-being, and performance of your Help Desk staff. They are working in what is often a very negative environment—complaints, angry customers, panic situations. Some of them have to sit in this kind of environment all day, without being able to leave their desks for any significant period of time. Anything you can do to improve their environment will work toward improving their physical well-being and their performance. Someone who has been sitting in a dark, cramped cubicle all day, away from other people, will probably react quite differently (and less positively) to the 50th complaint of the day than someone who is in an open, spacious, bright environment, close to other staff.

Actual physical comfort is one of the first things to consider. Your staff, especially those who sit answering the phone, need comfortable furniture, the best video display screens you can afford (with anti-glare screens), and headsets that allow them to have their hands free. Let them be involved in selecting equipment wherever possible.

Physical location is another thing to consider. People are like a lot of other mammals. They need light, air, exercise, and proximity to their own kind. You can't necessarily ensure that they get exercise, but you can give them the other things. Position your Help Desk in an area with windows, if possible. If not, make sure that the area is brightly lit. There are several alternatives to fluorescent lighting, which seems to bother a lot of people, and it might be worth your while to look into these. Ensure that ventilation is adequate. Too many office spaces are stuffy and dry. Plants, where possible, will also improve the environment. Large, potted plants that sit on the floor are better than smaller, shelf plants because they do not clutter shelf or desk space, they are larger and can be appreciated by more people, and they can be used as screens when necessary. Using a large plant as a screen often creates a more pleasant, open work space than having a solid partition there.

Help Desks of old were often isolated from the rest of the world, largely as a result of being associated with mainframes. Help Desk operators sat by their consoles in the confines of a cold, sterile computer room. Unfortunately, this is often still the case. The roles of Help Desk staff are changing as they need to be more in touch with other people—technical support staff, application support staff, network support staff. Having Help Desk staff situated near some or all of these groups creates synergy. Problems and potential solutions are discussed more readily, and information is passed more easily and naturally. People are closer to each other's environments and have a better understanding of what they entail. It's easy for a person to call across to an adjoining desk, "Hey, is anyone doing anything with the communications link to the mainframe? A few people are having problems." Help Desks should also, ideally, be located within sight of the Help Desk manager. The manager will be easily accessible to resolve any issues that might crop up, and will be able to keep a closer eye on Help Desk function.

One option that you might consider is allowing Help Desk staff to work from home. This is not for everyone, and it is not possible in all environments. It might be worthwhile, however, if you have Help Desk staff who want to work from home and are disciplined enough to work on their own, the technology necessary to set this up is readily available, and communication links can be set up between all necessary contacts. You will have to balance the costs of the technology against any benefits you feel could be realized. Benefits might include happier and more productive staff, and a decrease in office space requirements. Disadvantages might be less opportunity for informal communication and information exchange with peers, being excluded from team activities due to physical distance, being forgotten when information is being passed around to Help Desk staff, and perhaps missing information critical to effective Help Desk function.

Automation is probably the best way to achieve a more pleasant Help Desk environment. If you can automate a lot of the routine, repetitive work and give customers the ability to solve some of their own problems, then the actual work that Help Desk staff do will be more interesting and challenging. The number of uninteresting and repetitive problems coming in will drop, and Help Desk staff can focus on analyzing problem trends and eliminating the causes of more major problems.

Look at the environment that your Help Desk is in and ask yourself whether you would want to work there. If not, maybe you're not getting as much out of your Help Desk as you could be, and you should consider changing a few things. The people to ask for advice about this are the Help Desk staff.

Summary

The structure of a successful Help Desk is tailored to the needs of the business it supports and the environment it functions in, and these vary significantly from company to company.

The most important roles in a Help Desk are those of manager and of front-line staff—the staff who answer the phones. A manager (or supervisor) whose sole responsibility is the Help Desk is necessary to oversee the function of the Help Desk, look after staff, set objectives, plan for the future, and market the Help Desk to customers and management. Front lines can be set up as minimal-function or full-function. Dispatch front lines, the former, will take calls and pass them on for resolution; no problem solving will take place at the point of the call. A high volume of calls can be answered, but these can pile up if there are not enough dedicated resources to resolve them. A Resolve front line will try to resolve calls that come in, and will only pass on ones that take too long to resolve or that require specialized skills. It provides instant resolution on most problems and is a much more interesting place to work, especially if automation is employed to eliminate the mundane, repetitive processes. Analysts can be rotated through the Resolve front line to gain a wider knowledge of technology, exposure to various parts of the business, and a better understanding of the customers.

The Help Desk analyst resolves problems, analyzes trends, answers questions, and performs various tasks as required by Help Desk calls. Other roles that might be part of your Help Desk, depending on the services you offer, are those for technology selection, sourcing and purchase, hardware configuration and installation, hardware maintenance, software installation and testing, and network monitoring.

Traditionally, Help Desk staff have come from IS, but this need not be the case. Other sources for potential Help Desk staff are trainers or customers who are power users. Within IS, sources might be software developers, technical support staff, application support staff, and operations staff. If you want the Help Desk to be seen as a desirable career move, and you want Help Desk staff to be able to move easily into other areas, you have to ensure that jobs within the Help Desk build skills and knowledge and offer a challenge. Automate or outsource as much of the routine work as possible.

Help Desk staff need to be trained properly and should not be forced to learn on the job. Learning on the job might mean picking up other people's bad habits or learning only how a tool is used by the Help Desk, not what it is capable of and what it might be used for in the future.

The number of staff you will need on your Help Desk will be determined by several factors: the breadth of services you provide, the complexity of your technological environment, how standardized (or non-standardized) your environment is, how new your environment is, the sophistication and knowledge of your customers, and the automation you employ. You also need to consider any data you can get on the number and complexity of Help Desk calls that have been received in the past.

Having a consolidated Help Desk rather than two or more Help Desks generally improves consistency of service and information sharing, and makes more effective use of tools and people. It's also more cost-effective. Distributed Help Desks do have their place, but care needs to be taken to ensure that the needs of the customers and the business are being satisfied as effectively as possible.

Don't underestimate the importance of physical environment to the morale, productivity, and well-being of your Help Desk staff. Make sure they have good furniture, the best tools possible, and a bright, spacious and pleasant working environment, and that they can communicate easily with each other. Try to locate the Help Desk near other groups that the staff regularly interface with.

CHAPTER THREE

Problem and Work Management

Each call coming into the Help Desk means that a customer is working at less than optimal productivity. Your job, as a Help Desk, is to get that customer up to full productivity as soon as possible. When the calls start coming fast and furiously, this is not easy. You start working on one problem, and then you get a customer who is absolutely frantic and who demands your immediate help. How do you decide who gets served first? First come first served doesn't make allowances for the fact that some problems are more important than others. You decide that the second call must be more important because the customer sounds so frantic, and you put the first request aside to work on the second. Before you get started, another call comes in that sounds even more frantic than the previous one, and the cycle starts over. You find yourself with several things put aside while you work frantically on several more. Calls start coming in from customers asking why their work hasn't been completed. You haven't logged anything because you haven't had time.

Your Help Desk is now totally out of control, as illustrated in Figure 3.1. The problems have taken control and are doing a good job managing you. You don't have a chance to resolve one before you have to drop it and start on another one—a cycle that's difficult to get out of. The number of calls will keep increasing, because you won't be able to finish everything properly and you aren't doing anything to make things better. You aren't logging many calls so you don't have statistics that can help you get a handle on what you're dealing with. How do you get out of this cycle? By putting a program of problem and work management in place.

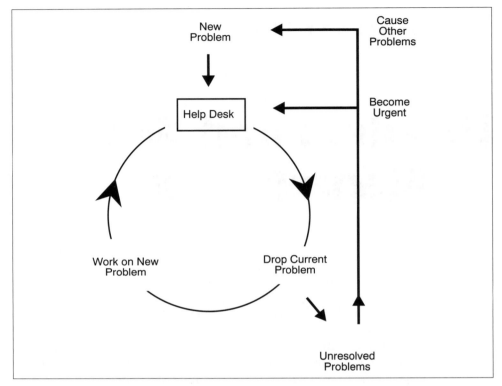

Figure 3.1 An out-of-control problem cycle.

There are several things you need to do to prevent problems from taking over:

- Know what is most important to the business and work on those things first.

- Set up and follow procedures to ensure correct and consistent service.

- Constantly evaluate Help Desk function to make sure that everything is working.

- Eliminate the need for as many of the calls as possible.

Those four points describe the most important components of effective Help Desk problem and work management: priorities, procedures, evaluation, and improvement.

If your priorities aren't well defined, Help Desk staff will work on the things that they think are important, which may bear no resemblance to what's in your plan, what you have committed to, or what is important to the business.

If your procedures aren't well defined, your customers will get different service depending on who answers the phone. A customer trying to type a letter might call up, extremely upset and frustrated, saying that the word processing software is not working properly. The Help Desk operator, intimidated by the upset customer, promises, "We'll get to it right away." Meanwhile, a customer who needs to do some stock trading via modem is waiting to get a problem with the transmission software fixed. The first problem gets priority over the second, even though the second is much more serious, and each of the customers gets a very different level of service.

Constantly evaluating how your Help Desk is working will ensure that any unbalanced priorities are quickly corrected and will address any issues with procedures that are incorrect or are not being followed. Evaluation also involves monitoring progress of planned work and making sure it gets done.

Planning improvements should be an ongoing function of your Help Desk. You have to be constantly looking for ways of reducing the number of calls and improving service to the customers. You want to be able to keep the number of calls under strict control. If the numbers start creeping up, you need to address the situation immediately and not wait until it is out of control.

Priorities

Somehow you need to ensure that your Help Desk resolves the problems that are most critical to the business before all others. At the same time, you want to make sure that the work you have planned to improve service to your customers gets done. Priorities will help you address both of these requirements. They will prevent the scenario of having every call become an emergency based on how upset the caller is, and having work started and then dropped midstream when something perceived as more important comes along. How angry a customer is should not play a part in the priority a problem gets, and there should be no "perceived" priorities—only clearly defined, well-understood ones.

Calls that are resolved by the Help Desk at point of call are commonly called incidents. They are resolved in the order that they are received. Calls that need to be passed on, or are not resolved right away for whatever reason, need to have a priority assigned. These calls can typically be broken down into the following categories:

- Problems:
  Problems are interruptions in service to customers. Something is wrong with hardware, software, or procedures, and as a result, the technology is not working as it should. Customers are prevented from achieving optimal productivity at their jobs.

- Requests:
  Customers making requests are asking for services that are part of the Help Desk's advertised list of services. These might include training, ordering PCs, and so on.

- Questions:
  Questions are queries about how to perform specific tasks using technology. Application questions are of the type, "How do I pull my spreadsheet into my word processing package?" Procedural questions are of the type, "How do I download a file from the mainframe?" or "How can I send this document to someone who is not on the LAN?" Consulting questions might include "What software should I use to create a newsletter?" or "Is there anything that can help me do this on a PC?"

Calls coming into the Help Desk are not the only thing you need to set priorities for. You need to make sure that work that you have planned, and perhaps some that you have not planned but that has become necessary, gets done. You have to be able to prioritize work, planned and unplanned, against everything else going on in your Help Desk.

- Planned work:
  Planned work is work that the Help Desk has committed to in its objectives. This might include upgrades to software or hardware, and work to eliminate problems or automate solutions.

- Unplanned work:
  Unplanned work is work that has not been planned for, but that has been made necessary by unforeseen circumstances. Often, unplanned work is necessary to prevent future problems. For example, an unexpected and significant increase in the number of users

storing information in the public files on the LAN server means that something needs to be done quickly to prevent a service interruption caused by lack of storage. Adding to or reorganizing storage may not have been planned for, but in these circumstances it takes priority over planned work.

In order to ensure that all of your Help Desk resources are not pulled into resolving problems, leaving you with no resources to do anything else that needs to be done, you need to set your priority structure so that your work and services have a priority at least equal to nonemergency problems, and you need to stick to it. This won't work, however, if you simply have too few staff. The problems, requests, questions, and planned work will pile up, unfinished, while Help Desk staff struggle to get out from under it all.

Your priorities also need to be in line with your strategy and objectives. They need to be working for you, not against you, in your efforts to carry out your strategy and reach your objectives. For example, if your strategy is to make customers self-sufficient, then you might want to place a lower priority on questions or problems of a learning type, and a higher priority on requests for training or coaching. If one of your objectives is to install a voice response unit, then that needs to have a priority at least as high as that of training and coaching requests. Figure 3.2 illustrates how a Help Desk might assign priorities.

Determining What's Important

Before you can establish priorities, you need to know what is most important to the business. Specifically, you need to know which systems or applications are most critical to the business and who the people are who use them. You also need to know what hardware is most critical to the business.

Critical systems or applications are those that the company you support needs to do its daily business. For example, shipping and receiving systems are critical for warehouses, point of sale systems are critical for stores, and airline reservation systems are critical for airlines. When any of these systems fail, there is no easy bypass. Large stores cannot function without their cash register systems—pulling out a calculator and tallying customer purchases by hand just wouldn't be practical, not to mention that inventory and sales activity information would be lost. Similarly, warehouses cannot ship anything when the systems that put

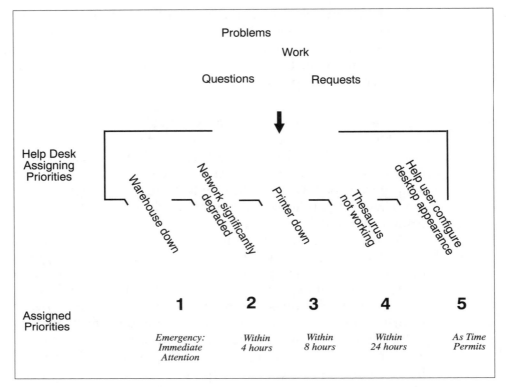

Figure 3.2 **Assigning priorities.**

their loads together and pull stock are down, and airlines have no way of tracking reservations without their reservation system. Each minute that these systems are nonfunctional means significant losses in revenue to the businesses involved. Problems must be fixed quickly.

Anything that prevents a user of a critical system from using that system also needs to be a high-priority problem. If a ticket agent's terminal goes down, that agent becomes inactive and cannot take calls. Fewer calls can get through, and therefore fewer reservations can be made. Business is impacted. If one cash register system is down in a store, the lineups at the other registers will be longer—store customers will have to wait in line longer and will be annoyed. Again, business suffers. Each of those users needs to be brought back up as soon as possible.

Critical hardware is hardware without which the business cannot function. For example, a server that runs a local area network supporting a function that takes in advertising for a daily paper would be considered a critical piece of hardware. Mainframes are critical by definition.

A good place to find this kind of information is in a company's disaster recovery plan. All of the most critical systems, hardware, and users will be there.

A Priority Scale

In defining priorities, you will need some kind of scale. A commonly used scale is one with values ranging from 1 to 5, where 1 denotes the highest priority and 5 the lowest. Sometimes priorities are built from a combination of scales and based on values such as impact and impairment, where impact indicates the impact of the problem on the business, and impairment describes the usability of the problem component (system, application, hardware). Regardless of the values used, what is most important in a scale is the clarity of the definition. The definition should make it clear to the person assigning priorities what the priority should be. Often, the priority will be obvious. "The warehouse is down," "no one can take any ads," or "the mainframe is down" is a pretty good indication that you have a serious, top-priority problem on your hands, while "the colors on my screen look kind of washed out" probably won't have you pushing the panic button. Other times, the priority will not be as easy to determine, and this is when a clear definition will help. If the definition refers to critical or noncritical components, then a list of critical components should accompany it. Response times are often tied into priority definitions to further clarify what each priority means. Service-level agreements use this kind of priority–response relationship to define and measure service levels.

Getting Support for Priorities

In order to honor priorities, you will need the cooperation of your customers, the rest of IS—specifically those areas within IS that work on resolving some of your calls—and your vendors. Customers must accept the fact that if an application more critical to the business than the one they are using goes down, then it will get priority over any problem they might have. They must accept that they cannot call the Help Desk up and whine or shout their way to a higher priority. The needs of the business must come first. IS areas that support the Help Desk—for example, application support areas—must be willing to abide by established priorities and allocate the necessary time and resources to fixing high-priority problems as quickly as possible. Vendors must understand your priorities when you call for help. They need to know how seriously you are affected by a problem and must be willing to respond to high priorities quickly, to honor service agreements.

To get this kind of cooperation, you need to communicate priorities so that everyone understands what the priorities are, the reasoning behind them, and their importance to the business. In fact, in setting up a priority structure, you should be getting input from or working with your customers, the rest of IS, and your vendors. The more involved they are in the original process, the more they will understand and buy into it. Figure 3.3 shows the ingredients required for a good priority definition.

Who Sets Priorities?

Part of the communication about priorities to customers, the rest of IS, and vendors should be information on who decides what priority a problem should have. Choices include the Help Desk, the customer, or the Help Desk and customer together. One Help Desk supporting a live retail environment gives the responsibility for setting priorities completely to the customers. When customers call in to report a problem to

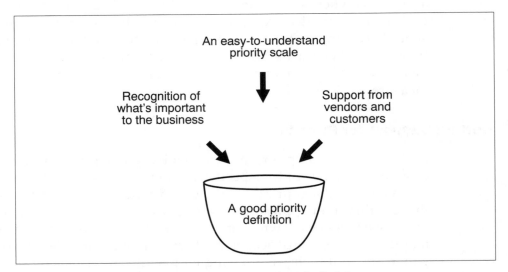

Figure 3.3 Ingredients for a good priority definition.

the voice response unit that front ends the Help Desk, they are asked to enter a priority from 1 (highest) to 5 (lowest). Priorities are clearly defined, well communicated, and understood by all customers. Another Help Desk within the same company has a clear understanding of the most important systems, applications, and users, and has chosen to set priorities itself. This seems to be the commonest choice for assigning priorities among Help Desks. According to the Help Desk Institute's 1993 Survey of Help Desk Practices, in approximately 47 percent of Help Desks, priorities are assigned by Help Desk staff or by persons that the call is passed on to. Another 31 percent of Help Desks assign priorities jointly with customers, and only 3 percent of Help Desks rely on customers to set priorities. The remaining Help Desks either do not prioritize calls or handle calls in the order in which they are received.

Establishing a Priority Structure for Problems

Along with information about which components (i.e., systems, applications, and hardware) and users are most critical to the business, a priority structure for problems needs to take into consideration the nature of the problem and the users and business it affects. Specifically, a priority structure for problems will take the following into account:

- The number of users affected and the criticality of those users.
- Whether service is degraded or completely shut down.
- Impact on the business.

Users Affected

A whole department, warehouse, or network that has lost service is a problem that needs immediate attention, much more so than a single user who has lost service. The more people who are affected by an outage, the more cost there will be in terms of time lost and work not done, and the greater the chance of impacting the business. There are exceptions, however, as not all users perform tasks of equal business importance. If the function a user performs is critical to the business, and a problem is stopping that user from performing that function, then that problem might merit a higher priority than one that affects several noncritical users. A critical user might be someone who relies on a PC with specialized software and communication links to do money management—buying and trading bonds. If this configuration is shut down for any length of time, the company could stand to lose a significant amount of money. Critical users are individual users who have a significant impact on the business when they cannot do their jobs.

Shut Down vs. Degraded Service

If service is still available, but slower than usual or limited in some way (e.g., some components are not working), the problem will get a lower priority than service that has been completely cut off. Degraded means that you are running, but not at full capacity. Shut down means that you are not running at all.

Impact on Business

Overriding all other considerations is impact on the business. If a business-critical function cannot be performed—for example, banking machines cannot be used, or the mainframe that runs everything is down—then its resolution must have the highest priority. Impact on the business involves potential income lost. If a newspaper can't take ads, or a stock broker can't buy or sell stock, there are severe financial repercussions involved. If a cash register can't function, sales can't be entered, and customers that are waiting impatiently might be lost forever. If, however, the result of a problem is that performance reports will be a day late, the financial impact on the business will be negligible. Having an impact on the business is defined as having a negative financial effect on the business—whether it be directly and immediately, or further into the future, such as by losing customers now. Operational systems such as order taking tend to have the biggest impact on the business, while administrative systems such as accounts receivable, although important, have less.

Using these three factors, along with information about which components and users are most important to the business, priority definitions can be built. These definitions will vary depending on how widely they apply (i.e., how general they must be), the scale chosen, and all of the factors that make each particular Help Desk environment unique. Following are three examples of different priority definitions, varying in width of coverage and in scale.

    The first example, shown in Table 3.1, is a priority definition for all problems coming into the Help Desk. In reality, this definition would be accompanied by a list of critical components and users.

Table 3.1 Priorities for Problems, Example 1

Priority	Definition	Example
1	Critical user(s) or component(s) down. Business is affected.	Warehouse systems have crashed. No merchandise is going into or coming out of the warehouse. As a result, business is severely affected.
2	Critical user(s) or component(s) degraded. Business is affected.	Response time on the local area network supporting staff responsible for taking ads has doubled for some reason. Number of ads that can be taken has decreased. Revenue is being lost.
3	Multiple noncritical users down or degraded. Business not affected.	One ring on the local area network has lost access to the company's electronic mail system.
4	Single noncritical user down or degraded, or noncritical component down or degraded. Business not affected.	A programmer is unable to print consistently.
5	Little or no impact. Problem could be cosmetic.	A customer is missing some of the standard Windows background patterns ("wallpaper").

The second priority definition, shown in Table 3.2, is one with a much narrower application: a single system (a cash register system). The definition for each priority is much more specific than in the previous example.

The third example, shown in Table 3.3, is designed for wide use and deals with a different kind of scale, which is based on impact and impairment. Impact is a measure of the business impact of the problem, while impairment describes how serious the problem is in terms of the remaining functionality of the problem component. A list of components classified as "critical" and "very critical" would have to accompany the definitions of impact. Help Desk action and final problem priority would depend on the combination of impact and impairment. For example, an impact 1, impairment 3 would get a lower priority than either an impact 1, impairment 1 or an impact 2, impairment 1.

Table 3.2 Priorities for Problems, Example 2

Priority	Definition
1 System Failure	Cannot use the registers to process customer transactions.
2 Off-line Registers	Registers are working but are off-line to the controller. Price lookup is not available.
3 Controller Functions	Certain controller functions such as cash balancing are not working—can continue with other daily functions. or Credit authorization is not available. or Sales cannot be transmitted to the store back-end computer (if this lasts for more than two days it becomes a priority 1). or Controller printer is not working. or Backup did not end successfully.
4 Register Hardware	Register hardware such as the printer, cash drawer, or keyboard is not working.
5 General Questions	Have a question about system operations. or Require general information.

Establishing a Priority Structure for Questions

Questions are a bit of a dilemma for the Help Desk. You want to help your customers with their questions, but you want them to be as self-sufficient as possible, both for their own good and for the good of the Help Desk. The better they understand the tools they are using, the better use they can make of them. For example, customers using word processing software will not be getting the most out of the software or making the best use of their time if all they know how to do is to enter and spell-check text. They won't know about time-saving features such as linking and embedding data from other software packages and creating templates for entering data. Customers who do understand their tools will make fewer calls to the Help Desk, lessening the Help Desk call load and leaving resources free for more serious issues.

Table 3.3   Priorities for Problems, Example 3

Impact	Definition
1 Severe	Component is very critical to the business; multiple users are negatively affected.
2 Major	Component is critical to the business; multiple users are negatively affected.
3 Limited	Component is not critical to business; few users are negatively affected.

Impairment	Definition
1	Component is shut down; no bypass or alternative available.
2	Component severely degraded. Limited function.
3	Component degraded but usable, or bypass or alternative available.

What you want to discourage, as a Help Desk, is having customers try to learn how to use a tool through calls to the Help Desk. This is a waste of time for the Help Desk, which should be spending its time on more serious problems, and a waste of time for the customer, who is spending a lot of time trying to figure the tool out. What would make much more sense, from a cost and effectiveness point of view, is for the customer to take the appropriate training. Priorities should discourage these kinds of calls.

There are exceptions, however. If you are dealing with a critical user who needs a question answered in order to perform a business function, then that question needs a higher priority, regardless of whether it is the result of lack of proper training. In this case, the question of training can be addressed later, using information gathered from call tracking. (This is one example of why it is important to log everything).

Using the same scale of priority definitions for problems as in Table 3.1, a sample priority definition for questions is shown in Table 3.4.

Establishing a Priority Structure for Requests

Your Help Desk should only be responding to requests that are included in your list of services. If you receive requests for services not on your

Table 3.4 Sample Priority Definition for Questions

Priority	Definition	Example
2	Critical user can't get business done.	User needs to know how to download critical financial data from the mainframe so that it can be transmitted via PC and modem.
5	Everything else.	"How do I put a border around my document?"

list, then you need to refuse them by suggesting where customers might go to get the service required. Tracking such requests will indicate whether you should think about changing or adding to your services. Requests that are on your list of services will require a priority, but they may be channeled off to specific areas—such as PC ordering—that will be setting the priority, possibly with the customer's input.

Regardless of who is assigning them, priorities for requests must be flexible enough to handle any exceptions and emergencies that come up. For example, someone might ask, "Please change my profile to allow me to access the figures I need to prepare a special performance report for the president. It's needed ASAP." A critical business decision might be waiting on that report.

You need to be flexible, but you also need some method for controlling "emergency" requests. If all the requests coming in are emergencies, then 99.9 percent of them probably aren't. You can try explaining to your customers that their emergency means that someone else loses priority—some other part of the business might have to wait for something. If this isn't enough to get them to downgrade the importance of their (nonemergency) requests, you will have to go to some other kind of control, such as management sign-offs or having the customers speak to the groups that will be affected by their "emergency" priorities. For example, if department A calls and asks for ten PCs "in a hurry; this is an emergency," you might tell them that you will service their request if they get approval from department B, who has also ordered some PCs but is ahead of them in the priority queue. Letting the customers sort out the priorities in this way usually means that the real priority emerges. (Telling a Help Desk that this is an emergency is one thing, but having to explain it to the manager of a department who will have to wait for PCs is quite a different

Table 3.5 Sample Priority Definition for Requests

Priority	Definition	Example
2	Emergency requirement.	Install special software ASAP to allow the business to put on a special promotion to respond to the competition.
3	All other requests for services supported by the Help Desk.	Order a PC.

thing.) It also means that the Help Desk is not trying to prioritize for the business. The business is performing this function itself.

If customers are having a hard time accepting priorities, you might want to take the issues off-line and visit the specific customers or groups individually. You can take the time to explain how much lead time is necessary for the Help Desk to service their requests. You can also show them how their "emergencies" affect the business, and how additional or improved planning on their part would ensure that their requests get serviced without a negative impact on other parts of the business that might have problems or requests of higher priority.

A sample priority definition for requests is shown in Table 3.5.

Establishing a Priority Structure for Work

Planned work needs to get a high enough priority to ensure that it gets done, especially if the resources doing the work are the same as those taking care of the problems, questions, and requests. You have objectives and service-level agreements to meet and improvements to make, none of which will get done if you give work too low a priority. Problems, questions, and requests will drain away your resources. If the staff members you allocate for planned work are different from those handling the day-to-day calls, you most likely won't have the problem of staff being pulled away to work on calls. What you might have to face, however, is resource drain from unplanned work: work that the Help Desk has not planned for in this time period (usually a quarter). Some unplanned work is inevitable. A technological environment rarely stands still, and things change at a pace that cannot always be planned. You may need to do some work to stop a recurring problem that is causing a lot of calls, or you may need to do some maintenance to prevent problems in the near future. Other unplanned work does not have as much business value—for example, Help Desk staff spending time investigating interesting software, or upgrading Help Desk software to get the new features, regardless of the fact the work was not scheduled until next quarter. You may find that staff don't even tell you about unplanned work, preferring to do it on the side, not considering that it is ultimately interfering with the business. Unplanned work should take precedence over planned work only if it is in the interests of the business for it to do so.

Planned work and unplanned work that must be done in the interests of the business should get the same priority as problems not affecting the business (a 3 in our previous examples). Other unplanned work should be put off until it can be included in a plan.

A sample priority definition for work is shown in Table 3.6.

Table 3.6 Sample Priority Definition for Work

Priority	Definition	Example
3	Planned work.	Upgrade the local area network operating system.
	Unplanned work that is necessary to prevent serious problems.	There has been an unexpected increase in the number of users putting data on a shared server, which has resulted in increased network traffic and a decrease in available space. In order to prevent potential problems that may bring individual users or the whole network down, a server upgrade is required. The server upgrade was not planned for in this quarter.
	Unplanned work that will resolve recurring problems that are putting a strain on Help Desk resources.	Customers using DOS applications often have problems printing. When this happens, Help Desk staff must reset the printer interface. In order to get rid of this problem, which is causing an increasing number of Help Desk calls, upgrading the DOS applications to the Windows versions has been moved forward and will replace some other planned work.

Putting It All Together

If the same staff are handling problems, work, questions, and requests (or some combination of these), you'll need to ensure that the priorities make sense in relation to each other. Your resulting priority structure might look something like Table 3.7.

Table 3.7 Sample Priority Structure

Priority	Problems	Work	Questions	Requests
1	Critical user(s) or component(s) down. Business is affected.	N/A	N/A	N/A
2	Critical user(s) or component(s) degraded. Business is affected.	N/A	Critical user can't get business done. Business is affected.	Emergency requirement. Business is affected.
3	Multiple, noncritical users down or degraded. Business not affected.	Planned work. or Unplanned work that is necessary to prevent serious problems. or Unplanned work that will resolve recurring problems that are putting a strain on Help Desk resources.	N/A	All other requests for services supported by the Help Desk.
4	Single, noncritical user down or degraded. or Noncritical component down or degraded. Business not affected.	N/A	N/A	N/A
5	Little or no impact. Problem could be cosmetic.	N/A	Everything else.	N/A

Changing Priorities Once They Are Set

Occasionally, you may want to change priorities of problems, requests, or work. Priorities may have been entered in error, or they may be upgraded to a more severe level as time goes on. For example, something that is down for an hour may not affect the business, but if that same thing is down for half a day, it may. (An example of this is a function that has to be performed in the morning, but when in the morning does not matter.) You might want to change priorities when you put in a temporary fix that lessens the problem's severity but leaves the problem still outstanding. For example, if you run out of direct access storage (DASD), you might borrow a pack from somewhere else to use while you clean up existing DASD or purchase more.

How long something has been in a queue is often used as a factor in deciding when to change priorities, but you want to be very careful about this. If something has been in a queue for too long, that might be an indication that it is of such a low priority that you shouldn't be doing it, that you don't have enough staff to handle your workload, or that your priorities are unbalanced for your environment. Rather than unthinkingly upgrading priorities of older problems and requests, you should address the cause of their being in the queue for so long.

Changes in priorities need to be controlled carefully to make sure that they do not interfere with your priority structure and the distribution of work. If you are constantly changing priorities, then your priority structure is not working and should be revised. Changing priorities should be an exception, not a regular occurrence.

Flexibility is key to making your priorities work. You don't want your priority definition to add needless red tape or to become a bottleneck, but you do want to make sure that the important things get handled before all others. Be sensitive to the needs of your customers and the business you support.

Procedures

Procedures are necessary to ensure Help Desk success, especially in the following areas:

- Consistency and correctness of service. Help Desk staff aren't making up the rules as they go along. If customers know that they're going to get the results that they need when they call the Help Desk, they're going to keep calling the Help Desk. They won't be tempted to go elsewhere to get help.

- Procedures also help customers make better use of the Help Desk. If the Help Desk asks for specific information each time a customer calls, customers will start having that information ready when they call. This will save the Help Desk time and get the customer's call processed faster.

- Having documented procedures in place also makes automation easier and use of Help Desk tools more effective. A process that is documented is much easier to automate than one that exists only as hearsay or in several versions. A Help Desk tool that routes logged Help Desk calls into various queues depending on who will be resolving the calls is useful only if procedures are in place to ensure that the calls are picked off of the queue and resolved.

Figure 3.4 shows how quality and accuracy improve as definition of procedures increases. Automation is considered the highest level of procedure definition.

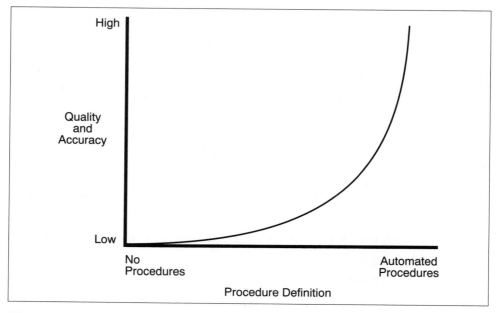

Figure 3.4 How procedures affect quality and accuracy.

Procedures are most effective when developed and documented by the people who currently perform them or who will be performing them. Internal procedures for tasks such as taking calls, resolving problems, and handling requests should be set up by the Help Desk staff who do these tasks on a day-to-day basis. Any procedures that involve other departments should be set up jointly with people from those departments. People who will be using procedures have a vested interest in making sure that they make sense, are easy to follow, and can be updated easily. Documenting procedures gives the people doing the documenting a greater understanding of the procedures, and can lead to identification of possible improvements, inconsistencies, and errors.

Customers need to be informed of any procedures that they need to follow when calling the Help Desk—any sign-offs they need when purchasing a PC, for example. You may want or need to involve them in developing these procedures, as well.

Documenting procedures in a way that ensures they will be used and can be easily updated is often difficult. Getting them down on paper (or on-line) is the easy part. Getting people to use them is the challenge. The only way to guarantee that a procedure is followed consistently is to automate it. Assuming that you have not automated all of your procedures, there are some things you can do to help ensure that your procedures are referred to and used:

- Keep procedures as short and simple as possible.

- Keep procedures in a central library accessible to all staff. In the same place, keep information that your procedures might refer to, such as priority definitions and routing information.

- Have regular reviews and revisions of your procedures—keep them current and alive. Assign someone responsibility for both reviewing and revising procedures. You can rotate this task.

- Integrate your procedures into any Help Desk tools you use, wherever possible. Let the tool prompt staff through the procedure, or use the tool to automate the procedure.

- Have Help Desk staff create procedures. Give them ownership.

- Make sure Help Desk staff understand what role they play in each procedure.

There are also some things you should avoid doing when setting procedures:

- Do not duplicate information that is stored and maintained elsewhere. Cross-reference it, instead. The duplication of what already exists will create a maintenance nightmare. This means that a set of notes on how to use software, or any form of software documentation, has no place in procedures. It makes more sense to go to the original documentation for that information.

- Don't attempt to train people in the use of tools in your procedures. This is ineffective as a training method, and leads to ungainly procedures that are hard to maintain. The same applies to skills such as communication, dealing with customers, and so on. People should not be learning skills from procedures—they should be getting those skills from training programs. Training programs will teach people what tools are capable of, not just how tools are used in a specific procedure. Training in skills such as communication and dealing with customers will involve practice and feedback—a much more effective way of learning a skill than reading about it.

You need to have procedures in place to describe how to deliver each of the services you offer. These will vary from Help Desk to Help Desk, depending on the services offered, but some common ones may include:

- Handling a call.
- Resolving a problem.
- Answering a question.
- Servicing a request.
- Responding to emergencies.
- Informing customers of system problems.
- Reporting.
- Disaster recovery.
- Communicating with other Help Desks.

If your Help Desk makes use of some kind of Help Desk software, then you may not need procedures for many of these. They can be programmed to happen automatically.

You also need procedures for those internal processes specific to your Help Desk. These might include any activities that need to be performed at the beginning and ending of Help Desk shifts, work status reporting, getting fill-in help for staff that call in sick, and so on.

Handling a Call

Information necessary to describe call-handling procedures includes:

- Greeting to be used
- Call logging
    What to log (everything!)
    How to log
- Assigning a priority
- Routing a call
    When to route a call
    How to route a call
    Where to route the call

Your Help Desk software can probably be set up to prompt you through logging and routing a call so you won't need to document any details on these tasks. Information on whom to route calls to can exist in a central procedures library (see Table 3.8). Depending on the Help Desk system you have, you might be able to store and update this information in the system itself.

Resolving a Problem

Procedures for problem resolution include details on:

- Picking up a problem
    How to take ownership of a problem
- Checking for trends
- Getting help
- Closing a problem

Checking for trends could be accomplished by your Help Desk system, depending on its sophistication. "Getting help" could suggest whom to go to, or what systems or documents to reference for further help in specific areas.

Handling Questions

Procedures for questions might include:

Table 3.8   Example of Routing Information

Situation	System	Route to
EMERGENCY: Call immediately!	Hardware	Operations: x4236 Pager: 334-7701
	Software	Software Support: x3345 Pager: 334-9901
	Network	Network Support: x4334 Pager: 334-9978
	Not sure	Operations Mgr.: x2909 Software Mgr.: x4443 Pager: 334-8890
Problem	Hardware	Hardware Maintenance Queue HM1
	Standard PC desktop software	Help Desk Analysts Queue HD1
	Distribution systems	Application Support Queue DS1
	Accounting	Accounting Support Queue AC1
Question	Standard PC software; PC-related processes	Help Desk Analysts Queue HD1
Request	Purchase PCs	Help Desk: PC Purchase Queue HD4
	Move PCs	Help Desk: Hardware Maintenance Queue HM1
	Change PC configuration	Help Desk Analysts Queue HD1

- Checking for trends:
  See whether this customer had called previously with questions and perhaps required some training.

- Making recommendations:
  Recommend training to customers. This includes referencing courses available and giving (or sending) the customer all of the

required information. If your Help Desk is really cracking down on training questions, this procedure might involve something a little more formal, such as sending a memo off to the customer's manager.

- Getting help:
  Where to get further information on specific subjects.
- Closing a question.

Servicing Requests

Procedures for servicing requests (that are on the Help Desk list of services) include information on what the Help Desk must do and provide and what is required from the customer. For example, in the case of PC purchases, the customer might be required to get senior management sign-off on a purchase requisition before submitting a request for PC purchase to the Help Desk. In turn, the Help Desk would place the order and give the customer an estimated installation date.

Handling Emergencies

Emergencies are a priority of 1 or better. Procedures for handling emergencies need to include information on how to set escalation procedures into motion, and on whom to keep informed at what stages of the emergency.

Informing Customers of System Problems

Procedures to inform customers of system problems typically include information on whose responsibility this communication is, what media to use to broadcast information, and to whom to broadcast it.

Reporting

Reporting procedures contain information on what to report on, how frequently, and to whom. Depending on the sophistication of your Help Desk software, you may be able to set your system up so that reports are generated at preset intervals and even sent to the appropriate people automatically and electronically.

Disaster Recovery

Disaster recovery procedures are usually part of larger, company-wide procedures (and documents), and are best set up in conjunction with any dedicated disaster recovery groups.

Communicating with Other Help Desks

Communicating with the other Help Desks (if any) within your organization is necessary to ensure that all Help Desks are kept informed of what is going on in the technological environment so that they can resolve customer problems more effectively. They can maximize the problem-solving information at their disposal and minimize duplication of effort. Things that your Help Desk may want to communicate to other Help Desks include:

- Major problems in your area of responsibility.
- Major problems in their areas that have come to your attention.
- Problems that were reported to you but that need to resolved by other Help Desks.
- Changes in your Help Desk environment, including new or up-graded technology and services.

Other Help Desks would have corresponding procedures to make sure they communicated the same information to you.

Evaluation

Evaluating the activities of your Help Desk on an ongoing basis is necessary to ensure that your Help Desk is functioning effectively. Evaluation checks that:

- Procedures are correct, understood, and being followed.
- Priorities are balanced and are being followed.
- Service delivered is accurate and is accomplished within an acceptable time frame.
- Planned work is completed.

Procedures

Written procedures are in constant danger of being ignored and forgotten. You have to make sure that your procedures are alive, that they are updated constantly, and that they change as your environment changes. You can assign someone the task of reviewing procedures with the Help Desk team every month or so at one of your team meetings. If you have procedures with other departments—they may be providing second-level support—you need to review those with the people in those departments to make sure that the procedures still make sense. You also have to make sure that procedures are being followed, both within your team and in other departments. There will be a better chance that this is happening if your procedures make sense, are understood, and change with the environment. Your Help Desk system will give you an indication of whether people are following procedures. It will report on logs not closed properly, problems not fixed properly, information missing, and so on. A daily or weekly review of the status of the Help Desk logs should bring these situations to light.

Priorities

When priorities are unbalanced, or are not being followed properly, you could find yourself with too many high-priority calls or calls that are waiting too long for service. Help Desk staff might be assigning too high a priority to calls that do not merit it. This could be the result of anxious users convincing the Help Desk staff that the problem is really severe, or just of a lack of understanding by Help Desk staff of what constitutes a high priority. You might also have a situation where the priorities assigned are too low. The logged call might sit in a queue forever, waiting to be serviced. You need to use your Help Desk system statistics to keep an eye out for these situations so that your customers get service based on what is most important for the business. If your priorities aren't working, change them—as your environment changes, they may need to be updated. Make sure that Help Desk staff, other support staff, vendors, and customers understand the priorities.

Service

When a problem is resolved and a log closed, you need to make sure that the customer was satisfied with the resolution—that it was performed correctly and within an acceptable amount of time. One way to do this is to send your customers notices when logs are closed, informing them that the problem was resolved and telling them to call the Help Desk if they were not satisfied. Your Help Desk system may be able to do this automatically. You want to take all customer complaints seriously and look for trends. There could be a problem with a particular staff member not understanding or following procedures, or you could have problems with a specific customer who feels that his or her priority should be higher than anyone else's. Either way, the Help Desk manager needs to get involved to rectify the situation. A customer might need an explanation of the priorities, or a staff member might need an update on procedures or some training.

Planned Work

Amid all that is going on in the busy Help Desk environment, you need to make sure that your planned work is not buried under a pile of problems. Have weekly updates with the people doing the work so that you are kept abreast of any roadblocks. Adjust your other Help Desk activities as necessary to make sure that your work gets done. This might involve some negotiations with management for more staff or tools. If you have been logging all calls, you will have the statistics to back you up.

Figure 3.5 shows an evaluation checklist to help evaluate Help Desk performance on an ongoing basis.

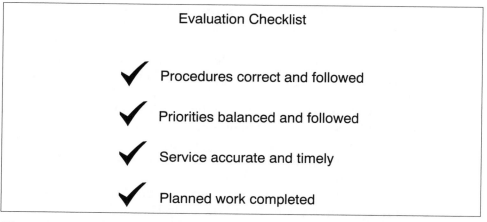

Figure 3.5 Evaluating the performance of your Help Desk.

Improvement

As well as making sure that your Help Desk is working as it should, you need to look constantly to improvements, to the future. Wherever possible, you need to stop problems before they happen:

- Be part of the implementation and change management process. Know when new systems are being implemented and when existing systems are being changed.
- Get involved in setting standards. Be on any standards committees that exist.
- Be part of disaster recovery planning. Make sure that procedures are in place for short-term disasters, such as failure of major hardware or software.
- Keep the Help Desk up to date on new tools, customer applications, and so on. Make sure that staff know what's happening in the Help Desk and the customer environments.
- Keep the Help Desk staff trained.
- Set up relationships with your vendors.
- Keep an eye on trends, good and bad.
- Listen to your customers and know what they need.

Change Management

Knowing when new systems are being implemented can prepare you for any initial problems. Better yet, you can be involved in the quality control of the new system. Be involved in any implementation meetings and make sure that the concerns of the Help Desk are heard. Also make sure that staff are available to support the application being put into place, and that they understand and will follow Help Desk procedures. Once the new system goes in, monitor calls and give the application people feedback as to how clean the system was. This will help them improve for next time, and will give you ideas on what to bring up at the next implementation meetings that you will attend. The same goes for changes to existing systems. If you are part of the change management process, you will know when systems are being changed, and can prepare accordingly and be part of quality control. Involve yourself and the Help Desk wherever possible—in acceptance testing if this makes sense, and in any promotion meetings. Send call statistics back to the maintenance group for change so that they can see what the quality was.

Standards

Standards generally make life on a Help Desk easier. They specify a finite number of products to support. Getting involved in setting and maintaining standards makes sense from a Help Desk point of view. You are close to the customers. You know the products they use and the problems they have with them, and you know what they want and need to do their jobs. You also know the problems that you are having with the performance of the hardware and software that you support. All of this information is extremely valuable for setting standards. You know what your customers need, what they do and don't like, and you know what technology is working and what is giving you problems. You will be able to help set standards that meet the needs of the customers, help ensure a stable technological environment, and help reduce Help Desk calls.

Disaster Recovery

When disaster strikes and a critical hardware or software component goes down, you will be on the line to get the problem fixed as soon as possible. You need to have recovery procedures in place for every critical component, and you need to make sure that everyone involved understands these procedures—Help Desk staff, other IS support staff, vendors, and customers. If this is not a Help Desk responsibility, you should be involved in making sure that it happens. Critical hardware should be covered by stringent service-level agreements with vendors, or a backup should be available on site. Critical software and data should have easily accessible backups should it get corrupted. You should also be involved in Disaster Recovery planning to help ensure that everything is covered. Your Help Desk experience will give you an understanding of impacts of outages, who is affected, and how long recovery takes. This kind of information is vital to recovery planning.

Keeping Up to Date

The technology environment changes very quickly; new products and processes are constantly being introduced. Keeping abreast of these will help ensure that the Help Desk is aware of and can take advantage of products that will improve service, solve a particular problem that the

Help Desk is having, or cut costs. A good way of keeping up with this kind of information is to send Help Desk staff, in turns, to conferences, user groups, and trade shows, and ask them to report on what they saw. This will not only bring valuable information back to the Help Desk, but will give staff some added interest to their jobs, and exercise their communication skills. As well as keeping up to date on the Help Desk environment, Help Desk staff should know what is going on in their customer environment. They need to know what their customers do, what business initiatives are taking place, and what systems are in the works. This information will affect what needs to be supported, and may affect selection of Help Desk tools. It will also give staff a greater understanding of problems when customers call in. They will have an idea of what the customer does, what the system does, and what impact problems have. If it is not possible for staff to meet with customer areas regularly, make sure you get them this information. Share it in team meetings. Have customers come into team meetings and explain what their areas do and how the Help Desk affects them.

Training

Training is just about the easiest thing in the technology world to put off. Yet lack of training is a great productivity reducer. If you don't get trained on how to use a software package properly, chances are that you aren't using it properly. If you don't get trained on how to handle customer calls, then maybe you aren't handling them as well as you could be. Make sure you don't fall into this trap with your Help Desk. Don't accept from people that they don't have time for training. It is their job to provide the best service possible, and they can't do that if they haven't been trained properly. Set training plans and make sure that they are adhered to.

Relationships with Vendors

Vendors can be valuable allies and resources. If you foster good relationships with them, keep them up to date on what is happening inside your company, and take the time to set up service-level agreements where possible, then you will have a better chance of getting a quick response when you have a problem. If you don't do any of these things, then there is no guarantee that you will get any kind of response when you have a problem and need their help.

Trends

Trends are a good barometer for helping to determine Help Desk direction. Keep a close eye on all Help Desk call reporting and constantly look for trends. Be aware of why calls are increasing or decreasing so that you can do something to stop the trend or encourage it. If the number of calls increased significantly because of a software upgrade, find out why. Was it lack of customer training? Were customers notified? Was the quality of the upgrade poor? Was it installed properly? When you have your answer, you can make sure that the same thing doesn't happen again for the next upgrade. If the number of calls decreases because of a training program you sponsored, then you may want to consider sponsoring other kinds of training programs as well, or offering this one again for people who didn't take it the first time.

Listening to Your Customers

Finally, listen to your customers. If you give them a chance, they will tell you, loudly and clearly, what they need, what they're satisfied with, and what they're not satisfied with. You can use this information to improve your Help Desk, to make it more valuable to the business. You can also take this information to other areas—areas that develop or maintain systems, areas that train customers. If a system does not do exactly what a customer needs, or is too slow or too cumbersome, the customer may, in frustration, let you know. You, in turn, can take this information to the IS area responsible for the system. They may not be aware of the problem; they may be able to solve it without much effort. Customers might also be asking for expanded Help Desk services. Perhaps they are working later hours and need the Help Desk to be there for them during those hours. You can use their input to help justify the cost of additional Help Desk hours. If you listen to your customers, they will tell you how to improve service.

Figure 3.6 summarizes the components of improvement. Looking ahead, continuously planning for the future and for improvements, will help ensure that your Help Desk will be able to continue handling the support requirements of your customers and the business as those requirements grow and change. You will be improving the technological environment for your customers, making them more self-sufficient and more productive. The Help Desk will be recognized as an integral and essential part of the business.

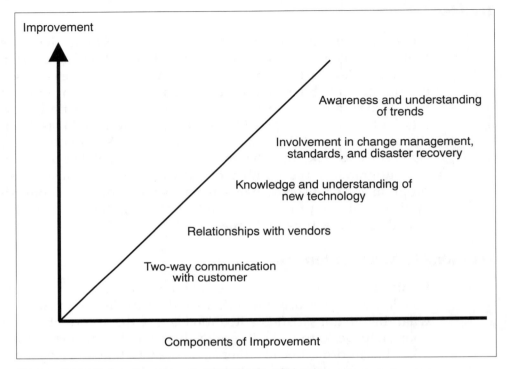

Figure 3.6   Ensuring ongoing Help Desk improvement.

Summary

You need effective problem- and work-management techniques on your Help Desk to ensure that you are not being managed by your problems. The most important components of effective Help Desk problem and work management are:

- Priorities: know what is most important to the business and work on those things first.
- Procedures: set up and follow procedures to ensure correct and consistent service.
- Evaluation: constantly evaluate Help Desk function to make sure that everything is working.
- Improvement: eliminate the need for as many of your calls as possible.

Priorities will help you ensure that your Help Desk resolves the problems that are most critical to the business before all others, and that the work you have planned to improve service to your customers gets done. Priorities need to be established for problems, requests, and questions that cannot be immediately resolved by the front line of the Help Desk. They also need to be established for planned work, and for work that has not been planned for but that has been made necessary by unforeseen growth or changes. Before you can establish priorities, you need to know what is most important to the business: critical systems, critical users, and critical hardware.

A priority structure for problems needs to take into account the number of users affected by a problem and the criticality of those users, whether the problem has degraded service or completely shut it down, and the impact of the problem on the business. Priorities for questions will tend to be low except when the customer needs the answer to a question to perform a vital function. Priorities for requests (such as purchasing a PC) will typically be determined jointly by the area handling the request and the customer. Planned work needs to have a priority at least equal to nonemergency Help Desk calls. Changes in priorities should be the exception, rather than the rule, and need to be controlled carefully to make sure that they do not interfere with your priority structure and the distribution of work.

Establishing Help Desk procedures for each process involved in providing service to the customers will help ensure consistency of service and correctness of action. Procedures will also help customers make better use of the Help Desk, make automation easier, and make use of Help Desk tools more effective. Procedures should be developed and documented by the people who currently perform them or who will be performing them. Documented procedures should be concise, reviewed regularly, integrated with Help Desk tools where possible, and created and understood by Help Desk staff. They should not duplicate information or attempt to train people in tool use.

Evaluating the activities of your Help Desk is an ongoing process that is necessary to ensure that your Help Desk is functioning effectively. It ensures that procedures are correct, understood, and being followed; priorities are balanced and are being followed; service delivered is accurate and accomplished within an acceptable time frame; and planned work is completed.

As well as making sure that your Help Desk is working as it should, you need to look constantly to improvements and to the future. Wherever possible, you need to stop problems before they happen:

- Be part of the implementation and change management process. Know when new systems are being implemented and when existing systems are being changed.
- Get involved in setting standards. Be on any standards committees that exist.
- Be part of disaster recovery planning. Make sure that procedures are in place for short-term disasters, such as failure of major hardware or software.
- Keep the Help Desk up to date on new tools, customer applications, and so on. Make sure they know what's happening in the Help Desk and the customer environments.
- Keep the Help Desk staff trained.
- Set up relationships with your vendors.
- Keep an eye on trends, good and bad.
- Listen to your customers and know what they need.

Looking ahead, continuously planning for the future and for improvements, will help ensure that your Help Desk will be able to continue handling the support requirements of your customers and the business as those requirements grow and change.

CHAPTER FOUR

Tracking

Tracking information might seem tedious, but the paybacks are tremendous. The information you can get from your Help Desk operation contains the blueprint you need to improve your level of service, and to improve the technology environment of your customers. Tracked information can tell you everything from how many front-line staff you need at any point during the day to how many and which PCs need to be upgraded in order to support a client/server system that is being planned for release on the network. If you want to operate a successful Help Desk in an environment of any appreciable size, you have no choice but to track. In a complex environment you simply cannot know what is going on without tracking; tracking tools can see things that you need to know but that you cannot possibly see. For example, a network management system can detect a faulty cable in a very complex network and tell you exactly where it is before anyone even notices a problem. If you were not tracking network performance, it might take significantly longer to find and resolve the cable problem. First, you would have to know that a cable was defective, and you could not know this until problems started occurring. You might not suspect that a cable was causing the problems—you might spend a significant amount of time checking other components. Once you realized that the cause was probably a cable, you would have to find out which cable was malfunctioning. You could be in the network for a long time, pulling cables, testing equipment, and wishing you had listened to your mother and become a doctor.

Tracking information cannot possibly be done manually. Gone are the days of keeping lists on paper or in SPF datasets—today's environments are just too large and too complex. You need tools to do the tracking for you. Tools range from simple standalone components, such as network "sniffers" used to detect cable problems, to completely integrated net-

101

work management systems that take an ongoing automatic inventory of hardware and software assets, monitor all components of the network, notify Help Desk staff of any problems, and even recommend solutions.

What Can Tracking Do for You?

Before you even think about what kind of information you should be tracking, you need to decide what you want to accomplish by tracking. Some possibilities are as follows:

- Identify trends in hardware and software performance.
- Manage hardware and software assets.
- Manage network performance.
- Manage vendor performance.
- Identify candidate processes for automation and outsourcing.
- Identify customers needing training.
- Build a problem/solution database.
- Identify recurring problems for elimination.
- Identify major problems before they occur.
- Manage Help Desk function.
- Keep customers informed.
- Provide the information necessary for charge back.
- Measure Help Desk performance.
- Justify improvements.

Identify Trends in Hardware and Software Performance

If you are tracking hardware involved in problems, you will be able to identify specific brands and models of hardware that keep appearing as causes of problems. For example, if a specific type of monitor keeps appearing as a problem, you will be aware of it and will be able to do something about it. You can notify the vendor for some kind of resolution, and you can stop future purchases of this kind of equipment. Customers who have that brand of monitor but have not yet experienced a problem can be notified, and if necessary, their equipment can be replaced. If you weren't tracking this information, each incidence of the problem hardware might be treated as a separate problem, and it might be awhile before any trend was noticed. Purchases of the defective hardware would continue, and customers owning that hardware would not have any idea that it was defective until a problem happened. You couldn't take advantage of the your statistics to negotiate a resolution with the vendor.

In the same way, software involved in problems needs to be tracked so that trends are identified. If a software release is installed with an undetected bug, and several people start running into that bug, the Help Desk will know. The specific software will keep appearing in problem logs, and the trend will be noted in reports or queries. The vendor can be notified that the software needs fixing, and other customers can be notified that the problem exists and told what is being done about it. They can also be notified of any bypasses available. Customers won't have to call the Help Desk, and won't be nearly as upset (if at all) about the problem because they were prepared for it. This would be true of software developed in-house, as well. The problem information could be fed back to the development group so that they could make a fix and look at improving their testing and quality control. In fact, the number of calls logged against the software would be one measure of the quality of job that was done.

Trends can be positive also. If you're tracking hardware and software involved in problems, you will know, by default, which hardware and software were not involved in any problems. For software, this is positive feedback to the quality control of the implementation. For hardware, these are components that you might want to recommend that you keep buying.

Manage Hardware and Software Assets

Businesses have a lot of money invested in their software and hardware assets. In order to safeguard this investment, they need to know what each asset looks like, where it is at any point in time, how much it is costing, and what value it is providing. They want to make sure that assets are maintained properly and upgraded when necessary so that they are getting as much value as possible out of them. Asset management is not something that IS does for its own good—it is a business requirement.

Managing assets involves keeping track of hardware and software inventory. Since the advent of PCs and all of the related hardware and software that came with them, this has become a distinctly nontrivial task. PC equipment is small and light and can go wherever you go—which means that it can go out the door with a thief, who might even be an employee. If you aren't tracking it regularly, you won't know what you have, where it's supposed to be, and what might be missing—stealing might be going on for quite a while before you notice it. Software is easy to install on PCs, and there is an abundance of it. It is also easy to copy. If you aren't tracking what is on your PCs, you could one day wake up to find your environment infested with viruses or your company charged with software piracy.

Keeping track of inventory will provide you with the vital statistics of your hardware to help you plan for upgrades. You will be able to find all of the PCs in need of memory, processor, or hard drive upgrades before a new system that needs these is installed. You can prevent people from running into problems that are due to inadequate systems. If your hardware performance tracking has identified a piece of hardware that you are consistently having problems with, you can find out where the rest of that hardware is and who is using it. You can notify these customers and, if necessary, replace the hardware. As time goes on, you will be able to find and upgrade or replace PCs that are outdated. You will be able to recycle PCs that have been replaced by more powerful ones.

Keeping track of the software in your systems will help you monitor and get rid of unauthorized software. You won't be in danger of having software in your organization that you are not authorized to use, or perhaps have not even paid for. This has become a serious issue for software vendors, who are losing significant revenue through pirated copies of their software. They are serious about prosecuting offenders, and you want to make sure that your company won't be facing charges of software piracy—an expensive and embarrassing experience. Knowing your software and where it is will help you plan for upgrades and ensure that all occurrences of a version of software are upgraded. It will keep you aware of whether standards are being followed. It will also let you take advantage of volume to negotiate more advantageous licensing agreements. You can keep software costs at the absolute minimum for the number of users that you have.

Tracking hardware and software assets will also help you with disaster recovery planning, purchasing and maintenance, and financial planning. For disaster recovery planning, you will know what your critical components are and where they are. Having a central database of hardware and software facilitates centralization of purchasing and maintenance so that economies of scale can be realized. It also allows you to reconcile true inventory with cost and depreciation information from your company's finance area. This will give your company a more accurate picture of asset value and will make your budgeting easier.

Manage Network Performance

Tracking network performance information will alert you to any changes that put your network in danger. For example, network traffic might be increasing at a rate much higher than you anticipated. Your performance information will reflect this, and you can do something about it before the situation becomes an emergency and the network grinds to a halt. Without network monitoring statistics, you would have no easy way of knowing there was a problem until the network actually ground to a halt, inconveniencing the customers and the business.

Tracking network performance will help ensure that you aren't surprised by any major network problems. You can monitor software usage, storage usage, network traffic, and performance of individual network components such as servers or cables.

Knowing how many people are using specific software on the network will help you plan for software license upgrades before they become an issue. You will know when the number of customers using a product is increasing so that you can increase the licensing before people are stopped from using the product. If you notice that no one is using a piece of software, you can take steps to remove it and stop paying for any maintenance or licensing. Monitoring use of space will allow you to plan for server upgrades before you run into space problems. If customers are putting more data on the servers than anticipated, you will be able to reorganize space or upgrade the server to prevent people from having problems when they try to store something there. If you notice that the number of users and transactions on your network is increasing faster than you expected, you will have the chance to do something about it before service starts getting degraded and people start calling in with problems. Monitoring network performance will also let you know when a specific component is malfunctioning, so you can replace it before it becomes a major problem affecting the whole network. Sometimes you will be able to fix the problem before anyone even notices there was a problem.

Monitoring network information might not be a function of your Help Desk, but even if it is not, it would be to your advantage to have constant access to it.

Manage Vendor Performance

If you track instances when vendor support is required in resolving problems, the corresponding resolution times, and the quality of the resolution, you can see how well the vendor is supporting you. You will have the statistics that will tell you whether the vendor is meeting any service-level agreements that have been set up. You can use these statistics to back up your discussion if you need to talk to the vendor about service. You can then continue to use them to monitor improvements, or lack thereof, and to justify breaking a contract with a vendor if it becomes necessary. You can also track overall performance of products supplied by that vendor to see whether you should continue purchasing them.

Identify Candidate Processes for Automation and Outsourcing

Tracking the calls you get to the Help Desk will tell you what things people call the Help Desk about most often. This, in turn, will tell you what things you need to automate or outsource to get the largest decrease in Help Desk call load.

If people are calling the Help Desk frequently asking for terminal resets, then automation in the form of a voice response unit that allowed people to reset their own terminals would eliminate all of those calls. Automating as many of the routine calls you get as possible will have a big impact on the number of calls that your Help Desk receives. It will free up staff to focus on more complex calls and to make improvements to Help Desk service.

In the same way, information about the calls you get can also show you where outsourcing might help you. If you are getting a lot of calls for packaged applications—how to interface with other applications, how to perform specific complex functions, how to use an application—then you may want to outsource this support to an external organization that provides this kind of service. You could then integrate this service into your Help Desk in such a way that people wouldn't even realize that they were accessing an external Help Desk.

Identify Customers Needing Training

A common complaint of Help Desks is that customers don't know the technology that they are using. Rather than taking the training on how to use a software package, or spending time looking for the information they need in a software manual, customers will call the Help Desk with their questions. Flooding the Help Desk with how-to questions is not the worst of their sins. Customers will use the software incorrectly because they don't understand it, and this can cause them to get incorrect results, to lose data, or to think that their computer isn't working properly. They waste a lot of their own time and the Help Desk's time.

Keeping track of these kinds of calls to the Help Desk will give you an indication of any customers or groups of customers that need training in specific software. For example, if someone calls up with a spreadsheet problem, and when you check the history for that customer, you see that this is the fourth call about spreadsheets, you have a pretty good indication that this person needs some training. You can recommend training right on the phone, as is illustrated in Figure 4.1: "I see that this is your fourth call about spreadsheets. There's a course being offered on that software. It will help you with your work and may save you some time." You can also do call-backs—run reports against your call logs that highlight repeat calls and then call the customers highlighted with training recommendations. If you weren't tracking callers and call information, you might not

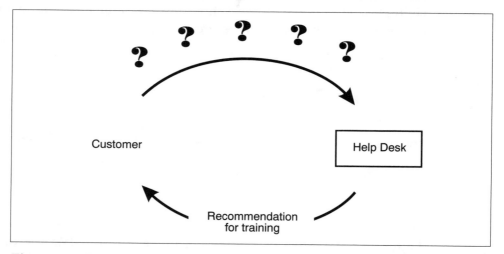

Figure 4.1 Tracking can show which customers need training.

be aware of this information. The customer might have spoken to a different Help Desk person with each call and, since the frequency of calls had not been noticed, would just keep calling, using up valuable Help Desk time. Decreasing these kinds of calls will lighten the Help Desk load and make customers more productive with their technology.

Another advantage of tracking this kind of information is that it will give you evidence to back up your assertion that these people need training. They can't really argue with you when you present statistics that detail how often they called and what they called about. They also know that you will be monitoring their future calls. They might just try to get some training before calling you next time.

Build a Problem/Solution Database

If you keep track of how you solve specific problems, you will be able to use that information if other customers experience similar problems in the future. From the problem and solution information you collect from tracking calls, you will be able to create some form of problem/solution database. As Figure 4.2 shows, when a customer calls, you can scan this data for information on similar past problems. This will help you resolve problems more quickly and for a wider variety of areas. For example, if someone is experiencing a problem where the display disappears from the monitor, the system might suggest a loose power cord as the problem. Help Desk staff could suggest this solution to the customer even if they had never seen this problem before. They might not know a product very

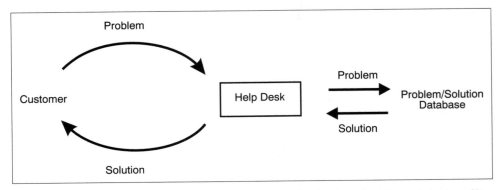

Figure 4.2   Tracking can provide a problem/solution database to expedite problem solving.

well, but if the problem has occurred before and its solution is documented, they can use that information to suggest a solution. Systems that store and retrieve problem/solution history can range from simple relational databases to complex expert systems, and can stand alone or be integrated with Help Desk call management systems (see Chapter 6).

Identify Recurring Problems

If you have several people on the front line of your Help Desk, all busy answering calls, you may not be aware of recurring problems unless you track problem symptoms and causes. Each person might, at different times, get a call about a different occurrence of the same problem. Because none of these people knows that the others are getting calls for the same problem, each person fixes a particular occurrence without addressing the fact that there is an underlying cause making the problem recur. The problem will just keep recurring, eating up valuable Help Desk time and costing customers time and inconvenience.

Tracking problem symptoms and causes will give the Help Desk the data it needs to identify problems that recur. They can be resolved as soon as they are identified so that customer inconvenience and Help Desk calls are reduced.

Identify Major Problems before They Occur

Being aware of trends in both problems and technology performance will allow you to stop more severe problems before they happen. As the graph in Figure 4.3 shows, early detection and correction of problems tends to lessen their severity.

If you notice an increasing number of problems with a specific software system, this may be an indication that the system needs to be replaced or rewritten so that it will be more stable in the future. Perhaps limits in the software are being reached and if something is not done to rectify the situation, the software might just stop working altogether.

If you are monitoring the performance of the network and notice degradation in any of the components, you can get them fixed before the degradation turns to complete failure and affects the whole network.

Manage Help Desk Function

The more you know about what is happening with your calls, the better you can manage them. You can ensure that calls are being handled

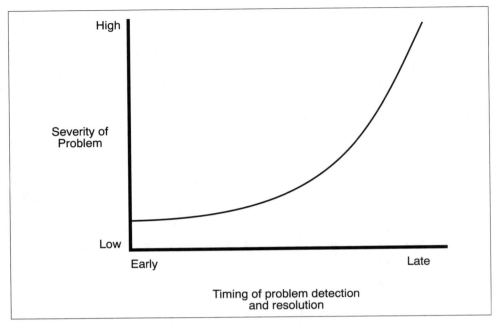

High

Severity of
Problem

Low

Early

Late

Timing of problem detection
and resolution

Figure 4.3 Tracking can facilitate the early detection and correction of problems.

efficiently, priorities are working, procedures are working and are being followed, staffing levels are adequate, and you can monitor staff performance. Tracking call data will allow you to do this.

If Help Desk staff have access to logged call information, then they will know whether a problem coming in has been logged already. This will prevent a situation in which two or more customers call into the Help Desk about the same problem and, because each speaks to a different Help Desk person, Help Desk staff do not realize that the same problem has been reported two or more times. The problem might be worked on by more than one Help Desk person—effort is duplicated, and valuable Help Desk time that could have been spent helping other customers is wasted.

If your Help Desk is receiving too many high-priority calls, or logged calls are sitting in the assignment queue too long, priorities either are not being enforced properly or are out of balance. Information from your call tracking system will make you aware of this situation and help you determine the cause. You can then, as required, either reeducate your staff and customers in priorities, or adjust your priorities in order to balance them.

If logged calls are not getting allocated or completed, if problems are marked completed but customers call to complain that they have not been completed satisfactorily, then you might have a problem with your procedures—they may be incorrect or nonexistent, or your staff might be either ignoring them or ignorant of them. Looking at statistics for unallocated problems, outstanding problems, and reopened problems will make you aware of any of these situations and will give you the data you need to find the cause and come up with a solution.

Statistics pertaining to call volumes and times to resolve calls will tell you if there is just too much work for your Help Desk to handle. If the number of calls you receive in one day is constantly increasing and the number of calls you are actually resolving each day is decreasing, you know you have a problem. Your backlog is going to skyrocket if you don't do something about the situation. Call statistics will give you the data you need to find out why your calls are increasing and how you can get them down. Automation may be indicated, or you may have to ask for more staffing, but you will have the data to back you up. You can also check volumes for different times to see whether you are staffing appropriately for peaks and valleys. For example, if 9 A.M. to 11 A.M. and 2 A.M. to 4 P.M. are your busiest times and Thursday is your busiest day, you want to be sure that you have enough staff working during those times to handle the volumes. Call statistics will tell you when your busiest and slowest times are so that you can staff most effectively for each.

If you keep track of who was assigned to each call, resolution time, and quality of resolution, you will have some good information about the quality of work that each person is doing. If poor quality is indicated, you can address it; if good quality is indicated, you can reward it. Staff will appreciate this. They will also realize that their work is reflected in the statistics, and may take more care to complete everything in a quality manner.

Keep Customers Informed

If you are monitoring the network and tracking Help Desk calls, you can notify your customers of any problems, unplanned maintenance, or unscheduled shut downs. This way, they can prepare for them, rather than being logged off suddenly while in the middle of something important.

You will be able to pass on information about trends to your customers. If you know that you are approaching license or storage limits, you can let them know so that they can use both software and storage more judiciously while you get them upgraded. You can even use this data to help make customers more aware of limits and costs of upgrading so that they will use resources more carefully. The more your customers know about their technological environment, the more effectively they can use it.

Your call tracking data will also allow you to keep customers informed of the status of their Help Desk calls. When they call to inquire, you will have the required information for them. Better still, if you are tracking this information in a database, you can give them the facility to get this information for themselves—via phone, by using a voice response unit, or via a PC or terminal, by using an interface to your database.

Provide the Information Necessary for Charge Back

Call tracking data will give you the usage information you need to bill your customers if your Help Desk charges back for services. Inventory information will also be required if you bill by PC or terminal. You can give each department an accurate breakdown of how it used the Help Desk over a specific period of time, including number of calls, types of calls, and so on. This information not only provides each department with billing information, but can serve as a departmental audit of Help Desk use. Managers can see what their staff are calling the Help Desk for, if there is any misuse such as calling with questions that should be addressed by training, and if there is enough use. They can check to see whether staff who seem to be spending too much time trying to solve problems on their own are calling the Help Desk, and then can address the situation as required. They can also check for trends in types and numbers of calls. If staff attended training, this information might give an indication of how effective the training was. If productivity was down, this information could show whether technology problems were contributing to the situation.

Measure Help Desk Performance

You can use information that you track to measure the performance of your Help Desk. How many calls you handle, how you handle them, your rate of successful resolution, the number of users you are supporting, the hardware and software you are supporting, and so on, will together give you an excellent idea of how you are performing. You can communicate this information to management and customers to show the value you are delivering. If you are not doing well or are just starting up, you can use these same statistics to show what you plan to do to improve. For example, if you are taking too long to resolve calls but are planning to eliminate the causes for many of your calls, you can show the difference this will make in your call volume and how you will use that difference to resolve calls more quickly. (Staff will be getting fewer calls, so they should be able to spend more time on problems, and resolution time should improve.)

An important part of Help Desk performance is customer satisfaction. You may be doing everything right, but if your customers aren't happy, if they are going to places other than the Help Desk for support, then you are not succeeding. For example, your calls may be going down, but the reason may be that your customers don't think much of your service and have stopped trying to get help from you. They have found their own ways to get help—either by asking people around them who know more than they do (a very expensive use of people's time) or by going elsewhere. Tracking calls will tell you who is using the Help Desk, who is not using the Help Desk, and who is misusing the Help Desk. You can address the misuse and talk to areas not using the Help Desk to find out the reasons. You want to make sure that you are giving your customers what they need.

Call data can also be used to measure performance against customer service-level agreements to see whether those agreements are being met and what areas need to be addressed.

Justify Improvements

If you have the statistics to show how a lack of improvements is affecting the Help Desk, then you improve your chances of getting the funding you need to make them. You could show the current situation, what you would like to change, and how it will improve things. For example, if your problem is lengthy resolution times, then you can show volume of calls, resolution time, and the resulting backlog. You can project what would happen if you decreased the volume of calls or increased staff. You could also show how you could decrease calls—you would have already identified the most frequently occurring reasons for calling, and how you could automate or get rid of them.

Keeping track of trends would show you unfavorable trends before they started affecting your service, so that you could go after funding before the fact. For example, knowing that your call volumes were creeping up while your resolution times were also creeping up would give you an indication that you needed to either decrease calls or increase staff to prevent severe degradation of your Help Desk service. The same applies to trends in technology. If the business were planning to roll out client/server systems, and your network monitoring and asset management systems told you that network equipment and PCs needed to be upgraded in order for this system to be able to run successfully, you could go after funding for the upgrades. You would know exactly what had to be upgraded, so you could make very accurate cost estimates and ensure that everything was in place before the system was rolled out.

Data Required for Tracking

Table 4.1 shows the (minimum) information that needs to be tracked to perform each of the functions discussed above. Information includes hardware and software inventory, customer information, call information, and network monitoring information.

Hardware and Software Inventory

A hardware and software inventory consists of a database of detailed information about each hardware and software asset in your company. Each asset is typically assigned an asset number and tracked that way. Stickers containing the asset number are put onto each piece of hardware before it is put into use so that it can be easily identified. Bar codes are sometimes used on the stickers in place of asset numbers for easier recording of information. Inventory information includes details such as component type, make and model, serial number, date of purchase, vendor, and warranty information. Table 4.2 shows an example of what the inventory data might look like for a few hardware components.

Tracking inventory manually is an onerous task. Someone has to go to each PC, record serial numbers of the PC and all attached components,

Table 4.1   What Tracking Can Do for You

	Hardware & Software Inventory	Customer Information	Call Information	Network Monitoring Information
Identify trends in hardware & software performance	X		X	X
Manage hardware and software assets	X	X		
Manage the network			X	X
Monitor vendor performance			X	
Identify processes for outsourcing or automation	X	X	X	X
Identify customers needing training		X	X	
Build a problem/solution database	X	X	X	X
Identify recurring problems			X	
Identify major problems before they occur	X		X	X
Manage Help Desk function	X	X	X	X
Keep customers informed	X	X	X	X
Provide the information necessary for charge back	X	X	X	
Measure Help Desk performance	X	X	X	X
Justify improvements	X	X	X	X

Table 4.2 Example of Inventory Data (P&L=Parts & Labor)

Asset #	Component	Make/ Model	Description	Serial #	Date of Purch.	Vendor	Warranty Info
101	PC	Compaq 486	33MHz 8M mem 245M hard drive Fax board Network card	A12355532	1/5/93	PCs Inc.	1 yr P&L
223	Monitor	MAG	VGA 14"	C122342334	2/4/93	Monitors Inc.	2 yr P 1 yr L
443	CD ROM	NEC Intersect		X34445901	3/3/93	CD-ROMs Inc.	2 yr P&L

open up the PC to see what cards are inside, and then check to see what software is on the machine. All other components, such as printers and servers, also need to be checked and recorded. In an environment of a thousand users, this is going to take awhile—and when you have finished, you have to start over again, because the inventory is out of date. People have loaded new software onto their hard drives, and perhaps swapped some of their equipment with someone else so that the equipment is no longer where you think it is.

A better way to get an inventory is to use asset management software, which will automate much of this process for you. It can run off of the network at regular intervals, gathering detailed information about each PC on the network and storing it in an inventory database. It will also run on standalone PCs so that the PCs needn't be opened up. Hardware and software data is gathered automatically. (See *Asset Management* in Chapter 6.)

Hardware and software information is useful on its own, but it becomes even more valuable when you link it to other data. For example, linking customer information to inventory will tell you where your hardware and software assets are, and will allow you to bring inventory information up automatically when you are handling a call from a customer. Linking inventory information to the company's asset system will mean more accurate asset accounting. Financial asset information will be more accurate, depreciation can be calculated more accurately, and the budgeting process will be simplified. Including hardware and software in call information will allow you to track performance of hardware and software.

Network Performance

Network performance information consists of information on how well (or poorly) the network is functioning, with details on specific network components. It can include information on network traffic levels, software usage, storage usage, component performance, and problems with any components such as cables or routers. It gives you the information you need to manage your network: to make sure that you can handle the growth you are or will be experiencing, to keep tabs on software usage so that you can ensure you have adequate licensing for the number of users using the software, to monitor storage usage so you can upgrade as required before people start running out, and to monitor component function so that you will be made aware of problems as soon as (or even before) they occur and can take appropriate action to prevent network degradation.

It would be impossible to gather much of the network data mentioned above without network management tools. Network management systems typically incorporate several tools so that they can offer wider functionality than individual tools, which might only manage one specific component of the network, such as cables. A network management system might offer a graphical representation of the network that shows any problem areas, a component that facilitates software distribution across the network, and a problem notification facility that calls or pages appropriate people when a problem occurs. (See *Network Management* in Chapter 6.)

Customer Information

Customer information that is of interest to the Help Desk includes details such as name, phone number, location, employee number, department, and user ID. Customer information needs to be included in call information and inventory information, but should not be duplicated. It should be picked up from where it is sourced—perhaps an employee database—

so that it is kept current. It can be linked to inventory through an asset management system, and to calls through a call tracking system. This will ensure that the Help Desk has current customer information and not an out-of-date copy.

Call Tracking

Call tracking data consists of the details of each call that comes into the Help Desk. These details cover the time period from when the call was logged until the call was closed. For calls that are still open, this data will allow the Help Desk to manage the calls, making sure they are assigned and completed within a reasonable amount of time. For calls that are closed, this data offers a valuable problem/solution history, which can be used to track trends and to help find solutions to problems that have occurred before. Problem/solution data collected from call tracking systems is used to build problem/solution databases or expert systems. Trends that can be tracked include hardware/software performance, vendor performance, recurring problems, and customer knowledge of products.

Call tracking data is collected by call management systems, which have a central database where all call information is logged. Functions exist to route calls into queues for resolution by analysts, and to do various reporting on the information. Call management systems are often called Help Desk systems and can contain various modules for managing different aspects of Help Desk functions. These might include an expert system to aid in problem diagnosis and an inventory management system that tracks hardware and software inventory. Table 4.3 contains an example of the kind of information a call management system might keep track of for each call logged.

In order to get the greatest benefit from call tracking data, all calls coming into the Help Desk should be logged. Otherwise, valuable trend information could be lost.

Information that is typically tracked for each call is as follows:

- Customer information
- Date and time of call:
  This will also tell you how long the call has been outstanding, so that you can track calls that are in the queue too long.

Table 4.3 Call Management Information

Customer:

Name: Mary Lake   **Emp#:** 36721   **Phone:** 451-3309
ID: MAL   **Locn:**   5th floor, East

Hardware:

#442	Monitor SVGA MTR 14"		**Ser#:**	144323221
#465	PC VIP		**Ser#:**	D435A144
	486 33MHz			
	8M / 245M			

Software:

Standard LAN software only

Call Information:

Date/Time:	4/24/93	11:31 a.m.
Call#:	1403	
Type:	Problem	
Description:	Monitor constantly flickering	
Priority:	3	
Component:	Monitor	
	#442	
Assigned to:	CLS	Chad Simson
Date/Time:	4/24/93	11:50 a.m.
Status:	Waiting	
Work Notes:	Needs new power supply.	
	Part ordered 4/24/93	
	Customer given loaner monitor 4/24/93	
Resolution:		
Date/Time:		

- Call type:
  This will vary by Help Desk, depending on the kinds of calls each gets. This might be something like problem, request, question, or incident, or it could be broken up into finer categories.

- Components involved:
  Hardware and software
- Reason for call (description):
  Includes key words for searches
- Priority
- Person assigned to problem
- Date and time problem assigned
- Current status
- Work notes—a history of what happened to this problem
- Resolution (including key words for searches)
- Date and time of resolution

You may also want to track what happens to calls before they come into the Help Desk. An automatic call distribution system (see *Telephone Technologies* in Chapter 6) will give you information on the number of calls coming in, the number of calls abandoned, the number of calls sent to phone mail, time spent in the hold queue, and so on. This will tell you how many calls are not even reaching you and what customers are experiencing in their attempt to get to the Help Desk.

Integration

The information you track is most valuable when you can integrate it. The more that systems know about each other and can talk to each other, the more powerful they become. For example, in Table 4.3, call tracking information contains reference to the hardware owned by the customer. If the information is integrated, the Help Desk person can just key in the customer ID and all of the customer information and inventory information will come up automatically. In the call information, under "component," the Help Desk person just has to specify "monitor" and the system will fill in the rest, because the system knows which monitor the customer owns. The monitor has been flagged as a problem, and searches on call information looking for problems with monitors or that specific monitor will pick that call up, so trends in monitor performance can be tracked. Help Desk staff can go into the inventory database, select a component such as a brand of monitor, and ask if there have been any problems

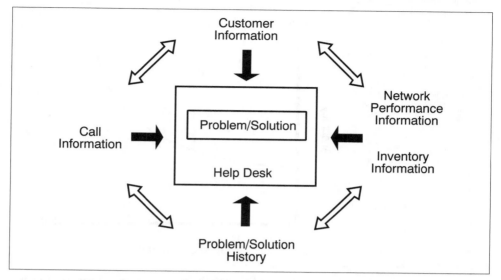

Figure 4.4 Integration in the Help Desk.

recorded against it. The system will be able to find all occurrences of problems with that brand of monitor cited as the component causing the problem. The integrated system knows inventory information, customer information, and call information. You can get customer or inventory information from a call; you can get customer and call information from inventory; and you can get call and inventory information for a customer, all without duplicating any information. (See Figure 4.4.)

If the information were not integrated, recording a call would happen somewhat differently. The customer would call in, and customer information would have to be taken and keyed in. Things might be keyed in incorrectly. Then the customer would give the inventory numbers of the configurations being used. The Help Desk person would go to the inventory system, check what the configurations were, then key them into the call tracking screen. This presents more chance for error. Under "component," the monitor information would have to be rekeyed. If any information is keyed in incorrectly, searches will be of no use. If a name is spelled wrong or a model number is omitted, valuable trending information can be lost. On top of all this, it took the Help Desk person a long time to key everything in, especially compared to having it all happen automatically.

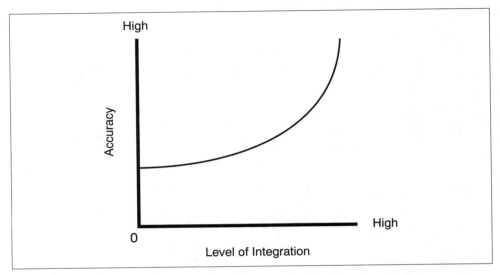

Figure 4.5   As level of integration increases, so does accuracy.

The more integrated a system is, the less data you have to keep duplicate copies of or rekey, and the less chance there is of error (see Figure 4.5). Systems are talking to each other to get information; error-prone human intervention is limited. Systems know more, so they can be more intelligent. A network management system that can see all components of a network and how they interact, and can thus flag problems or potential problems, is much more powerful than several individual network tools that do not talk to each other but monitor their own network components in isolation.

When you are tracking data, the more integrated that data is, the more useful it will be to you. Keep this in mind when you are selecting various tools for your Help Desk.

Getting at the Tracked Information

Today's technology environments are just too complex to do any kind of tracking manually. You will need tools to help you (see Chapter 6). How you get the tracking data out of these tools will vary from one to another. Some will generate standard reports; others will let you customize reports; some will let you run canned queries against the tracked data;

others will let you write your own queries against the data. Some will notify you (by paging you or sending you an electronic mail message) when there is something that needs looking at, while others will simply present the data and let you decide whether there is anything that needs attention.

You will have to decide what is best for your environment, and what you can afford. The three things to keep in mind when deciding how you will do your tracking are as follows: the more integrated a system is, the more powerful it is; the easier information is to get out of systems, the more it will be used; and what's best for the business is what's best for you.

Summary

The paybacks to tracking information are tremendous. The information you can get from your Help Desk operation can tell you everything from how many front-line staff you need at any point throughout the day to how many and which PCs need to be upgraded in order to support a client/server system that is being planned for release on the network. Tracking information cannot be accomplished manually because of the complexity of our technology environments—you will need tools to help you.

Some of the things that you can accomplish through tracking are:

- Identify trends in hardware and software performance:
  You can get the hardware or software fixed before it becomes a problem.

- Manage hardware and software assets:
  You will be able to improve planning for upgrades, ensure that software licensing is up to date, get rid of unauthorized software, provide more accurate figures for valuation and depreciation of assets, facilitate disaster and recovery planning, and facilitate the centralization of technology purchase and maintenance so that economies of scale can be realized.

- Manage network performance:
  You will be alerted to anything that might endanger your network and will have the ability to monitor software usage, storage usage, network traffic, and performance of individual network components.

- Manage vendor performance:
  You will know if your vendors are offering poor service or poor products and can take corrective measures.

- Identify candidate processes for automation and outsourcing:
  You can identify processes that will bring the most benefit by being automated or outsourced.

- Identify customers needing training:
  You can make sure that customers are offered the training they need to use their technology properly and to best advantage.

- Build a problem/solution database:
  Keeping a history of problems and solutions will prevent you from having to rethink a problem each time a similar one happens.

- Identify recurring problems for elimination:
  Tracking causes for calls will alert you to problems that keep recurring so that you can get a proper solution put into place and reduce calls.

- Identify major problems before they occur:
  Negative trends, such as increasing number of calls accompanied by increasing resolve times, can be noted and addressed before service grinds to a halt. Degradation in the performance of network components such as cables can be brought to light and resolved before network performance is significantly affected.

- Manage Help Desk function:
  You can ensure that calls are being handled efficiently, priorities are working, procedures are working and are being followed, and staffing levels are adequate.

- Keep customers informed:
  You can provide your customers with information about problems, unplanned maintenance, and unscheduled shutdowns as early as possible so as to minimize impact on them.

- Provide information necessary for charge back:
  You can provide each department with information on how often and how effectively it used the Help Desk.

- Measure Help Desk performance:
  You will know how effectively you are handling and resolving calls and which of your customers are or are not using your services. You'll know where you need improvement.

- Justify improvements:
  Tracking will give you the statistics to show how a lack of improvements is affecting the Help Desk. This will improve your chances of getting the funding you need to make them.

The data you need to track to accomplish the above is hardware and software inventory, network performance data, customer information, and call details.

A hardware and software inventory consists of a database of detailed information about each hardware and software asset in your company. Automated asset management systems are available to simplify the very work-intensive process of taking and maintaining inventory.

Network performance information includes details on network traffic levels, software usage, storage usage, component performance, and problems with any components such as routers or cables. This information can be provided by network management systems, which monitor performance of the network.

Customer information is required in almost every aspect of tracking. It should be picked up from where it is sourced—perhaps an employee database—so that it is kept current.

Call tracking data consists of the details of each call that comes into the Help Desk. It allows the Help Desk to manage calls, making sure they are assigned and resolved within a reasonable time, and offers valuable problem/solution history data for reference.

All of the tracked data mentioned above is valuable on its own, but its value increases exponentially when it is integrated. The more that systems know about each other and the more they can communicate, the more powerful they become. Errors will decrease, and rekeying or duplication of data will become unnecessary.

CHAPTER FIVE

Toward Automation

The concept of automation has been around for a long time. Ever since the dawn of thinking and reasoning, people have looked for ways of making life easier for themselves. The wheel, tools, carts—these were all early attempts at automation. They improved the quality of the lives of the people who used them. Each of them eliminated some measure of drudgery.

People are still thinking, reasoning beings. They should not be wasting their time and effort on tasks that require little thinking and that could be automated. Why go through the tedious effort of adding columns of numbers together to balance accounts when a computer can do it for you, faster and more accurately? Why go through the drudgery of washing stacks of dishes by hand when an automatic dishwasher could do it for you? Why cook in a wood stove when you can cook in an oven that has perfect and even temperature control, and does not require any wood chopping? Why go through the tedious and repetitive process of resetting terminals for customers who call the Help Desk when you can automate the process using a voice response unit? Why indeed. That's what this chapter is about: making sure you aren't wasting valuable human resources on Help Desk drudgery that could be automated. This chapter was written with the input of Arnold Farber and Rosemary LaChance of Farber/LaChance, Inc., industry-recognized experts in the field of automation.

Automation isn't about losing your job. It's about keeping yourself in business, and you can see proof of that over and over in the history of automation. Refrigerators may have eliminated the ice block business, but they created a whole new business that needed even more people: the business of cold food storage, or refrigeration.

Automation isn't about automating existing processes, either. It's about examining the existing processes to see if they make sense or if there is a better way. The inventors of refrigeration didn't look at automating getting ice blocks out to customers, they looked at providing automated cold food storage. Automation is about rethinking processes and asking, "Do we need to be doing this?" or "Could we be doing this better?"

The same applies to the Help Desk. Automation on the Help Desk is about keeping it in business, and keeping the business it supports in business. Humans cannot do everything that is required on the Help Desk today manually—not with the speed, volumes, and accuracy demanded by businesses. Technology is just changing too rapidly and becoming too complex to be supported manually. The car service industry is in a similar situation. Mechanics can no longer service a car with only a box of tools and a few spare parts. Cars have become so complex that mechanics need automation in the form of diagnostic computers to even figure out what's wrong.

Automation on the Help Desk is also about examining Help Desk processes and seeing if they make sense. For example, instead of automating fixes to JCL errors, why not install software that eliminates the errors? Instead of accessing a database when customers call with requests for information and then passing that information on to them, why not let them access the database themselves and get the information they want whenever they want it, without having to rely on a human? Credit card companies have followed this reasoning, and they now use automated systems that allow customers to call in and retrieve information about their accounts using only their touch-tone phones.

The technology is the easy part in automation efforts. The people are the challenge. Management, staff, and customers may all feel threatened by automation, perhaps refusing to understand it or even fighting it. Most of the focus in automation projects needs to be on the human side, so that the automated system is supported by management, promoted and championed by Help Desk staff, and used by customers.

What's in It for the Help Desk?

In today's world of cost cutting and paring down to the bone, automation is more important than ever in making your Help Desk successful. It will allow you to improve your service to your customers, increase the number of services you provide, or serve more customers, without the corresponding increases in resource costs. Automation can result in:

- Faster and more accurate service.
- Handling of higher volumes.
- More effective use of staff.
- A more stable technology environment.

Faster and More Accurate Service

An automated system is given a set procedure to perform and does it time after time, perfectly, without fail. Humans don't have this ability. They're just too . . . human. If someone calls the Help Desk up with a request for a terminal reset, the Help Desk person will get the required information, put the customer on hold, key in the appropriate instructions, and then ask the customer to try to log on. "Still can't do it" is the customer's response. The Help Desk person tries again, figuring that perhaps an instruction was missed. "Nope . . . still doesn't work" is the customer's response when asked if the reset worked. Finally, realization dawns. The user ID is wrong. "Is your ID BAL?" asks the frustrated Help Desk person. "No, it's DAL!" answers the equally frustrated customer. Finally the problem is resolved. The terminal is reset, the customer logs on successfully, and the Help Desk call is over.

If a voice response unit were set up to handle terminal resets, the process would be significantly different. The customer would call the Help Desk number, select the appropriate function for terminal resets, and enter the required information on the telephone key pad, and that would be the end of it. The customer's terminal would be reset quickly and without any intervention from Help Desk staff. Both the customer and Help Desk person would agree that this is the more favorable scenario.

Routine tasks that require no reasoning are perfect candidates for automation. If there is a procedure in place to do something, chances are that it can be automated—and be performed faster and more accurately than before.

Handling of Higher Volumes

Use of technology is increasing, and technology itself is changing and becoming more complex—and it's all happening at warp speed. Calls to your Help Desk will probably be increasing, and you're going to have to find ways of handling them without increasing staff, because staffing budgets are not increasing at warp speeds. Consider the example of an appliance manufacturing company that is expecting the yearly total of calls to its Help Desk to reach 9 million by the end of the century. No one could afford the staffing that would be necessary to handle that many calls manually. Most calls are inquiries about use and care of products and scheduling of service. The company is putting together a sophisticated and highly automated Help Desk system with a goal of satisfying each customer's request or solving each customer's problem at first call. The customer should not have to call back about the same request or problem. Automation will allow the company to handle the projected high volumes and improve customer service at the same time.

More Effective Use of Staff

What would you rather have your Help Desk staff working on: a call from a customer asking for the status of a PC order, or a call from a customer who is responsible for taking ads for the newspaper you both work for and who is having trouble with the ad-taking software? The weekend deadline is approaching, the phones are ringing, and each ad not taken means revenue lost—in a very slow economy.

You'd probably rather have your Help Desk staff working on the call that was more important to the business—the customer who was unable to take ads. Yet what if the PC status call were answered first, and while the Help Desk person searched the call database to find the order, the customer with the ad problem called in and got voice mail, because all Help Desk staff were busy? In this Help Desk environment, you couldn't ensure that the most important calls got answered first because you wouldn't know what the call was about until you answered it.

Automation can get rid of the ordinary calls, such as the PC status request, so that your staff can focus on the more complex calls. In the example above, it could provide your customers with a function that would give them the ability to get PC order status information themselves. This would make your staff more available to respond to problems such as the one experienced by the customer working with the newspaper ads.

A More Stable Technology Environment

Automation allows you to be proactive. If you wait for your network to go down and then worry about fixing the problem, your business is going to suffer. Being reactive just isn't good enough to keep a company competitive. You need a system that will alert you of potential network problems so that you can do something to prevent them. Network management systems can do this. They monitor the components of a network and alert you to any degradation in performance or any unusual conditions. They can call or page specific people at the first sign of something unusual, and they can suggest resolutions to problems to speed the problem-solving process.

Any sign of degradation or unusual network behavior can be addressed before it becomes a major problem. Problems will be brought to light immediately, and the appropriate staff alerted so that they can be resolved as quickly as possible.

Being able to react quickly, to take care of problems as soon as or even before they happen, will lead to a more stable environment with fewer network shutdowns.

Automation Tools

Are the automation tools that Help Desks need available? Absolutely. They're not all perfect, but there are certainly enough to choose from to make a substantial positive impact on your Help Desk. For skeptics who are reluctant to trust any part of their Help Desk processes to automation, Rosemary LaChance has this answer: "Doctors have been using automation to monitor patients in intensive care for years. If doctors are willing to trust patients' lives to automation, surely we can trust our systems to it."

Tools for automation on the Help Desk include Help Desk management systems, expert systems, voice response units, remote diagnostic software, asset management systems, and network management systems.

What Can You Automate?

There are several areas within the Help Desk that can be automated, or partially automated:

- Call tracking and management.
- Problem resolution.

- Routine procedures.
- Asset tracking and management.
- Network monitoring and management.

Call Tracking and Management

Call management systems can simplify call entry by filling in data fields automatically—all you need to do is key in a customer identifier, and the corresponding customer information and hardware and software configurations are filled in. The systems can automatically put the call in a queue for resolution once you assign it, and can generate messages to customers once the call has been resolved. The systems can also flag undesirable situations, such as calls that have been in a queue for too long, or calls that have been open too long. Calls won't be allowed to fall through the cracks. Call management systems work off of central databases, which can be queried. These databases can be used with a voice response unit to let customers check the status of their calls.

Problem Resolution

Expert systems provide a knowledge base of problem/solution data that helps Help Desk staff resolve problems. Some expert systems are based on complete problem/solution cases that have occurred in the past. For example, one of the cases might be a flickering monitor that was the result of a loose cable between a monitor and a PC. If this situation should occur again, the Help Desk person would feed the expert system the symptom of flickering monitor, the system would do pattern matching through its cases, and it would bring back the suggested solution of loose cable. This kind of expert system is very helpful to people who do not have knowledge of all products being supported, or are just learning. It is very good as a learning tool and requires little product knowledge to use. Other expert systems ask for clarification as they attempt to diagnose and narrow down the problem. They need to make choices, and often need information from the Help Desk person in order to make a choice.

Expert systems expand the knowledge base of people on the Help Desk. The people can diagnose problems on the basis of more knowledge than they alone have. People who have knowledge are the ones who provide the information for the expert systems. The more problem/solution data that expert systems contain, the more powerful they become.

Another aid to problem solving is remote diagnostic software. This is software that allows a Help Desk person to take over a customer's PC without leaving the Help Desk workstation. The Help Desk person can look through configuration files, see exactly what was going on in the customer's PC at the time of the problem, and run through the problem scenario. The Help Desk person would have all of the information possible about the problem and could resolve it more quickly, all without leaving the Help Desk area.

Routine Procedures

Just about any procedures that are routine, that follow specific steps, can be automated. A script might be written to perform a procedure so that it could be automated via a voice response unit, or a program could be written (or purchased) to automate it. If a procedure can be written down, chances are that it can be automated.

Asset Tracking and Management

Taking inventory of hardware and software—and keeping this inventory up to date—is tedious, to say the least. It takes too much time and too many people to be practical. Asset management software will do this automatically. It will, via the network, record details of your hardware and software assets attached to the network and store them in an inventory database. Not only is this a time saver, but it will ensure a more accurate and up to date inventory that can be used to plan software and hardware upgrades, keep software licensing up to date, and track hardware to make sure that it is safe, maintained properly, and upgraded as required.

Network Monitoring and Management

Network management systems can monitor all parts of the network, reporting on all problems and usage. Problems with power, cables, or any network component can be detected, and a solution suggested. The monitoring software will notify staff as soon as a problem or unusual situation occurs.

Automated Help Desk tools vary in complexity and power (and price). For example, some network tools monitor only specific components of the network, while others monitor the whole network. Some network management tools include automated asset management software. Call management systems frequently include inventory tracking and expert system components. Often, companies will purchase several separate tools and integrate them into a complete network management system.

Automated Help Desk tools also have their limitations. For example, expert systems typically require a lot of work at the front end to get them set up, and then a lot of maintenance to keep the knowledge up to date. Asset management software does not yet recognize all types and makes of hardware components. The tools may not be perfect, but they could still be of great help to you in decreasing your workload or providing better service. For example, even if asset management cannot do all of your inventory, what it can do you won't have to worry about. Your total inventory will be more accurate than before, and as functionality of the tool expands, you can simply add it in. You will have the knowledge to use the tool and you will have already started using the data that it generates. You'll be a step ahead of companies that waited for the tool to become perfect. For more detailed explanations of Help Desk tools available, including their features and their limitations, see Chapter 6.

Tools for automating Help Desk functions are constantly being developed and improved in response to customer demand. Vendors are always looking for ways to automate more aspects of providing customer support. To keep ahead of your competition and to make use of tools as soon as they are available, you should consider being a beta test site for Help Desk tools. You will learn, get ideas, and have the benefit of giving the vendors suggestions for improvements. Technology is just going to keep expanding and getting more complex. You can't sit back and declare that you're finished. You have to keep looking for new ways to improve, to automate. Being a beta test site will help you do this.

Success Factors

When you are putting automation into your Help Desk environment, your success depends on several factors, as illustrated in Figure 5.1. You have to make sure that you address all of them so that they don't become obstacles. When implementing automation, your success will depend on

Figure 5.1 Success factors for an automation project.

- Help Desk performance data
- Business need
- Management support
- Adequate budget
- Communication to Help Desk staff
- Training for Help Desk staff
- A comprehensive plan with milestones
- Communication to customers

Help Desk Performance Data

Before you can start thinking seriously about automation, you need to gather some data about what goes on in your Help Desk environment. You need to know how you can improve Help Desk performance and service through automation, and in order to do that, you need to know what that performance is. Call information needs to be tracked, and trends—such as reasons for calling—need to be noted. This information is also necessary in order to make a business case for your automation project so that you can get funding for it.

Business Need

If you are putting in automation, you want to make sure that it is offering something that the business needs and is not just perceived as an IS toy. Tasks being automated should offer a visible and measurable payback. For example, if you are automating terminal resets and this will reduce your call load by 10 percent and make it easier for customers to get their terminals reset, then the benefits of the automation will be clear. It will be easier for you to get support for future automation. If, however, you choose to automate an obscure process that has no impact on call load, but was something that Help Desk staff hated doing, then you're not going to get a lot of support for it. Management will want to see payback, in business terms, for the money you have spent.

Management Support

You will need support from management to get the funding you need for automation, but also to help get support from customers and staff. If people feel that the automation is a company initiative, not just an IS thing, they're going to be more enthusiastic about it and more willing to give it a try. If the message is coming down from the top, people are more likely to listen to it. Management support will also be required to handle any staffing and restructuring issues. If staff are going to be moved around in any way, you will probably need management approval.

Adequate Budget

If you can't get the funds to cover all of the expenses involved in automation—hardware, software, staff, training—then you can't do your automation project. An automation project has a lot more overhead than the cost of the automation tool. It needs staff that are dedicated for a specific period of time, and it needs training. Don't be tempted to skimp on staff or training—if the tool isn't put in properly, not supported adequately, or not promoted adequately, then your automation effort will fail. Your cost justification should show that staff and training are just as important as the tool itself. An automation tool cannot be implemented with any success by someone who is working on it only part time and who has not been trained properly on it.

Communication to Help Desk Staff

Committed staff are staff that support automation, that see its benefits, and that work willingly and eagerly to improve and automate processes. If you are willing to invest time and effort in two-way communication with your staff about automation, you will have a greater chance of having committed staff. Help Desk staff may initially be afraid of automation: of how it will affect their roles, of losing their jobs, or of not knowing enough. They may be skeptical—they may not believe that automation will bring benefits. You need to address each of these fears and the skepticism. You need to make the staff see that automation is not really just about the Help Desk—it is about the business, and about staying in business.

Staff that are not committed can sabotage automation attempts, even unintentionally. Their lack of interest will prevent them from seeing and taking advantage of opportunities for dispelling fears and concerns about the system, and from encouraging and helping customers to use the new system. They won't be looking for further opportunities for automation. Their lack of interest may be seen by customers as a sign that the system is not really worthwhile.

Training

If staff don't know how to use the automation tools properly, they might not be using them to their full potential. They may only be using half of a tool's features because they don't know about the others or don't know how to use the others. If they don't attend formal training, then they won't have this information—manuals will simply not give them the information they need to use the tool to its full potential. Even if the tool is already being used in your environment, each person working with it should attend training. Learning on the job won't teach staff how to use the tool properly, it will only teach them what the tool does in the limited circumstances in which it is being used. Knowing how the tool works, how it integrates with other tools, and what it is capable of is far more valuable than just knowing how the tool is used in your organization.

A Comprehensive Plan

An automation project that is going to succeed needs a plan with clear and measurable milestones. The plan should be published to management, staff, and customers alike, in whatever form is appropriate in your organization, so that they can all see and measure progress. Skeptics might start being convinced when they see that the automation you are implementing is going in as planned, is being used, and is working. Plans will help you keep the momentum going. Continuous small steps will get you there faster, and with less pain, than a few giant leaps. Continuous steps will let you adjust to feedback from customers and staff as you progress so that you are sure that you are really improving things for your customers. This will help your project gain acceptance from customers and staff, and will reassure management that the automation is really working. Small steps will help you keep the customers involved—will let you get their feedback, change things to meet their needs, and show them that you are listening. The customers will feel more involved, and this will help ensure acceptance.

Communication to Customers

Customers who are prepared for your automation effort will be more accepting of it. If you go to customers, get feedback about what you're trying to do, communicate continuously, and promote the automated system constantly, especially in its early days of implementation, you are going to be a lot more successful than if one day you simply announce that you have implemented an automated system and everyone should start using it. If customers won't use your system, it won't work, no matter how good a system it is.

The Human Element

The most challenges in your automation effort are going to come not from the technology but from the people. Getting and keeping the support of management, staff, and customers will make dealing with the technology look simple by comparison.

Management

In dealing with management, your most useful allies are a good business case and a comprehensive implementation plan. Your business case is necessary to ensure that you can justify the funding you need. Your comprehensive implementation plan will increase management confidence in your ability to carry the project out, and will provide a tool with which management can measure your progress and success.

Things you may have to contend with are executives who have had bad experiences with automation in other companies, or who are simply against automation, and executives who are afraid of losing a measure of power through automation. They may not be willing to give up head count, or they may be afraid that if automation continues and spreads—as is probably already happening to some extent in the data center—they will soon be managing nothing but machines.

You can't do a lot about politics and empire building, but you can address fears about automation not working. Make sure your business case is comprehensive, and take advantage of any communication opportunities to answer concerns and even elicit suggestions. Management will be more comfortable with automation and less likely to try to stop you if they know you are listening to them and are taking steps to ensure that the failures they may have seen in other places won't happen in your environment.

Customers

Customers want service—they want it now and they want it to be accurate. They should love automation—what they want is exactly what automation delivers. If you can get customers over their initial fears of using the system, and if your system works properly, giving them what they want faster and more consistently than a human, then they will use it.

Initially, customers may not want to use the system. They just may not believe that the automation works, they may be afraid of pushing the wrong buttons, or they might just not want to deal with a machine. In order to dispel any fears they might have, you need to communicate. Before the automation is turned on, they should know the business reason for the automation and how to use the tool, and they should be encouraged to collect and give feedback. The business reason should be clear enough that they can't really argue about the necessity for the tool. Instructions on tool use should be as clear and as simple as possible. Have a few customers run through them before you distribute them so that you are sure that they are understandable and that they work. Encouraging customers to collect and give feedback will tell them that you are listening, and they will therefore be more inclined to try the tool out.

When you are setting up an automation tool such as a voice response unit, make sure the voice scripts are appropriate for your customers. People setting scripts up have a tendency to oversimplify, which can be very irritating to customers. Don't treat your customers as dimwits. Instructions that are repeated over and over can be very annoying to a customer trying to use the system. An option to repeat would be preferable.

In the early days of operation for your automation tool, you are going to need a lot of support for your customers. Many customers are going to push the option for a human Help Desk person and will want to know more about the automation. What you need to do is to be responsive and positive, and to encourage them to use the automated system. You can say, "I will do this for you, but did you know that you can do it yourself? You just select the option you want and push your user ID in on the telephone pad. We really want to know how it's working, so we would really appreciate your trying it out and giving us your feedback." This approach will go a lot farther with a customer than "We don't do that any more. Use the automated system." The former scenario will probably get that customer into the automated system. The latter will have that customer complaining to other customers and to management. Respond to all customer concerns and questions, and take every opportunity possible to encourage customers to use the system. A customer who is satisfied with your service and is comfortable using your services will do more for your marketing than just about anything you could do.

Staff

If Help Desk staff don't want your automation effort to succeed, then it won't. There are an infinite number of ways to sabotage a project, some of them quite passive and even unintentional. If your Help Desk has installed a voice response unit to handle a specific problem, and a customer bypasses the unit to call in directly to your Help Desk to have the problem solved by a human, your Help Desk staff will be hurting your automation project if they simply respond to the request as usual. They may be thinking, "Customers don't want to use the unit. They would rather talk to me. The Help Desk still needs me to do this." The customer won't have been given a reason for trying the new system. What staff should be doing is encouraging customers to try the automation and give their feedback. Staff should be enthusiastic and always on the lookout for opportunities to market the system to customers. Not doing this is passive, yet very destructive to the project.

Ensuring that your staff wants the project to succeed is largely a matter of communication. If you can make staff see the benefits to the business and to themselves, you will be well on the way to getting them committed. Perhaps the business is unable to support increased head count, yet is demanding more from the Help Desk. Eliminating mundane repetitive tasks from the Help Desk will make it a much more interesting environment for the staff. They will be working on more complex, interesting problems and they will be learning to use various automation tools. They will be more marketable as employees.

If your automation effort is such that people might be redeployed or might even lose their jobs, then you need to do a lot of work up front before you even start your communication. You need management commitment that every effort will be made to redeploy staff within the company, and that if staff do have to be laid off, they will be compensated and helped in their search for another job. If you don't have this kind of commitment, you are going to have a hard time getting commitment to automation from your staff.

Communication needs to be two-way. The staff may have a lot of concerns that they will need to express, and you should make sure that these are addressed to as great a degree as possible. Their first reactions on hearing about automation efforts might be concern for keeping their jobs, worrying about what their jobs will look like after automation, or worrying that they don't know enough to do other things. Encourage questions about job security and answer them as honestly as you can. Be positive. You may not have all of the answers, but if you can communicate that management cares about the staff and that the staff won't be dispensed of at the drop of a hat, then you have made a good start at your communication effort. If you have training plans, this is the time to talk about them. Reassure staff that they will receive the training they need to acquire the new skills they will be expected to have. You also need to communicate the needs of the business and how important they are: when the business fails, no one has a job.

This does not mean that you should go out and use a brute force method of communication. Farber and LaChance tell of one company that launched a major effort to automate its data center by telling the employees that 75 percent of them would lose their jobs. This may have been brutally honest, but it was extremely nearsighted. They didn't spend time explaining the automation, the processes involved, the length of time the project would take, the business benefits, and the efforts that would be made to find jobs for people. The communication effort need not have been approached as a giant leap. A much more effective method would have been a series of small successive steps, with management handling the staff issues with each step, and management committed to making those issues easier for the people involved. Many times, people don't need to be laid off—they can be redeployed, and staff savings realized through attrition. In the example above, IS management did not take into account the fact that the data center staff were needed to plan out and do the automation. Without their support, the efforts would not succeed— and their support would certainly not be forthcoming with the kind of communication they had just received. What motivation have staff for planning and implementing automation when they have just been told that 75 percent of them will soon be out of a job? In fact, the staff, who were frightened and resentful, made the automation effort move so slowly and offered so few results that the company executive got fed up and decided to outsource the whole data processing department, putting the entire IS staff and management out of work. This situation was a lot worse than the original estimate. Management learned too late the importance of taking care of the human element. The computer won't really care what you subject it to, but the people certainly will.

When your automation project is ready to start, you should give it to your staff. Give them ownership for the project and for its success. You may need to keep a close eye on the project at first and offer a lot of support, but ownership should remain with your staff. They should create or have direct input to the plan and any milestones, and they should evaluate and select any tools required. The more ownership you give them, the more committed they will be to seeing the project through.

Training is also necessary to ensure staff commitment. Training will give them the knowledge to use the tool properly and the confidence to use it in new ways and to try new things. It will also help them to realize that management is committed to making sure they have the skills they need to do their jobs.

Fostering a climate of innovation will also work toward getting staff committed. If they know they are allowed, even encouraged, to try new things, to look for better ways, to make mistakes, then they will enter into the project with a lot more enthusiasm. You are giving them permission to have and follow ideas, to think.

Effects on Structure

The more you automate your Help Desk, the more routine and repetitive tasks will disappear. The calls you get and the work that will need doing will be challenging. Your staff will require product knowledge, analysis and problem-solving skills, and innovation. The front-line staff on the Help Desk need to be experts. If, prior to automation, you had a front line that simply routed calls, or that solved only simple calls, you're going to have to change that.

Your front-line staff are going to need training. How much and what kind depend on what they were doing before automation and what they will be doing now. The tendency is for companies to think that people can't be retrained, that it's easier to lay off current staff and get someone else. You're doing a big disservice to your staff if you think that way. Don't put staff aside until you've given them a chance. Give them the training they need and assign other staff as coaches. You may be pleasantly surprised by the result. Not only will you have more knowledgeable and skilled staff, but they will already be familiar with your environment and they will be totally committed to and enthusiastic about the project. Also, how you treat your front-line staff will set an example for the other staff. If they see you investing training time and effort in the staff, they may be less concerned about their own jobs and more inclined to believe any assertions you may have made about keeping or finding jobs for people.

If your staff responsibilities change significantly, compensation should also change. Make sure that salaries are adjusted accordingly. Don't pay them for a lower-level job than they are actually doing. That speaks a lot louder than words about how you value them.

The Automation Project

When your automation project is ready to start—you have management approval and funding and you have communicated to your staff—you need to put an automation team together. That team needs to get down to details of what to automate, and in the process, it needs to look at Help Desk procedures with an eye to eliminating unnecessary ones and improving inefficient ones. A plan needs to be put together, and staff need to be trained on the new tools and in any other new skills they require.

Once a new tool has been tested and is ready to be put into production, you need to ensure that it is rolled out in a way that ensures maximum acceptance by your customers.

Putting Together the Team

Your project should be run by a team of Help Desk staff. How many depends on how big your initial automation effort is. When you put the team together, give them responsibility for the project. Take time to ensure that they understand what this responsibility is and what you expect of them. If you haven't communicated clearly what you are expecting, then the only way you're going to get it is by coincidence—if your staff just happen to do what you expect. Make sure that the team understands what the automation initiative means to the business, and that all decisions that are required should be business-driven.

Give the team responsibility for investigating and selecting the tool(s) necessary for the automation of the procedure. Have the vendor interface with the team, not with yourself. They will learn about the product, and about the whole process of negotiation. They will also have established the contacts that will be necessary throughout the implementation of the product. The more involved they are, the more committed to the project they will be, and the more they will learn.

Finally, give your team time to work on the project. Make the work part of the Help Desk objectives and allocate enough staff for enough time. The team will soon be discouraged if you keep having to pull them off of the project to work on other things.

Deciding What to Automate

When you first start to automate, you want to automate something with the biggest bang for the buck: something that will make a difference to Help Desk service or performance, that will be noticeable, that can be held up as an example of what automation can do. You also want it to be something relatively uncomplicated, because it is your first effort and your team is just learning.

The best place to look for what to automate is in the Help Desk data you are tracking. Look at the reason for the highest number of calls you are getting. This is most likely something fairly routine—your staff know it inside and out because they've performed it so often—and is often the perfect candidate for automation. You know with a good degree of accuracy what kind of impact it will have on Help Desk performance: all of the calls that used to come in for it will be eliminated.

Don't Pave the Cow Paths

Be careful not to automate existing processes that don't make sense. Automation of the Help Desk often involves reengineering so that inefficient or incorrect processes are eliminated, and existing processes are improved. Only the processes that make sense are actually automated.

Before the team starts looking for ways to automate, it should examine Help Desk processes and see which ones can be eliminated. This includes resolutions to problems. Why automate the fix to the problem if you can eliminate the problem? One company chose, as its first automated Help Desk process, the retransmission of sales data. Data was supposed to be sent each night from retail outlets to the head office, but often there were transmission problems and the head office did not receive the data. The next morning, the Help Desk received numerous calls asking for retransmission, which is why they chose this function for automation. The reasons for the problems in transmission were that the technology being used was inappropriate and the processes were faulty. Fixing those would have eliminated the problem and saved everyone a lot of time and trouble, more so than just giving customers the ability to get their data retransmitted.

The Plan and Milestones

Let your Help Desk team develop the plan for the automation project, or at least have significant input to it. Your plan is a map of your route to project completion, and you should have frequent milestones to measure progress along that route. Report on this progress frequently to management to maintain their confidence in the project.

In your plan, take small, frequent steps rather than fewer large ones. Deliver less, but deliver more frequently. This will allow you to adjust for feedback from your customers and from the Help Desk as you go along. What you deliver at the end of each step will keep getting better, because you are adjusting your route to the feedback you are getting at the end of each step. With each step, your customers will be more used to automation and will accept it more easily.

The whole automation process will be ongoing: find the best thing to automate, then automate it. Find the next best thing to automate, then automate it—and so on, as illustrated in Figure 5.2. You will always be on the lookout for processes to automate, for possible improvements. You will have a plan for each process you decide to automate.

Training

Make sure the team members receive the training they need when they need it. Training staff long before the automation tool is installed will be wasted training. They will need a refresher course once the tool arrives. Have the team draw up training requirements as part of their plan so that they can put together a training schedule. This can be included in milestones so that it will be measured.

Training not only helps staff make better use of tools, but gives them confidence to solve problems themselves and the incentive to try things themselves that they wouldn't have thought of before.

In your plan, include attendance at Help Desk conferences or product user groups. The staff who attend these can bring back valuable tips on using the automation tools that they have selected. This information can

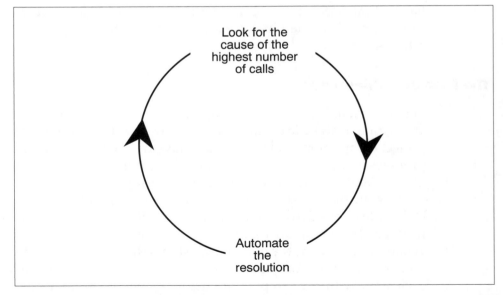

Figure 5.2 Automation is an ongoing process.

often save staff from making mistakes that others have already made, and can provide ideas for most effective use of the tool and acceptance of the tool by customers.

Rolling Out the Product

Before an automation product is rolled out, the customers must be prepared. Help Desk staff must communicate what is going to happen and how it will affect customers' use of the Help Desk. Electronic mail is a good way to notify customers, if they are all electronic mail users. Try to make your communication clear; otherwise, you will be deluged with calls by customers who want to know what is happening.

When the tool first goes out, customers might still choose to talk to the Help Desk rather than using the automated tool. They might be apprehensive of using a new tool, or they might not understand it. If this happens, you should suggest that they give the new way a try, and then talk them through it. Tell them you want their feedback. Help Desk staff must be positive and encouraging about the automated process. They must not be content to allow staff to use the old way. Walking people through the new process is how telephone operators (who used to make long-distance phone calls for everyone) handled customers who were leery of dialing their own long-distance calls. The operators would walk customers through the procedure so that the next time the customers could do it themselves.

Small Steps, Big Result

Start small, but don't think small. Rosemary LaChance estimates that as many as 90 percent of calls to the Help Desk can be automated. Only 10 percent of the calls are new problems that Help Desk staff haven't seen before. Once a problem has happened, the solution or fix should be automated if possible. It shouldn't happen again.

When Are You Finished?

You're never finished with automation. As new technology comes along, new problems will come along and you'll have to find new solutions to automate. New automation technologies will be introduced that can improve Help Desk service and the technology environment even further.

Keep searching for solutions, keep innovating, keep improving. Help Desk automation isn't a project with a beginning and an end, it's an ongoing endeavor.

Summary

Automation is not about losing your job. It's about keeping yourself, and the business you support, in business. It's also not about automating all existing processes, but rather about examining the existing processes and seeing if they make sense or if there is a better way.

Automation is also about leaving the mundane, repetitive tasks to computers, and giving the more challenging tasks to thinking and reasoning humans. The technology is the easy part in automation efforts. People have a hard time accepting automation. Your focus needs to be more on the people than on the technology.

Some of the benefits of automation are:

- Faster and more accurate service.
  Automation can perform procedures over and over at much-faster-than-human speeds, and without making mistakes.

- Handling of higher volumes.
  Automation can handle volumes that simply cannot be handled by humans.

- More effective use of staff.
  Automation can free Help Desk staff from routine tasks and allow them to focus on those more important to the business.

- A more stable technology environment.
  Automation will allow you to monitor the network for any signs of degradation so that these can be addressed before they become problems. This will result in an environment that has a higher availability and fewer problems.

Automation tools are available for the Help Desk. They may not all be perfect, but they can certainly have a positive impact on your Help Desk. There are several areas within the Help Desk that can be automated, or partially automated, with the use of Help Desk tools:

- Call tracking and management.
  Automation can facilitate call tracking by filling in tracking information automatically, and by routing calls automatically. The call database can be accessed by customers so that they can inquire about the status of their calls.

- Problem resolution.
  Problem resolution can be greatly enhanced by expert systems, which suggest solutions to problems. Remote diagnostic tools allow Help Desk staff to take over customer application sessions without leaving the Help Desk.

- Routine procedures.
  If a procedure is performed routinely by the Help Desk, then chances are that it can be automated.

- Asset tracking and management.
  Automated asset management systems can eliminate or lessen the need to do manual tracking of hardware and software inventory by tracking all software and PCs on the network.

- Network monitoring and management.
  Network management systems monitor components of the network and notify staff of any degradation or unusual activity, and may even suggest solutions.

When you are putting automation into your Help Desk environment, your success depends on several factors:

- Help Desk performance data.
  Before you can improve, you need to know where you are now. You need to gather some data about what goes on in your Help Desk environment.

- Business need.
  Tasks being automated should offer a visible and measurable payback so that the benefits of automation will be clear.

- Management support.
  Management support is required to get the funding you need for automation, to get the buy-in of customers and staff, and to handle staffing and restructuring issues.

- Adequate budget.
  You need to make sure that your budget is adequate for staff and training.

- Communication to Help Desk staff.
  Investing time and effort in two-way communication with your staff about the automation and their concerns gives you a greater chance of having committed staff.
- Training for Help Desk staff.
  If staff members don't know how to use the automation tools properly, they might not be using them to their full potential.
- A comprehensive plan with milestones.
  A plan should be published to management, staff, and customers alike, in whatever form is appropriate in your organization, so that they can all see and measure progress.
- Communication to customers.
  Customers who are prepared for your automation effort will be more accepting of it. You need adequate communication.

The most challenges in your automation effort are going to come not from the technology but from the people: you need to get and keep the support of management, staff, and customers. In dealing with management, your most useful allies are a good business case and a comprehensive implementation plan. You need to address any fears about automation not working. Customers want the immediate, accurate service that automation gives them, but they may have initial fears about dealing with the technology. You can dispel these by walking them through the automated process when they try to use the manual one.

If Help Desk staff don't want your automation effort to succeed, then it won't. Through two-way communication, you need to ensure they understand it and are committed to it. You need to address any concerns that they might have about their jobs or their futures. Your front-line staff will need to have greater product knowledge, and greater analysis and problem-solving skills. If your staff don't have these skills, don't discard your staff, train them.

Your automation project should be run by a team of Help Desk staff who have complete responsibility for the project, including selection of tools. Give them time to work on the project and the training—they need it.

When you're looking for what to automate, look at the reason for the highest number of calls you are getting. This is often something fairly routine, and thus a perfect candidate for automation, but be careful not to automate existing processes that don't make sense.

Let your Help Desk team develop the plan for the automation project, or at least have significant input to it. The plan should deliver smaller results frequently, rather than larger ones less often. This will allow for constant feedback and adjustment.

Before rolling out the automation, make sure the customers are prepared. Help Desk staff must communicate what is going to happen and how it will affect customers' use of the Help Desk. If customers are leery of using the tool at first, walk them through it.

Start small, but don't think small. You're never finished with automation. It is an ongoing endeavor.

CHAPTER SIX

Help Desk Tools

Help Desk tools are the tools that allow Help Desk staff to track and manage calls, solve problems and answer questions, monitor the network, and manage technology assets. Without tools, and given the complexity and range of technology being supported by most Help Desks, many of these tasks would be impossible. Humans simply cannot store, process, or retrieve data as quickly, as accurately, or in the volumes that a computer can.

Tools allow Help Desk staff to become more self-sufficient. With tools, staff have the information and functions at their disposal to resolve more of the problems that come into the Help Desk. They don't have to pass as many calls on to experts. Tools can also help customers become more self-sufficient. Customers can retrieve their own information and can even solve some of their own problems.

Help Desk tools help ensure consistent responses to customers, and they allow the Help Desk to be proactive in detecting and preventing potential problems. Processes can be automated so that they will be performed consistently and correctly. Problems that have been solved will be kept track of so that they don't have to be solved again.

Some of the advantages of Help Desk tools can also be dangers. When working with tools that help you find and even automate solutions to problems, it becomes easy to fall into the trap of accepting problems because you know how to solve them. The fact that you can solve a problem quickly with the tools you have at hand does not mean that you should be content to allow that problem to keep happening. It would be preferable to either eliminate the cause or automate the solution so that the customers can invoke the solution themselves.

153

Help Desk tools also facilitate the integration of information. Integrated tools such as network management systems allow individual components to share information and talk to each other. As a result, these systems become more powerful, and their information becomes more accurate. They are able to diagnose and flag situations that the individual components would not have had enough information to find on their own.

What does all of this mean to the business? Technology will become more stable and employees will become more productive. Tools will allow the Help Desk to become more proactive in managing the network. Degradation or unusual activity can be detected and addressed before it becomes a problem, and problems can be resolved quickly. All of this means a more stable network. Customers get their problems solved quickly and accurately, so they have less down time. Calls are tracked, so training needs can be identified and the appropriate training administered. Customers will be making more effective use of their technology. The business can become more competitive.

Types of Tools

Help Desk tools include everything that facilitates the jobs of Help Desk staff and allows them to offer their customers better service. These include:

- Reference tools
- Forums for learning and idea exchange
- Tools for communication
- Telephone technologies
- Call tracking and management
- Asset management
- Network management
- Problem solving
- Use of multimedia
- Self-help for the customer

There are a myriad of vendors involved in the development and sale of these tools. Some market their version of the tools as standalone modules, while others offer totally integrated systems. The Help Desk Institute, an organization devoted to Help Desk improvement, puts out a yearly Buyer's Guide describing the various Help Desk tools available and listing where to get more information on each. Ziff Communications Company puts out a product called Computer Select, a CD-ROM of magazine articles and related information that can be searched for product announcements, reviews and descriptions, and information on each vendor. Other sources of product information include organizations such as Data Pro Information Services Group and on-line bulletin board services.

Degrees of sophistication and integration have a big effect on price, and the ranges in price are as wide as the range of products available. Selecting products is a matter of carefully determining the requirements for your particular environment and balancing those with your budget.

Reference Tools

Reference material for Help Desks is material that allows the Help Desk to keep up with changes in technology, stay informed of fixes or problems in software and hardware, access technical manuals and documentation for help in resolving problems, and give customers information on where to go for services that the Help Desk does not provide.

Reference material used to mean binders and binders of documentation, which was not updated and was often misplaced. It meant software and technical manuals that sometimes disappeared when they were needed the most. Today's reference material should seldom be on paper and should require very little manual updating. Help Desk reference tools include:

- Phone lists
- Phone numbers and contacts for services that the Help Desk does not provide
- CD-ROM
- Electronic bulletin boards

Phone Lists

A phone list is perhaps the simplest Help Desk tool and one of the few that may need to be manually updated. The Help Desk should have phone lists for key contacts in case of problems, and for vendors and suppliers. Wherever possible, this list should be integrated into the Help Desk software being used. Customer phone numbers should not be kept on a separate list but should be part of the customer information accessed from the Help Desk system.

Phone Numbers and Contacts for Services the Help Desk Does Not Provide

If there are services that you do not provide but occasionally get requests for, a service that you *can* provide is letting people know where they can get the service. A table of services, contacts, and phone numbers—available to all Help Desk staff and integrated into the Help Desk system if possible—will make sure that this information gets passed on to customers consistently and quickly.

An even better solution might be to provide this information directly to customers so that they don't have to talk to a Help Desk person to get it. If you front-end your Help Desk phone system with a menu, you might add this information as an option. Alternatively, you might have a central base of information that customers could access via their PCs or terminals.

CD-ROM

- CD-ROM for magazine articles

    Databases of articles and abstracts from hundreds of computer magazines are available on CD-ROM. These are an excellent reference tool for researching a product that you are considering buying, or for obtaining more information on technology directions or specific processes. Databases that can be accessed include magazine articles, hardware products, software products, and computer companies. Search and access is quick, accomplished by entering keyword search text. Subscriptions are purchased for a year, and a new CD-ROM is sent every month. Each CD-ROM contains twelve months' worth of information.

- CD-ROM for support information

    Technical information for supporting networks and applications is available for easy search and access on CD-ROM. Material includes books, manuals, technical notes, and related materials, all of which are useful in solving problems or research. Instead of thumbing through journals or reference manuals, you can let the system do it more quickly by keying in appropriate key words or search text. This material will help Help Desk staff answer application questions they might get. Subscriptions to these CDs are typically purchased for a year, with updates issued monthly.

Implementing one of the CD-ROM reference tools mentioned above is relatively inexpensive compared to other Help Desk tools, but reference tools do have limitations. The databases of information provided are static. You cannot add site-specific information.

Electronic Bulletin Boards

On-line bulletin board services provide information on products, product upgrades, problems, and fixes. You can download upgrades and fixes directly. They also provide comprehensive news on what is going on in the industry, support information, and various technical forums. If you have a problem that you cannot resolve or an idea that you want to air, or if you just want to get some ideas, you can join a forum and talk to other people in your field. Bulletin boards provide access to information and forums for a vast number of products and companies. The major bulletin boards vary somewhat in service provided and in cost, and you might want to join more than one. These are great learning and reference tools for Help Desk staff, available right at their desks.

Forums for Learning and Idea Exchange

One of the most valuable ways of keeping staff up to date with technology that is constantly changing, and to keep them innovating, is by sending them to conferences and trade shows and getting them involved in user groups. This will allow them to exchange ideas, get feedback on ideas, pick up new ideas, and avoid problems that others have run into. When budgets are being cut, this is usually one of the first areas to feel the blow, but that can be a mistake. When technology is changing as rapidly as it is today, when competition in business is as great as it is today, you cannot afford to be left behind. You need to take advantage of anything that makes you better, and often that means improving technology. Keeping up to date will allow you to do this; it will give you the information you need to select and purchase a tool that will help your particular environment.

Help Desk Institute

If nothing else, you should join the Help Desk Institute (HDI). HDI is a membership organization devoted to the improvement of Help Desks. It sells reference material on how to set up and improve Help Desks, puts out a newsletter, offers a wide variety of training given by experts in the field, and hosts a variety of seminars and conferences around key topics in the area of Help Desks. Membership in the institute, paid on a yearly basis, allows discounts on reference material and courses. Membership spans 11 countries. HDI also helps set up local Help Desk Institute chapters, which function as user groups—they meet to discuss Help Desk issues and bring speakers in. Topics of seminars offered include communication with Help Desk customers, problem solving, supervisory skills, quality, management and improvement of the Help Desk, and how to design and set up a Help Desk.

Trade Shows

Trade shows showcase new and existing products. They give staff an opportunity to attend seminars on various products, and to talk to vendors about product potentials and any problems they have experienced. Staff can get an idea of product direction.

Conferences

Conferences such as the International Help Desk Conference (put on by the Help Desk Institute) allow professionals to get together, talk about what's new, identify trends, and discuss what is required in the Help Desk field. These conferences are also a good opportunity to let vendors know what you need in the way of Help Desk tools. Vendors attend to listen to requirements and problems, and they get feedback on products.

User Groups

Various vendors have their own user groups and hold their own conferences for their specific products. These are valuable forums for information exchange.

Tools for Communication

Communication tools include those being used to facilitate communication within the Help Desk and those that are used to communicate with customers and other support staff.

White Boards

Sometimes the simplest tools are the most effective. If Help Desk staff become aware of a serious problem, they might write a note on a central white board, visible to all other Help Desk staff, to make everyone aware of the situation. The drawback? Someone has to remember to erase the message.

Voice Mail

Voice mail can be part of your Help Desk phone system. It can take messages when all Help Desk staff are busy, and can be used to broadcast messages about the system. It must be used carefully on a Help Desk—if you don't get back quickly to people who leave messages, then people aren't going to use voice mail. They will find another way to get help, and it might not be through your Help Desk. Voice mail can be integrated with Help Desk software and/or other telephone technologies. For example, a customer might initiate a Help Desk call by using a voice response unit that interfaces with Help Desk software to generate a trouble ticket automatically. As part of the problem initiation, the customer might leave a voice message describing the problem. The whole area of voice processing is looked at in more detail farther on in this chapter, in the section entitled "Telephone Technologies."

Electronic Mail

Electronic mail is not only a general-purpose communications medium, allowing communication with everyone who has a user ID for that system (usually all Help Desk customers), but can also be integrated with Help Desk software to allow customers to interact directly with the Help Desk system. Some Help Desk systems have interfaces that allow customers to log problems and generate trouble tickets automatically by sending an electronic mail message into the Help Desk. In the same way, when a log is closed, an automatic notification can be sent to the customer. Other Help Desk systems allow for even more integration of electronic mail into the Help Desk function. For example, when a Help Desk staff member enters a problem, it can be flagged as a problem relevant to another staff member's problem, and the details can be automatically routed to that person.

Electronic Displays

Electronic displays can be set up in customer areas to keep them up to date on system status. If there is a problem, the display will either flash or beep, and a message indicating the nature of the problem will be displayed. This will cut down on calls to the Help Desk. Customers will get information about system status when a problem occurs simply by looking up at the display.

Telephone Technologies

Telephone technologies for the Help Desk can manage phone traffic into the Help Desk, route calls, accept customer input entered via the telephone keypad, and interact with other technology based on input from the customer. Examples of these are automatic call distributors, automated attendants, and voice response units. Sophistication of these tools is increasing constantly, and functionality overlaps to the point that one tool will often include another.

An aspect of telephone technology that is currently experiencing explosive growth, and that is changing the face of voice processing, is computer telephony: the integration of computer and telephone technology. Computer telephony is giving voice processing greater flexibility and functionality, decreasing its cost, and making it easier to set up and use. It is making the resources and information on a LAN accessible via telephone.

Automatic Call Distributor (ACD)

At its simplest, an automatic call distributor is a phone system, or software within a phone system, that manages the flow of calls coming into the Help Desk. An ACD typically routes calls on a first-come-first-serve basis to the first available Help Desk analyst. If all analysts are busy, callers are put into a queue and played a recorded message, such as "All Help Desk staff are currently busy; your call will be answered as soon as a Help Desk analyst becomes available." The ACD monitors the queue and sends the caller who has been in the queue longest to the next available operator. Some ACDs allow for programming of the routing algorithm so that it can be customized to the requirements of each specific Help Desk, and can vary according to traffic and time of day. The ACD monitors routed calls to make sure they are being distributed evenly among staff. More sophisticated ACDs ask customers to select from a list of options depending on the nature of their problem so that their call can be routed into the appropriate area. The ACD also provides statistics for calls such as number of calls coming in, number of calls abandoned, time on hold, and time per call. If the statistics provided by the ACD are not satisfactory—that is, not in the format required, or not giving the information required—there are separate ACD reporting packages that will do the job. Some packages allow managers to pull ACD information up on their PCs and get the information in real time and in the desired form.

Automated Attendant

A basic automated attendant for the Help Desk answers a customer call with an automated greeting offering a selection of options, then routes the call based on the option selected. Options usually include transfer to a human operator. Automated attendants can also be much more sophisticated. They can anticipate a caller's needs—based on where the caller is calling from, for example—and can be integrated with other technologies to use networking and voice-response features to route calls and give out information. Such integration can give customers the ability to check on the status of their Help Desk calls by entering their trouble ticket numbers. It can also give customers the ability to select an option and get prerecorded responses to frequently asked questions. While customers are on hold, the automated attendant can play prerecorded messages. Some automated attendants can make use of automatic number identification to pass calls on to Help Desk analysts who are servicing specific areas. Companies frequently use automated attendants to provide a reduced level of after-hours support.

Voice Response Unit (VRU)

A voice response unit (VRU) is a combination of hardware and software that allows a customer to interface with other technology, such as a mainframe, a local area network, or a fax machine, to get information or to perform a specific function. The customer typically makes a selection from a menu of options and then enters any data required via the telephone key pad. The VRU takes that data and acts upon it depending on the function requested. A VRU can fax selected documents back to the caller, provide prerecorded information on a specific topic, give the status of a job, reset terminals and printers, and reboot local area network file servers. The VRU can also be set up to interface with a call management system to allow customers to report problems or make requests and to check on problem or request status. Entering alphabetic data on a telephone key pad has some limitations. One company implemented a voice response unit to automate several Help Desk functions, including user ID resets. Unfortunately, user IDs were only three characters in length, which was not enough to uniquely identify a person via a telephone key pad. The Help Desk decided to use employee numbers instead. A voice recognition feature for VRUs would eliminate such limitations. Although this technology isn't quite up to the required standard yet, vendors are working to improve it.

Computer Telephony

To date, most computer–telephone integration has taken place through mainframe computers. This is now changing rapidly, as the technology and standards necessary to allow integration of telephones with LANs and PCs are developed. Two of the most critical of these are the Telephony Services Applications Program Interface (TSAPI) developed by Novell for LANs and the Telephony Application Program Interface (TAPI) developed by Microsoft for PCs. Another prominent vendor that is working toward computer–telephone integration is Lotus. Lotus has developed an application programming interface called Phone Notes that will enable software developers to create applications in which callers can access and listen to information from a Lotus Notes database. This technology has great potential for Help Desk applications, especially in the area of allowing customers to get their own solutions.

Novell's approach to computer telephony is server-based. Calls are controlled through PC applications, but PC and telephone remain separate, joined only through background links. Application messages travel across the LAN, through the server, and across a link to the telephone switch. This configuration gives Help Desks the ability to control a call even when they are not part of it, which allows for the synchronization of calls with screens of data. Help Desks can receive or transfer a screen full of data along with a call.

Microsoft's approach is client-based. The applications are run directly from and within the PC, using special interface boards. There is a direct connection between PC and telephone.

Vendors are working with the standards developed to provide the technology building blocks for LAN- and PC-based applications such as automated attendant, voice mail, audiotex (allows callers to select and listen to frequently requested prerecorded information), fax-on-demand, and delivery of database information via voice. Figure 6.1 shows some of the functions that computer telephony applications will provide.

One of the most important applications coming out of computer telephony, from a Help Desk point of view, is Caller ID database lookup. When a call comes into the Help Desk, the telephone switch identifies the caller (through automatic number identification) and passes the calling number across the LAN to a Caller ID database. Information from the

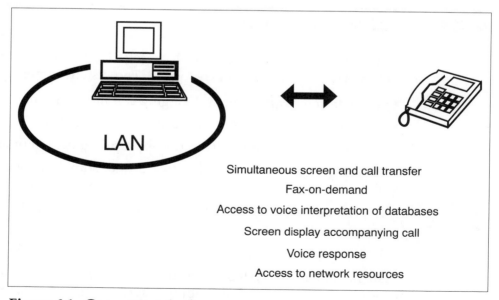

Simultaneous screen and call transfer

Fax-on-demand

Access to voice interpretation of databases

Screen display accompanying call

Voice response

Access to network resources

Figure 6.1 Computer telephony.

database is sent across the LAN to the analyst taking the call, so that when the analyst picks up the phone, the information for that caller is displayed on the analyst's screen. Information might include customer information such as hardware configuration, software used, records of previous calls and how they were resolved, and so on. This means a significant time saving for each call. If necessary, the analyst can pass the call on, along with the screen full of information, to a second-level support person.

Other computer telephony applications that bring increased functionality to the Help Desk include voice response and fax applications. The Help Desk might use a VRU that interacts with the customer to try to solve a problem by sending a fax, or by offering a selection of prerecorded solutions for the customer to listen to. Help Desk analysts can also initiate faxes from their PCs. If an analyst finds that explaining a solution is too complex or time-consuming, it might be easier for that analyst to simply fax the information to the customer using a fax server on the LAN.

Computer telephone integration brings client/server flexibility to the Help Desk and opens up a new realm of possibilities for service improvements.

Call Tracking and Management

Call management systems, also called Help Desk systems, track and manage all Help Desk calls that are logged. The systems typically include:

- A function for capturing and logging call information.
- A central database where all logged calls are stored.
- A function for routing calls to the appropriate person or area.
- A function for managing hardware and software assets, or the ability to interface with other asset management systems.
- A problem/solution database or expert system, or the ability to interface with one.
- Reporting and querying capabilities against logged data.

Call management systems can also have connections to electronic mail systems, automatic call distribution systems, automated attendants, voice response units, pagers, and fax machines.

Capturing and Logging Call Information

Call management systems allow for easier logging of calls by automatically filling in customer information, which is obtained by links to various databases and systems. This information might include customer hardware and software if the system has a link to the inventory database. When logging a customer call, some form of customer identification, such as a user ID, is entered into the system, and the system fills in as much information as it knows about that customer—for example, name, phone number, location, department, time of call, and hardware and software configurations. The system also assigns the call a unique identifier, often called a trouble ticket. The Help Desk person can then enter details of the call. These might include description, components involved, and priority. A logged call contains all details of the call, its status, and any progress that has been made on it. Notes are entered on the logged call by the person working on it. Progress on calls can be monitored from call initiation to call close.

Interfaces with voice response units and electronic mail systems give the Help Desk the option of having customers log their own problems. Customers can call in through a voice response unit and enter the relevant data using the telephone key pad. The call management system will capture the information and log the call, generating a trouble ticket. Alternatively, customers can send a problem to the call management system via electronic mail to have the call logged and a trouble ticket generated automatically.

Central Database

Logged calls, and all of the notes surrounding them from beginning to end, are stored in a central database from which queries and reports can be run. Customers can be given access to this database so that they can check on the progress of their calls. This database provides information that can tell Help Desk managers if their Help Desks are working as they should and point out problem areas. The data can be queried to find calls that have been outstanding for too long, calls that are receiving too high a priority, and calls that had to be reopened because they were not resolved properly the first time. It can give call volumes by type of call or reason for call, and can sort data by Help Desk analyst. Queries or reports can usually be customized as required and scheduled to run automatically. This data can tell the Help Desk manager if priorities are being used properly and are properly balanced, if procedures are correct and are being followed, and if there are staff who appear to be having trouble getting calls resolved. It can also alert the Help Desk to trends such as problems with specific makes and models of hardware or recurring problems, and can identify customers or groups needing training in a specific product.

Routing Calls

Call management systems can route calls electronically into a queue for a specified person or area. An analyst can then take ownership of the call by picking it off of the queue; that analyst's ID is automatically recorded against the call. The analyst fills in notes on the logged call as it is worked on to indicate what is being done, and then enters a description of the resolution when the call is completed. Completed calls are marked as closed, and some systems even automatically send an electronic mail message to the customer indicating that the call has been completed.

Managing Hardware and Software Assets

Some call management systems include a component that tracks hardware and software inventory. Others may not include the software to do this, but can get data from other asset management systems.

Problem/Solution Database or Expert System

Call management systems may include an expert system or problem/solution database, which can be used to help resolve problems, or may interface with such systems. Problem/solution databases can be built from the call management database with information from calls that have been logged and closed. The database itself can be queried with keywords used to search through problem descriptions and solutions.

Reporting or Querying Capabilities Against Logged Data

Standard reports and queries are supplied with most call management systems, but these systems often allow Help Desks to build their own reports or queries. These can be designed to flag specific trends. Reports

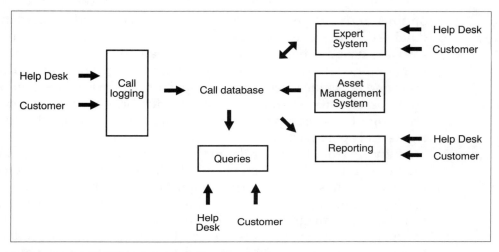

Figure 6.2 Call tracking and management.

or queries can be run against the database of logged calls on an ad hoc basis or at regularly scheduled intervals.

Call management systems are available for both mainframe and PC environments, and some can interface with both. They range from the very simple, with limited functionality, to the very complex, with high degrees of integration and functionality. Host-based systems tend to be slower, more cumbersome, and more difficult to modify. If the host is down, the Help Desk system is inaccessible. PC-based systems tend to be faster and more flexible, have more functions, and be less affected by problems with other network components. Figure 6.2 shows some of the key interfaces of a call management system.

The value of a call management system lies in its data, specifically the calls that are logged. The higher the percentage of calls that are logged, the more useful and powerful this data will be.

Asset Management

An asset management system automatically tracks hardware and software that is connected to a network. It collects extensive information, which includes details on applications and system software, hardware configuration, memory, hard drives, boards, hard drive utilization, setup options, and configuration files. Information collected is stored in an asset database. The system can remove illegal software and keep track of software usage to help ensure that adequate (but not excessive) licensing is maintained. It may also include a financial component that does some book and tax value calculations against the database of asset information. Some asset software makes provision for on-line vendor catalogs for ordering of new equipment or checking of prices. Even details on user rights and spare parts can be tracked.

Reports from the asset database can be issued by node, customer, or type of equipment, and can usually be heavily customized. Reports can be used to help solve network problems related to hardware and software configurations, plan upgrades, manage maintenance contracts, track warranties, and manage software licensing compliance.

Asset management software can be set up to run at predetermined times, and can do some or all of a network at any one time. Some versions have the ability to do portions of a PC each time the user of the PC logs onto the network. The system remembers where it was last time and continues. This way, the customer does not have to wait while the software does a complete inventory. The software can also be used on individual workstations that are not part of a network, to give the same information.

Asset management software largely automates a task that is tedious and time-consuming to say the least. Taking inventory manually means walking around from PC to PC, making note of software, hardware components, serial numbers, and opening each PC up to record the various boards and add-ons inside. By the time you finish a PC and go on to the next one, the inventory of the first is out of date. Software could have been added or deleted, configurations could have been changed, and the hardware itself might have been moved. It is next to impossible to keep an up-to-date inventory of hardware and software assets manually.

Some Drawbacks

Most asset management packages available work only with a limited number of models of PCs and cannot audit attachments such as monitors, printers, and modems. This limitation is due to the fact that there are no industry standards that allow for easy querying of hardware. To combat this, a consortium of vendors called The Desktop Management Task Force was formed in 1992 to address this issue of nonstandardization. This group has outlined a set of common application programming interfaces called the Desktop Management Interface (DMI), which is to be incorporated in such devices as microprocessors, hard disk drives, and network adapters, and in software such as operating systems and applications programs. The DMI will automatically gather data on all these elements, enabling companies to manage desktop systems across networks. With participation from top software and hardware vendors, the task force is developing a specification for a small memory-resident program that will reside on client PCs and report critical information, such as the name and serial number of an add-in board. DMI-compliant products were already in beta testing when this book was being written. Also under consideration are ways to retrofit pre-DMI PCs. PC component data would need to be reformatted into DMI format.

Conclusion

Automated asset management software is fairly new. With help from DMI, it will continue to improve in functionality and usefulness, and will change significantly over the next few years. In the meantime, even if the software cannot track all of your inventory, it will still save you the time and trouble of tracking what it can take care of. It will give you information that you could not get before, and you can start experimenting with various uses for this information. When you *can* track all of your inventory, you will already have the processes in place for collecting inventory information and for making best use of it to manage your assets effectively.

Network Management

Network management systems monitor the performance of all components, or specific components, of a network, and can flag occurrences of problems, degradation, or unusual activity. The more components your management system can monitor, and the more information it can integrate, the more useful it will be to you.

Network activity can be watched from a workstation, and a graphic representation of the network will show where any problems, abnormalities, or degradations occur. Network management systems offer functions such as traffic monitoring, software distribution, storage management, and software license management. Some include components for managing assets and security, and others go even farther and monitor workstation usage and application performance.

As a network management system runs, it continuously monitors a company's network looking for trouble spots. If it locates a problem, it can notify the appropriate person via electronic mail or beeper, and may even analyze the problem and use a case-based expert system to recommend a solution. Some network managers even take action to fix certain problems, or allow staff to fix these problems from the network management workstation. Problems that can be detected include power problems, defective or broken cables, damaged connections, incompatible network interface cards, and nonfunctioning software routers.

Network management systems need to know what normal network behavior is so that they can flag abnormal behavior. Staff can set thresholds defining normal behavior or, in some cases, the system can watch the network for a defined period of time and define for itself what normal behavior is. After the definition period, the system will flag anything it did not previously encounter—for example, variations from normal network traffic volumes, virus activity, security breaches, and improper or damaged connections.

Network management systems allow potential problems or negative trends to be flagged and fixed before the network is affected, suspicious or unusual activity investigated before it becomes a problem, and problems identified as soon as they occur. They ensure that the network is running as efficiently as possible, and that it is maintained and upgraded as necessary to handle any new software or increases in traffic. They make the network more stable and, as such, are a mandatory requirement for any mission-critical network.

Problem Solving

Help Desk tools that help with the problem-solving process are remote diagnostic software, problem-solution databases, and expert systems.

Remote Diagnostic Software

Remote diagnostic software products allow Help Desk staff to take over a customer's PC session from their own workstations, so that they can help resolve any problems that the customer is experiencing. Help Desk staff can see exactly what the customer was doing at the time of the problem and what the customer's PC environment looks like, including configuration files. With remote diagnostic software, staff can watch the screens and operate the keyboards and mice of any node on the local area network. This might cause some privacy concerns among Help Desk customers, and these would need to be addressed before any such tools were put into use. Remote diagnostic tools can typically be configured to give the customer some kind of indication that the customer's PC is being monitored.

One current disadvantage to this software is its negative affect on LAN traffic. When Help Desk staff are taking over a customer session, they must intercept the activities of the customer, who might be on a distant segment or ring of the LAN. This affects overall network balance and can slow traffic down considerably. Vendors are working to address this problem. Despite this disadvantage, remote diagnostic tools are well worth looking at. They give the Help Desk staff the ability to perform fast and accurate problem diagnosis without asking too many technical questions that the customer might not be able to answer, and without having to rely on the customer's version of what happened—all without having to leave their own workstations.

Problem/Solution Databases

Problem/solution databases are typically home-grown relational databases that provide a base of site-specific problem and solution knowledge. They contain a history of problems that have occurred at your site and the solutions that resolved them. Help Desk staff enter problems with appropriate keyword queries to look for matching problems and their solutions. Some databases support hypertext links (which link segments of text so that one can be accessed quickly from the other), so Help Desk staff can jump quickly to related material if they think they are close to an answer. These databases allow you to search for keywords in different contexts, so you may look at solutions you would never have considered. The databases do no screening for you—it is up to you to decide where to look next. The system has no intelligence; your judgment does the work. Problem/solution databases need frequent updating—as new problems happen, they need to be recorded. The database is only useful for problems that have already occurred previously.

Expert Systems

Although expert systems are referred to as *reasoning* systems, they are not really capable of reasoning, only of knowing. Humans find reasoning a time-consuming process, and what we tend to do is store the results of our reasoning for later reference. That stored information is what we put into expert systems. An example that Daniel Crevier uses to illustrate this in his excellent book *AI: The Tumultuous History of the Search for Artificial Intelligence* compares a biologist to a physician. Of the two, the biologist is better able to explain the workings of a human body, but is unable to recognize a specific infection and prescribe the appropriate drug for it. Recognition of the infection and prescription of a drug are often not a matter of reasoning, but rather of knowing which symptoms go with which infections, and which drugs are effective in eliminating each infection.

An expert system is composed of a knowledge base and a shell. The knowledge base can be structured in various ways, but always contains the knowledge—information that will suggest to the user of the system what to do or what conclusions to reach under a specific set of circumstances. The knowledge base is built by the experts who know how to solve the problems that might occur. The shell of the expert system is the part that contains the mechanism for accessing the knowledge base and the user interface. The knowledge base searching mechanism is sometimes called the *inference engine*. Several vendors offer expert shells, which companies can customize to their own requirements by providing the information. The shells contain logic that is the result of years of AI research, and that would take a significant time to recreate.

Expert systems tend to be PC-based, for reasons of speed and flexibility.

Two of the currently most popular formats for knowledge bases are rule-based and case-based.

Rule-Based Expert Systems

In rule-based expert systems, the knowledge base is made up of IF THEN rules. Each specifies what to do or what conclusions to draw under a specific set of circumstances. Rule-based systems are typically part of a decision tree that allows selection from a few options at a branching point; the option selected then branches into another set of options at the next point in the tree. For example, at the start the system can ask about the type of operating environment being used—DOS or Windows; after a selection is made (Windows), the staff member is shown the next level of questioning—which of three program groups was being used—and so on until a solution is reached. Rules can contain certainty factors, indicating the estimated probability of a given answer or situation. For example, the problem might have a 70 percent chance of being related to hardware and a 30 percent chance of being related to software.

Rule-based systems are updated by adding new rules. The person updating the system can correct errors in rules by asking the system how it reached a faulty conclusion. The defective rule will appear in the chain of inference cited by the system. Since the rules are usually self-explanatory, users of the tool can also follow the reasoning involved and satisfy themselves of the validity of the system's conclusion.

Case-Based Expert Systems

Case-based expert systems contain whole cases, rather than rules. They work on the basis of pattern matching. The knowledge base is built using information from prior cases. Each problem entered into the database is entered as a case: the problem and its solution as they occurred previously. Help Desk staff enter the various characteristics of a problem, and the system searches for similar previous cases. With a large enough knowledge base, even a relatively inexperienced Help Desk person can use this system to resolve known problems. Case-based systems are updated by adding new cases, and are only useful for problems that have occurred previously.

Drawbacks of Expert Systems

The work necessary to set up and maintain the knowledge base in an expert system can be, or can become, prohibitive. Maintaining a knowledge base can become a nightmare in an environment where things change rapidly and a large number of cases or rules must be maintained.

Expert systems tend to be useful only within specialized areas. When the knowledge base gets too wide, they start to break down. Things no longer relate to each other in the same way, and words might mean different things.

Conclusion

How useful an expert system is for you depends on the resources you have and the types of problems you tend to have. If you have the resources necessary to set up and maintain the knowledge base, expert systems can be a valuable Help Desk tool. They enhance the knowledge of your staff and allow them to solve problems that they would not have had the knowledge to solve on their own.

If the problems you get tend to be ones that you haven't seen before, or that involve new technology, expert systems may not be able to help you.

Use of Multimedia

Multimedia is not a tool on its own, but rather one that is incorporated into other Help Desk tools to make things clearer to help staff. For example, diagrams or pictures incorporated into Help Desk systems and expert software might make it easier for Help Desk staff to visualize what a particular hardware component looks like so that they can help the customer solve a problem, such as where to plug in a cable. Sometimes videos with voice explanations are included to explain more complex procedures.

Self-Help for the Customer

The more customers can do for themselves, the farther existing Help Desk resources can be stretched. Some of the functions customers can perform for themselves, as illustrated in Figure 6.2, include:

- Checking on the status of problems.

  A voice response unit connected to the call management database can provide the customer with problem status. The customer can call in, key in a trouble ticket number, and get the required information. Alternatively, the Help Desk can give customers restricted access to the call management system so that customers can check status themselves, directly on the system.

- Reporting problems.

  A voice response unit or electronic mail system connected to the call management system can give the customer the capability to log problems via phone or electronic mail. The call management system can pick up the required information, log the call, and generate a trouble ticket.

- Performing simple functions.

Simple and commonly requested functions, such as terminal or printer resets, can be programmed into a voice response unit, so that customers can call in and perform these functions themselves by selecting an option and keying in the requested data.

- Getting information and solving problems.

The Help Desk may be able to give the customer direct access to any problem/solution or information databases that it uses. A customer can search the database for the problem and try any suggested solutions before calling the Help Desk.

Prerecorded messages giving out commonly requested information can be offered as selections on a voice response unit so that customers can get the information themselves.

Linking a knowledge base to a fax-on-demand application driven by a voice response unit allows customers to request faxes containing current information on suggestions or solutions for problems, via phone. The documentation the customer receives is actual extracted data, so it is the most up-to-date information available.

Integration

Help Desk tools that are integrated, that can talk to each other and share data, are more powerful than those that stand alone. A case-based expert system on its own is useful. One that is integrated with a call management system and that will automatically use the information that you log for a call to search for a problem/solution match is more useful. Network monitoring tools that run on their own, each monitoring a different network component, are useful, but a network management system that integrates several such tools to monitor the whole network is more useful and much more powerful. Not only will the system be able to monitor individual components, but it will be able to see their effects on each other, and how their interactions affect the whole network. The system can make more intelligent suggestions for fixing problems, because it will have more knowledge to draw on. Reporting will give you a consolidated picture—you won't have to go to several different reports from several tools to get the information you need. Data will be more accurate because no duplication will be necessary. The systems communicate so data can be retrieved from the source.

Integrated tools can be purchased or built by combining individual tools and data. If you can't find one that suits your needs, you will have to build one. You may purchase a call management system and then buy separate components, such as an expert system and an asset management system, and integrate the three. You may buy a network management system and then purchase a separate component to monitor cables because the system didn't include one. You would integrate the cable component into the main system so that it would function as part of the system. You might also purchase an asset manager and integrate that into your network management system, so that your management system could check node hardware and software when trying to determine causes of problems and when looking for potential problems. Figure 6.3 shows how an integrated system might work.

With an integrated system, you might be able to realize the following scenario:

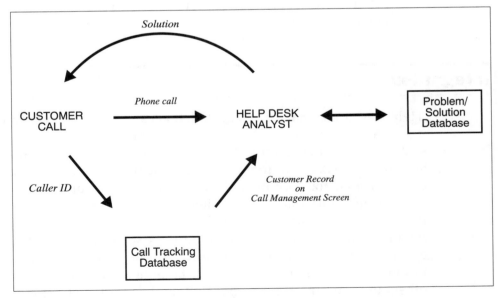

Figure 6.3   Integration of Help Desk tools.

A call comes through to the Help Desk. Your LAN-based computer telephony application picks up the caller's phone number, retrieves the customer information (including hardware and software configuration) from the call management database, and sends it to your PC in call management screen format, along with the actual phone call. Before you even talk to the customer, you know it's not a routine problem or request, because your voice response unit is taking care of those. Your call management application tells you that there is a potential problem with the brand of monitor that the customer is using, which is currently under investigation with the vendor. No problem with the monitor this time. The customer's PC was moved and now the PC won't even boot up. You ask your expert system for help, and it uses the data you have keyed in to suggest that the keyboard and mouse cables have been reversed. The system displays a detailed drawing of the back of that model of PC showing where connections need to be made. You use the drawing to walk the customer through the process of reattaching the cables. The problem is solved.

The next call comes in, and because the customer is having trouble explaining what the problem is, you use remote diagnostic software, which is also integrated into your call management system, to take over the customer's application to see what's wrong.

Before the third call comes in, you get paged by the network management system for a cable malfunction. You check the monitor, and sure enough, you can see exactly where the bad cable is. You pass the logged call to the hardware maintenance technician, who is alerted by pager of its high priority. It is resolved before you receive any calls about it. You are able to solve almost all problems using only the tools at your disposal.

This vision is a little idealistic, maybe, but it is certainly something you can start building toward.

Summary

Help Desk tools can help you track and manage calls, solve problems and answer questions, manage hardware and software assets, and monitor networks. They allow both Help Desk staff and customers to become more self-sufficient and the Help Desk to become proactive. Problems and problem trends can be identified and taken care of before they become serious. What this means to the business is more stable technology and more productive employees.

Tools for the Help Desk include those for reference, education and idea exchange, call distribution, call management, asset management, network management, and problem solving.

Reference tools include phone lists for vendors and suppliers, phone numbers and contacts for services that are not provided by the Help Desk (but that are requested by some customers), technical support information on CD-ROM, and databases of articles and abstracts from magazines on CD-ROM. Electronic bulletin boards are also valuable tools for reference. They offer news on products and services and industry events, and provide download services for upgrades and products. They also hold forums where people with similar interests can get together and discuss individual problems, suggestions, and issues.

One of the best ways of keeping staff up to date with technology that is constantly changing is to have them interact with vendors of Help Desk tools and other Help Desk professionals for education and idea exchange. Trade shows, conferences, and user groups all provide excellent opportunities for this kind of interaction. An organization that also offers these kinds of opportunities, and one to which you should belong, is the Help Desk Institute. It provides training, reference material, seminars, and conferences, all dedicated to the improvement of Help Desks and Help Desk professionals.

Communication within the Help Desk and to customers and other support areas is an important part of Help Desk function. Tools that help you communicate include white boards used in the Help Desk area for messages about serious or global problems, voice mail, electronic mail, and electronic displays. Voice mail can be used to take Help Desk calls when all staff are busy or absent. Electronic mail can be used for Help Desk requests or for communication with remote users, and can be integrated with other tools. Electronic displays can be used in customer areas to display system status so that customers can be kept informed of problems or unusual activities without having to call the Help Desk.

Automatic call-distribution systems control the call traffic into the Help Desk. They can use a variety of routing routines to make sure that callers get the fastest service possible, and to provide detailed statistics on the call traffic. Automated attendants offer customers an automated greeting and a selection of options, including speaking to a Help Desk analyst. They route each call based on the option selected. Voice response units accept input from customers via a telephone keypad and then act upon it, interacting with other technology in the process. Voice response units can provide specific information or status, fax selected documents to customers, and restart terminals and printers. A new aspect of telephone technology currently experiencing explosive growth is computer telephony: the integration of computer and telephone technology. It offers greater functionality and flexibility in telephone applications, and in a LAN implementation, it gives the caller access to other resources (such as databases) on the LAN.

Call management systems track and manage Help Desk calls. They include a function for capturing and logging call information, a central database where all logged calls are stored and from which reports and queries can be run, and a function for routing calls to the appropriate area. These systems can also include components for asset management and problem solving. Call management systems help ensure that the Help Desk is functioning properly, and they provide valuable trending information that can be used to prevent serious problems and improve service.

Asset management systems automate the time- and labor-intensive process of taking inventory of hardware and software assets. They track all assets attached to the network and collect detailed information on each, which they store in an asset database.

Network management systems monitor the performance of network components and of the network as a whole. They monitor traffic and detect component degradation, problems, or unusual activity so that these can be addressed before the whole network is affected. Some network managers include components for software distribution, storage management, asset management, and security.

Aids to problem solving on the Help Desk include remote diagnostic software, problem/solution databases, and expert systems. Remote diagnostic software allows Help Desk staff to take control of a customer's PC session from their own workstations to help resolve any problems that the customer is experiencing. Problem/solution databases contain a history of problems and their resolutions. Help Desks can search this database when they receive a call that they cannot resolve: they can see whether the problem occurred previously and what the solution was. Expert systems provide a knowledge base, which contains information that can be used to help solve problems, and a shell, which holds the knowledge base and provides the mechanism to get at the information. The knowledge base in expert systems requires significant effort to set up and maintain. Two of the most common types of expert systems are rule-based, in which the knowledge base is made up of IF THEN rules, and case-based, in which the knowledge base contains whole problem/solution cases. Case-based expert systems are useful only for problems that have already occurred.

Help Desk tools offer self-help for the customer. The customer can log calls, check on call status, search a problem/solution database, perform functions such as terminal resets that are provided as options on a voice response unit, and retrieve information in voice or fax form, to help solve problems or answer questions.

Each Help Desk tool is useful on its own, but becomes more useful and powerful when integrated with other Help Desk tools and other data. Tools that can talk to each other and share data have more knowledge to make use of, and therefore greater functionality. They can take more information into account as they do their processing, and they can provide more informed and more accurate data. A completely integrated environment may not yet be possible, but it's certainly worth working toward.

CHAPTER SEVEN

Measuring Performance

As a Help Desk manager, you must keep a vigilant eye on the perform-ance of your Help Desk. You need to take on the role of auditor, and be constantly checking for cost-effectiveness, business value, and the satis-faction of your clients. You can't afford to let performance slip. Corpora-tions are less tolerant today of unsatisfactory performance than they ever have been.

Measuring performance won't only tell you how successful you are, it will give you valuable information on how you can improve, and will help you plan for the future. It can point out areas that you aren't handling as effectively as you could be, and will show how the technology base you are supporting is changing and growing. It will make your planning process less painful and more accurate.

Help Desk performance isn't something that is only of interest to a Help Desk manager. It is information that should be shared with custom-ers, staff, and management. Customers will get a better understanding of how the Help Desk functions, how their use of the Help Desk affects its performance, and why they are getting the levels of service they are. They will be able to see service trends—hopefully improvements—and how their feedback is used to make changes to and improve Help Desk service. Staff will get a better understanding of how their individual performance affects the overall performance of the Help Desk. The more they know about the factors affecting Help Desk performance, the better informed and motivated they will be to make improvements. They will also appre-ciate knowing that their feedback makes a difference. Sharing Help Desk performance with management allows them to see the business value the Help Desk is adding and the kinds of services it is offering its customers.

Performance information shows the workload that the Help Desk is handling and the environment it is supporting. The greater understanding that managers have of Help Desk performance, the easier it will be for the Help Desk to get support (financial and otherwise) to justify the tools and resources that it needs.

Measuring performance isn't a matter of looking in one place or running a one-time report. It's about gathering data from everyone affected by the Help Desk, and using all of this input to create the big picture that describes overall performance. It is measuring performance continuously, to be able to see trends of improvement or degradation. Performance statistics for one period of time are a snapshot of performance. Several iterations of performance statistics, over several periods of time, provide a moving picture, showing changes in performance.

Perspective

In order to get a complete picture of how your Help Desk is performing, you need to look at its performance from several different perspectives: those of customer, Help Desk staff, Help Desk manager, and management. No one of these views will give you a complete picture of your performance. For example, if you ask your customers how your Help Desk is performing, they might think that you're doing a fabulous job. You're answering all of their WordPerfect questions quickly and correctly. They've started calling you more and more because your answers are so reliable. In fact, your call volumes are increasing because you are so good at answering these questions. If all you looked at was customer satisfaction, you'd think you were doing a pretty good job as a Help Desk. But that's just one point of view. Your staff might have something different to say about it. They might be getting pretty tired of answering WordPerfect questions—especially since the kinds of questions customers are asking show that they haven't bothered to take any training. They're using the Help Desk to learn the software. A Help Desk manager might have a different perspective again: the Help Desk won't be able to achieve its objectives this quarter because too much time is being spent on WordPerfect support. The management view won't be positive, either. Managers will not be quite as impressed as your customers. For what the Help Desk is costing, in terms of people and tools alone, it should be delivering a lot more than WordPerfect support. What management is looking for is evidence that your Help Desk is adding value to the business. And they aren't seeing it—WordPerfect support just doesn't cut it.

Together, these different perspectives on Help Desk performance provide a complete picture of the situation. In this case, they show a Help Desk that is not meeting objectives, not adding value to the business with its current focus, and not an interesting place to work—a dysfunctional Help Desk that has specific areas needing improvement.

If you don't take all views into account when you measure your Help Desk performance, you won't really know how your Help Desk is performing. You may not be able to spot trouble until it is too late, and you won't see all of the improvements that you could be making. Your planning for the future will be less informed, and therefore less effective, than it could be.

Customer Perspective

A customer takes a somewhat selfish view of the Help Desk: "What's in it for me?" Customers will measure how successful the Help Desk is against those things that are important to them:

- Are Help Desk staff knowledgeable and polite? Can the person on the phone usually resolve the problem?

- Are problems followed up on and resolved, or do customers have to keep calling back?

- Are problems resolved quickly?

- Are customers able to get a high priority when they have a real emergency?

- Are things done when promised—for instance, does a service technician arrive within the time promised by the Help Desk?

- Are customers given training opportunities when they need them?

- Are customers kept informed of the status of their problems?

- Are they kept informed of system changes—software upgrades, for example?

- Are they informed of planned down times?

- Do they have some way of finding out when the system is down, how long it will be down, and how serious the problem is?

- Are they getting the services they need?
- Are service-level agreements being met?

These are things that are important to Help Desk customers—things that will help ensure minimum down times and make dealing with the Help Desk a pleasure rather than a frustration. The more "yes" answers you have to these questions, the more successful your customers are likely to consider you.

Customers won't call the Help Desk to say, "You're doing a good job," but neither will they necessarily call to say that you're not doing a good job. Don't believe that everything is fine just because you don't hear from them. They may have given up and be getting their support elsewhere, or they may have decided to go higher up to complain. Either way, your Help Desk isn't going to benefit. You have to go after customers for their feedback. The sooner (and more often) you get it, the sooner you can start to adjust your service to better meet their needs.

Staff Perspective

Customers are very influential in determining whether the Help Desk is successful from a staff point of view. Staff talk to customers all day and are getting constant feedback—if not in actual words, then in tone of voice, or in the requests themselves. What customers think of the Help Desk is communicated to Help Desk staff every time customers call, and this will have a big influence on how staff think the Help Desk is performing (as well as on staff morale).

How well prepared staff are to solve problems will also influence how successful they feel the Help Desk is. Training, tools, and availability of support from other areas are all necessary and important to them. If they aren't there when they should be, then performance will suffer.

Questions that staff will ask themselves to determine how well the Help Desk is doing from their point of view include:

- Do callers appear confident in the ability of Help Desk staff?
- Do staff have a reasonable workload?
- Are repetitive, uninteresting tasks automated?
- Are staff getting the amount of training they need?
- Do they have the tools to do the job? Are the tools working properly? (For instance, is Help Desk software fast enough to allow staff to log calls when they occur?)

- Do they have the support required to do the job? Are second-level support areas handling passed-on calls effectively?

- Are vendors providing adequate service?

Staff on Help Desks care very much about what customers think of their capability. Negative feedback from customers will be tough on morale, but may provide motivation to improve. Positive feedback from customers will be a reward. Staff will feel they are performing well when customers trust and respect them, when their work is interesting and challenging, when they have the tools they need, and when Help Desk processes are working.

Help Desk Manager Perspective

Customer satisfaction, staff feedback, and performance against objectives, budget, and service-level agreements all play a role in determining how successful the Help Desk is from a Help Desk manager's point of view. A Help Desk manager also looks to the internal workings of the Help Desk to help gauge how successful it is:

- Are staffing levels appropriate? Is the Help Desk able to handle peak loads without being over staffed for times of lighter traffic?

- Are procedures correct and being followed? Are greetings appropriate?

- Are priorities working? Are the most critical issues being resolved before all others?

- Are there any negative or positive trends in the calls, by type? Are there other areas that should be getting involved?

- Are calls coming in and out at a reasonable rate? Is resolution time reasonable?

- Is the Help Desk meeting its objectives?

- Is it meeting service-level agreements?

- Are staff performing well? Are they managing workloads? Do customers speak positively about staff?

- Is the Help Desk going to be able to handle growth in the environment? What is the trend in technology purchase and use?

Management Perspective

Management has the broadest perspective on Help Desk performance. The management point of view takes all other perspectives into account.

Managers are looking for business value. They want to know whether the Help Desk is worth the investment. Business value will vary in definition from manager to manager, but generally it is determined by several factors, including Help Desk achievements (performance against objectives); cost of service; satisfaction of customers, including performance against service-level agreements; value of individual services being provided; volume of customer calls being handled; and growth of the technology environment. Questions they are interested in to gauge Help Desk performance are:

- Are objectives being met?
- Is spending within budget and being allocated as planned?
- Are service-level agreements being met?
- Are customers satisfied?
- Is the Help Desk bringing value to the business?

Management will probably always be assessing the Help Desk for cost-effectiveness: can they get the same or better (if they don't feel you are performing well) service elsewhere for a better price, without giving up anything of importance? If they think they can, then they will. Don't wait for them to come to you. Go to them with the information that will let them evaluate the performance of your Help Desk. Better still, make sure your Help Desk is delivering the business value they're looking for.

When you have all four of these perspectives, you can get a true picture of Help Desk performance (see Figure 7.1).

Measures

In order to measure performance of your Help Desk, you'll need both quantitative and qualitative measures. Quantitative measures give you actual quantities or numbers, while qualitative measures give you the characteristics or qualities of what you are measuring—the things you can't put a number to. For example, consider a Help Desk that is measuring itself against a service-level agreement. The Help Desk manager looks

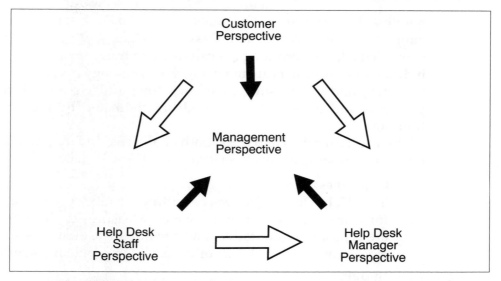

Figure 7.1   Management perspective of Help Desk performance takes all other evaluations into account.

at the numbers and thinks things look pretty good. Response times are being met 100 percent of the time. The manager decides to get some qualitative measures as well, and goes to customers and Help Desk staff for feedback. Customers think that the Help Desk is doing a great job and is meeting all aspects of the agreement. Staff, on the other hand, think it's failing. The response times aren't reasonable, and staff are working themselves into exhaustion trying to meet them. The Help Desk manager now has a very different picture of performance, and can address the situation before service is degraded or the staff drop from exhaustion. Another example is a Help Desk that has a problem resolution time that looks good on paper, but that is completely unacceptable to a specific group of customers who need a faster resolution time. They are doing critical work that the Help Desk might not know about, and the existing resolution times are affecting the business. A third example, and somewhat more drastic, is the Help Desk that is quite pleased to see the quantitative measure of number of calls decreasing. Customers, however, are simply fed up with inadequate service and have found another source of support. In each of these examples, just looking at the numbers would give a false impression. In the same way, just looking at qualitative measures would not give the whole story. Customers and Help Desk staff might be quite happy with the way the Help Desk is working, but the numbers might show that a large percentage of calls are of a training nature. This would indicate that customers are not using the technology properly or to its full potential, and are wasting their own time and Help Desk time with problems and questions that could be eliminated by the appropriate training.

Measures for the Help Desk, both qualitative and quantitative, can be taken from several areas of performance. These include:

- Objectives
  Your Help Desk objectives constitute a contract with management for a specific level of performance. Measures of this performance are typically quantitative, and include measurements such as decreases in number of calls or decreases in problem resolution time.

- Budget
  What your Help Desk spends is really half of a measure; the other half is the business value your Help Desk delivers. In looking at budget itself, you need to look at how much you spend (quantitative) and the business value of what you spend it on (qualitative).

- Service-level agreements
  Service agreements are contracts with customers for specific services, response times, and so on. They involve both qualitative and quantitative measures.

- Customer evaluation
  Measures within this category are primarily qualitative. You are measuring customers' perception of service.

- Help Desk staff evaluation
  In this category, you are measuring staff perception of service and their readiness and ability to provide that service (that is, whether they have the required tools and training). Measures are largely qualitative.

- Help Desk function
  This category is largely quantitative. Through statistics gathered primarily by your Help Desk call management system, you are measuring effectiveness of call handling and external support, and are looking for trends.

- Help Desk manager evaluation
This category takes all others into account. The Help Desk manager evaluates overall Help Desk performance using all of the data gathered. The manager then makes recommendations for changes or improvements, and summarizes the information to pass on to senior management (see Figure 7.2).

For each of the performance areas above, measures must be defined and taken, and the results interpreted, so that improvements can be made or further investigations undertaken. The more measures you use, the better performance picture you will have, and the more fuel you will have for improvement.

Objectives

When you're measuring your Help Desk against your objectives, you might be measuring the effectiveness of changes or improvements that you have made or the stability of existing service levels. For example, one

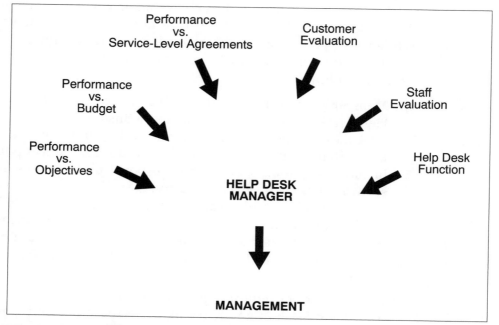

Figure 7.2 Help Desk manager evaluation.

of your objectives might be to reduce calls to the Help Desk by 20 percent. In order to achieve this reduction, you need to make some kind of change, such as installing a voice response unit to handle specific types of calls or eliminating recurring problems that are causing extra calls. Another of your objectives might be to maintain an average problem resolution time of four hours. You're already at the four-hour level, but you want to ensure that you stay there.

Regardless of whether your objectives measure change or stability, they should be focused on the business. If it is important to the business that all problems be resolved within four hours, then that had better be one of your objectives. If calls are increasing while the budget is staying the same, and you need to be able to maintain service levels to the business, then reducing the call load so that you can maintain service should be on your list of objectives.

So you can tell whether you've been successful at achieving objectives, your targets need to be clear and measurable. "Reduce calls by 20 percent" is precise and measurable, as is "Maintain an average problem resolution time of four hours," but "Start process of call reduction" is not.

Your targets also have to be achievable. If you say, "We will reduce calls by 20 percent," you should have done enough homework to be confident that your change will really eliminate that many calls.

Quantitative measures that you may want to use in your objectives include the following:

- Number (or percent) of calls resolved at point of call:
  Help Desks typically want to increase this number so that they can offer more of their customers total service with one call. Improvements that can increase the number of calls resolved at point of call include using tools such as voice response units, remote diagnostic software, or expert systems and giving staff training that will enable them to handle a wider variety of calls. This number can be measured easily by just about any Help Desk call management system. An example of an objective using this measure would be to "Increase number of calls resolved at point of call from 50 percent to 60 percent."

- Number (or percent) of a specific type of call:
  Your Help Desk might be trying to decrease certain types of calls: calls of a training nature, for example, or requests to handle tasks such as terminal resets. In the former case, you might be planning

to initiate a marketing campaign for training and offer several training courses; in the latter, you might be planning to automate terminal resets through a voice response unit. To know that your training campaign worked, you would need to see a decrease in the number of training-type calls into the Help Desk. Similarly, to know that your automation of terminal resets has been successful, you would need to see that calls for terminal resets were all being handled by the voice response units—none of these calls should be coming into the Help Desk. Call statistics from your call management system would tell you whether you achieved your target decreases. Examples of targets are: "Reduce the number of training type calls by 10 percent" and "Reduce number of calls into the Help Desk by 30 percent," where 30 percent of calls were terminal resets.

- Resolution times for problems not resolved at point of call:
  If resolution times are too high for problems that cannot be resolved at point of call, one of your objectives might be to reduce them. You might expect to do this through training, additional tools, improved procedures, outsourcing, or additional staff. Help Desk call management systems typically collect information on problem resolution times, and show whether you have been successful in reaching your target: "Reduce average problem resolution time for calls not resolved at point of call to 48 hours from 72 hours."

- Number of calls left unresolved:
  If your Help Desk is finding that problems are being left open too long, or are somehow falling through the cracks, one of your objectives will probably be to reduce or eliminate the number of calls left unresolved after a specific time—say, five days. In order to achieve this, you may be creating new procedures, providing training for staff, or purchasing new Help Desk software. Your objective might be to "Reduce the number of calls left unresolved after five days to less than 2 percent." Your Help Desk call management system can give you the data to tell you whether you've succeeded.

- Delivery time for services:
  For whatever services you provide, such as purchase and installation of PCs, you may be hoping to improve delivery time. Your objective might be to "Reduce the average time between PC order and installation to 14 working days." Your solution may be to outsource the whole activity to a vendor. If the vendor is using your

call management system, you can check your performance there, or you may ask your vendor to provide service-level information that you can check.

- Promised vs. actual:
  If the estimates your Help Desk is giving customers on when a service or solution will be delivered are consistently too low, you will want to set an objective to improve them, perhaps through training or improved procedures. As an example, if currently you meet your promised delivery date only 45 percent of the time, your objective might be to "Meet promised delivery dates 90 percent of the time." If your call management system tracks promised delivery time, it can tell you how successful you've been.

Other measures that you use will depend on your own individual Help Desk.

Performance against objectives isn't always as simple as "Yes, we achieved this" or "No, we didn't." Your achievements might look different from your objectives for various reasons:

- Circumstances can change quickly, as can he demands of the business. You may have had to change your focus on to something of greater business value.
- You may have underestimated the time required to achieve the objective. The objective may not have been realistic.
- You may have failed in some part of your change initiative.
- Staff may not be performing up to expectations.

In each of these cases of objectives not met, there is something your Help Desk can learn and improve from. You can improve your knowledge of what is required for a good estimate so that future objectives will be more reasonable. You can find and correct what went wrong in your change initiative and avoid the same mistakes in the future. You can identify and correct staff performance problems. You can turn any failures you have into learning experiences.

Table 7.1 shows a set of objectives and Help Desk performance against them.

In this example, not all objectives were achieved. Reasons included a problem with the support load, unrealistic objectives, and the way in

Table 7.1 Evaluating Performance Against Objectives

Objective	*Accomplished*	*Problems (if any)*	*What was learned*
Increase number of calls resolved at point of call to 80 percent (from 60 percent) with use of remote diagnostics software.	Achieved 68 percent	Some customers are refusing to let Help Desk staff monitor their sessions. Concerned with data security.	*Need to communicate the fact that users will be notified when their sessions are monitored; will only be used for diagnostics. A marketing effort is needed here.*
Upgrade all machines with less than 8 megabytes of memory to prepare for client/server.	85 of 110 machines upgraded	Taking longer per machine than planned. Ran into scheduling difficulties with customers.	*Next time, need to take this into account. This was an unrealistic objective.*
Install 15 PCs into the Sales area for the new Sales Promotion project.	Done on time; no major problems.		
Install new release of word processing.	Network Operating System required an emergency upgrade to fix response problems that happened when the 950th user came on line. This was successfully completed. Word processing upgrade was postponed.		
Research and select inventory management package.	Not done.	Support load was too high.	*Have to get this done. Need to reduce the load or get help.*

which a specific tool was implemented. There are (at least) three ways in which this Help Desk can improve from this information:

- It can improve its estimation skills. It has learned something about time required to carry out PC upgrades.

- It can focus its attention on the support load it is handling. The load is interfering with improvements, and investigation is required into the reason for the increased load and into ways of decreasing it.

- It can improve the way it is handling rollout of automation (in this case, remote diagnosis). More time must be spent with customers to make sure they understand it and are comfortable with it.

The installation of the word processing upgrade was not accomplished, but instead focus was switched to a network operating system upgrade, which had much greater business value at the time. This can be considered a successful accomplishment.

Budget

Budget isn't a complete measure on its own, but it's one that gets a lot of attention. It's really one half of a measure: the cost vs. benefit measure, which involves measuring what the Help Desk costs against the business value it is delivering. In order to help ensure that the cost side is lower than the benefit side, it is up to the Help Desk manager to make the best possible use of the budget, and that is the measure discussed here.

Staying within your budget goes without saying. No one has much tolerance for a manager who goes over budget. Performance against budget is not so much the amount you spend, but what you spend it on—how you handle the money that was allocated to you. As with objectives, if your actual spending varies from your planned spending in your allocation, if you bought added business value, your handling of the budget is successful. Just as overspending is not acceptable, spending less than you were allocated can be viewed as unacceptable. If you could have purchased a software package to improve Help Desk performance, but chose not to so that you could come in under budget (perhaps for political reasons), you may measure high on your own scale, but you won't measure high on anyone else's scale. Management will not be impressed when they hear customers complaining about poor service. Customers won't be impressed with this false economy—they are wasting more time than the package would have cost. Your staff certainly won't appreciate it, either. You want to maximize business benefits so that the cost vs. benefit comparison comes out in favor of the Help Desk.

One measure that you may want to keep track of is support cost per PC (or other technology component). Tracking this number will alert you to costs that may be out of line for the number of PCs being supported, will give you data to use for charge back purposes, and will help plan for PC growth. As you begin to understand this number, you may even want to include it in your objectives. Management will certainly be interested in this number. It can also be used to compare the cost of support by an internal Help Desk vs. cost of support by a third party. The wise Help Desk manager performs this comparison occasionally as a check of reasonableness (although a true comparison must take into account more things than just cost).

Table 7.2 shows an example of performance against budget.

Table 7.2   Evaluating Performance Against Budget

Item	*Budgeted Amount*	*Spent*	*Explanation*	*Observation*
Help Desk software upgrade	$12,000	$8,000	New version of support module is coming out in a few weeks. We will wait for it—it has extra functionality we could use.	*Good decision.*
Salaries	$58,000	$58,000		
General Office	$20,000	$20,000		
Software licensing for standard desktop software upgrades	$70,000	$0 on desktop upgrades; $70,000 on network operating system upgrade	Channeled funds into NOS to address performance degradation.	*Best use was made of the money.*
Cost per PC	$156, this quarter; $680 over last four quarters			

In Table 7.2, withholding spending for the new software upgrade (to wait for the new version) in this case was a good business decision—the new version is more suited to Help Desk needs. Channeling budget into an emergency operating system upgrade was also a good business decision. The cost of not upgrading (degraded performance) would have been greater than the cost of not making the software upgrades.

Service-Level Agreement

Service-level agreements not only define a Help Desk performance measurement, but also clarify both customer and Help Desk expectations. Each party understands what its responsibilities are and what to expect from the other party. The agreement contains both qualitative and quantitative measures.

A Help Desk might have a separate agreement with each customer area, agreements only with critical areas, or one agreement with all customers. A service-level agreement is most often developed jointly by customers and Help Desk, and can include:

- Help Desk responsibilities:
  What the Help Desk will be doing for the customer—for example, how each call is handled, or what monitoring or reporting is done.

- Customer responsibilities:
  Includes information the customer should have ready when calling the Help Desk, how the customer must report problems, and training the customer is expected to take.

- Hours of operation:
  Includes any after-hours service available.

- Help Desk services.

- A definition of priorities.

- Response times, usually by priority.

- Systems and components supported.

- Systems and components considered critical.

- Support fees, if any.

- Any additional "pay for as you use" services.

Following is an example of a service-level agreement between a PC Help Desk and the Classified department of a newspaper company.

Service-Level Agreement

Between:

The Corporate Help Desk and Classified

For period between:

March 1, 1993 and April 30, 1994

1. Help Desk Responsibilities

   - Provide dedicated phone number and electronic mail address for support: 222-4567, HELPD.
   - Take and log each call or electronic mail message.
   - Assign each call a priority based on priority codes.
   - Classify each call into one of the following categories: hardware, software, communications, training, general information.
   - Resolve problem or pass on for resolution to internal department or external vendor. Keep responsibility for each problem until it is closed.
   - Monitor and track problems, ensuring that they are resolved and closed.
   - Handle workload in order of priority.
   - Generate monthly Help Desk usage report to customer area.

2. Help Desk Hours of Operation

   - Regular hours of operation are Monday to Saturday, 6 A.M. to 8 P.M.
   - Off-hour support is provided for emergencies only, to the same number, by pager.
   - Hours of operation will be extended by four hours quarterly for a period of three days. Support will be provided 6 A.M. to midnight on the first three working days of each quarter.

3. Customer Responsibilities

   - Call 222-4567, or send electronic mail to HELPD for problems, questions, or requests. Problems will not be worked on unless they are logged into the system.
   - Provide customer number when calling.
   - Attend training on all software used.
   - Know how to use hardware.
   - Read and abide by all security and standards policies.

4. Services Provided to Classified by the Help Desk

- Hardware maintenance and inventory.
- Support of all hardware and software.
- Network monitoring and maintenance.

5. Priority Table

Response time is defined as the time between when you place the call and when work on it is started.

Priority Code	Description	Response Time
1	Critical system or component down	15 min.
2	Critical system or component degraded	45 min.
3	Noncritical system or component down	1 hr.
4	Noncritical system or component degraded	1.5 hrs.
5	General question	5 hrs.

6. Systems and Components Supported

Critical Systems:

- Ad Ordering
- Ad Creation

Critical Components:

- Ad server TIAD
- Local area network, ring 006
- All 12 PCs on the ring

Noncritical systems:

- Ad billing
- Ad reporting
- Ad search
- Standard desktop software
  - Microsoft Windows
  - Word for Windows

- Excel
- PowerPoint
- Microsoft Mail

Hardware Supported:

All hardware that meets Corporate standards (as per Corporate Technology Standards document) will be supported.

7. Additional Services and Fees

Training on standard desktop packaged software is available, and will be arranged by the Help Desk, for the cost of $250 per half day. Course dates and times are available from the Help Desk and are distributed to all customer areas quarterly.

Performance must be measured against each category in the agreement, and any recommendations for improvements made. Performance against a service-level agreement is a two-way measurement. In one direction it measures how the Help Desk meets its responsibilities, while in the other it measures how customers meet their responsibilities.

Performance against the service-level agreement can be checked using:

- Call statistics from your call tracking system (quantitative):
  Your call statistics will give you information on call volumes, resolution times, handling of priorities (order, resolution time), and types of customer calls.

- A survey of customers (qualitative):
  This will give you the customers' perception of how the Help Desk fulfilled its responsibilities: whether priorities were assigned appropriately, whether any prompting by customers was needed to actually get the work done, and so on.

- A survey of staff (qualitative):
  Help Desk staff will be able to give feedback on whether customers fulfilled their responsibilities: did they go through proper channels or did they try to cajole Help Desk staff away from their other calls to do work for them? ("Can you help me with this? It will just take a minute.") Did they provide the required information when they called? Did they take appropriate training, or were they using the Help Desk instead of taking training?

Table 7.3 shows a sample of service-level agreement measures.

Table 7.3 Measuring the Service-Level Agreement

Item	Statistics (Quantitative)	Customer Feedback	Staff Feedback	Observations
Customers must request support using Help Desk number or electronic mail ID.	N/A	Always done.	Customers still try to get support from staff who are en route to fix another problem.	*Need to market the cost of "stolen" support.*
Customers must attend training.	Percent of training-type calls = 30 (very high).	Don't always have time.	Still getting a lot of how-to calls on word processor.	*Need some marketing and a meeting with customer management.*
Help Desk must resolve problems within time frame specified.	75 percent of problems resolved in time frame.	Service staff took a long time to fix monitors.	Had problems getting ABC vendor to replace defective monitors as per warranty.	*Address this with vendor; also, are Help Desk staff communicating effectively?*

Table 7.3 indicates several areas for improvement:

- Customers aren't following regular channels for reporting problems. This must be stopped to prevent valuable statistics from being lost and to prevent disruption in priorities and staff workload.

- Customers are wasting their own time and Help Desk time with training calls. At 30 percent of calls, this is an area that has room for significant improvement if customers take the required training.

- Vendor management could use improvement. The Help Desk needs to either get this vendor working or find a new one.

- Help Desk communication of call status to customers seems to be a problem. The Help Desk needs to address procedures for this.

Customer Evaluation

A customer evaluation is a report card of Help Desk performance from customers. It provides the valuable customer perspective in overall Help

Desk evaluation. Customers evaluate the Help Desk against those things that are most important to them. These include:

- Speed and accuracy of service.
  Customer perception may be different from the quantitative measures supplied by a call management system.

- Provision of emergency service when required.
  Measuring customer perception would give an indication of whether the definition of emergency in Help Desk priorities was adequate.

- Quality of Help Desk staff (how knowledgeable they are).
  Just one customer who feels that the Help Desk doesn't know anything can do significant damage to Help Desk image and Help Desk success.

- Quality of training.
  How appropriate was it for the customer and environment? Was the topic covered adequately? How timely was it?

- Quality of services, such as PC purchase.
  Was the equipment delivered appropriate for the job being performed? Was it delivered when promised? Was it set up properly?

- Quality of communication.
  Are customers kept informed of progress on their calls? Are they informed of occurrences and durations of system outages or planned down times? Are they informed of training available, services available, how to use the services?

Getting customer evaluations of Help Desk performance can mean meeting with customer representatives to gather input on each of the performance categories, or sending out customer surveys such as the one in the following example. (This evaluation can be combined with performance against service-level agreement, if one exists.) Once surveys are collected and evaluated, results should be sent back to customers with any plans for improvements.

Specific areas, such as training and PC purchase, can be targeted separately for feedback. Perhaps all training attendees could be surveyed a few months after receiving the training so that they would have had a chance to use it and could give feedback on its relevance. Each person who received a PC might also be asked to fill out a quick survey form to give feedback on the whole process.

Following are a customer survey and sample results.

HELP DESK REPORT CARD

Customer Evaluation

You are a recent customer of the Help Desk. We would very much appreciate your input to help us rate our service. Please answer the following questions and return this card to the Help Desk by April 4th. Thank you for helping us improve!

Period: January 1 to March 31.

For each statement below, rate the Help Desk on a scale of 1 to 5, where 1: never true; 2: seldom true; 3: true half of the time; 4: usually true; 5 always true.

1. Staff are knowledgeable.
   If not 5, please explain: _____
   _____

2. Staff are polite.
   If not 5, please explain: _____
   _____

3. I have confidence that the Help Desk will help me.
   If not 5, please explain: _____
   _____

4. I have no trouble getting through to the Help Desk.
   If not 5, please explain: _____
   _____

5. My call is either handled on the phone or logged and resolved in a timely fashion.
   If not 5, please explain: _____
   _____

6. The Help Desk meets target dates and times that it gives me.
   If not 5, please explain: _____
   _____

7. The Help Desk keeps me informed of progress on calls that cannot be resolved immediately.
   If not 5, please explain: _____
   _____

8. The Help Desk keeps me informed of planned down times.
   If not 5, please explain: _____
   _____

9. The Help Desk informs me of changes in the environment (such as software upgrades, new software or systems, etc.).
   If not 5, please explain: _____
   _____

10. Using the Help Desk makes me more productive.
    If not 5, please explain: _____
    _____

Ways in which the Help Desk could make me more productive:

_____
_____
_____

Other comments:

_____
_____
_____

In this customer evaluation, you are looking for:

- The perception that customers have of Help Desk staff; any indications that Help Desk staff need training in either software products or customer service.

- How customers feel about quality and availability of service. If customers don't think that calls are being resolved in good time, yet call management statistics show that the average response time is good, perhaps the Help Desk definition of "good" is different from the customers', or perhaps there is significant deviation from the average. A service-level agreement might be indicated.

- How well the Help Desk is communicating to its customers; whether any changes might be needed.

- What value customers feel that the Help Desk is adding.

Table 7.4 indicates that customers feel that the Help Desk has a lot of room for improvement:

- There seem to be some products that the Help Desk is supporting but that staff aren't knowledgeable in—two products are specifically mentioned. You need to check with staff to ensure that they are getting the required training and that it is being administered on time.

- Getting through to the Help Desk seems to be a bit of a problem occasionally. You have to look at Help Desk traffic to see if there are any peaks that aren't being covered properly.

- Resolution times seem to be somewhat of a problem. You will need to check call statistics to see if response times are okay. If they are, you might need to clarify with the customers what constitutes an acceptable response time.

- Communication to customers seems to be a big problem. Customers aren't kept informed of call progress, planned down times, or changes. This needs to be investigated further. Perhaps new procedures are in order.

- The productivity comment needs monitoring—perhaps the variation is related to the fact that there was some lack of confidence in staff.

Help Desk Staff Evaluation

In evaluating Help Desk performance, Help Desk staff take both service-level agreements and direct customer feedback into account. Measures that Help Desk staff will use include:

- Customer attitude.
  Help Desk Staff are close to the customers. They talk to them all day, and they will notice if and when attitudes change. Customers calling the Help Desk aren't always in the best of moods, but staff can gauge changes to identify whether customers are satisfied with the service they are getting. If your Help Desk has a call-back program to check on the timeliness and quality of tasks, this will tell staff very clearly whether customers are satisfied.

- Legitimacy of customer calls.
  If the Help Desk is being misused, business value decreases, so this is not a trivial measure. If Help Desk staff notice an increasing number of calls that customers could have resolved easily themselves, this could signal misuse. If customers aren't bothering to look things up or to take training, then they are wasting time that the Help Desk could be spending doing things of greater value, such as making improvements. In addition, those customers probably don't understand the software, so they could be misusing it and making expensive mistakes.

Table 7.4 Customer Evaluation Results

	1	2	3	4	5	Customer Comments	Help Desk Manager Observations
Staff knowledgeable		10%	10%	80%			
Staff polite					100%		
Have confidence in staff		10%	10%	40%	40%	Don't seem to be up on latest release of Excel. Good in WordPerfect.	*Check with staff. Any new products rolled out? Training up to date?*
No trouble getting through to Help Desk			10%		90%	Hard to get through in the morning.	*Check traffic stats.*
Call handled in timely fashion		10%	15%	35%	40%		*Check call-handling procedures and re-sponse times.*
Kept informed of progress on calls	20%	30%	30%	20%		Very frustrating. I don't know when my problem will be fixed.	*Need to address com-munication.*
Kept informed of planned down times	75%	20%	5%			Poor communication.	*Ditto.*
Kept informed of changes in the environment	50%	30%	20%				*Ditto again.*
Makes me more productive		20%	40%	35%	5%		*Check vs. last quarter; keep an eye on this.*

- Adequacy of training received (for staff).
  If Help Desk staff feel that they aren't getting the training they need to handle the calls that come in (to deal professionally with the customers, or to use the tools that they have), then they won't feel that the Help Desk is doing as good a job as it could be.

- Availability and performance of tools.
  If staff don't have the tools to do their jobs properly, performance will suffer. In this measure staff will indicate whether they have the necessary tools, and whether those tools are working properly and are effective.

- Workload.
  Staff who don't have enough time to handle all of the work assigned them are staff who are going to be tired and stressed, and not nearly as effective as they could be on the Help Desk. Call statistics might not show this. Reports might indicate volume of calls, but if the staff are doing something else besides calls, the reports won't show this.

- Availability and function of second-level support.
  Help Desk staff will also evaluate interfaces with other support areas that they may have to pass calls to. If staff have to do a lot of calling or reminding to get the calls handled, then their jobs are more difficult and they are wasting time unnecessarily.

- Value of tasks performed.
  As well as quantity of work, staff are going to look at the value of the work that they do. If they find themselves doing simple tasks, over and over, or are constantly interrupted in their work by time-wasting administrative tasks, they aren't going to attach much value to their jobs. This measure can also identify candidate processes for automation or outsourcing—are the staff doing something that should be automated?

- Vendor performance.
  Help Desk staff might have a lot of contact with vendors, and will be able to report on qualitative measures such as responsiveness, quality of service, willingness to help out in the case of problems, how warranties are honored, and so on.

These are all things that affect the function of your Help Desk and that you need to know about. Report cards for staff, for evaluating Help Desk function, might be a good idea for your Help Desk. They would formalize the evaluation process and perhaps give it a greater value to staff. You may find this unnecessary if you have frequent meetings with your staff and a routine of sharing all of this information regularly. A checklist of areas to talk about might serve you just as well.

If you do choose to go with a report card, you will probably find that having the information summarized on report cards is useful when you do your overall evaluation. You won't forget anything that was just mentioned at a meeting. As well as using this information to audit Help Desk performance, share it with your staff. Let them know what it is being used for, what changes you will be making because of it, and that it does make a difference. This will help ensure that you continue to get a good response.

Quality of staff evaluations will vary depending on the quality of staff. Staff who are really interested in improving the Help Desk will give you good feedback. Staff who are just putting in time may not (although a Help Desk seems a rather tortuous place to be putting in time). You will have to recognize this and sort it out.

Following are samples of a staff evaluation and evaluation results.

HELP DESK REPORT CARD

Help Desk Staff Evaluation

For period: January 1 to March 31.

For each statement below, rate the Help Desk on a scale of 1 to 5, where 1: never true; 2: seldom true; 3: true half of the time; 4: usually true; 5 always true.

1. Customers are generally pleasant to deal with.
   If not 5, please explain: _____

   _____

2. Feedback from customers has been positive.
   If not 5, please explain: _____

   _____

3. Customers call for legitimate reasons.
   If not 5, please explain: _____

   _____

4. My workload is reasonable. I can accomplish all of my work without overtime and I am not left without something to do.
   If not 5, please explain: _____

   _____

5. I receive upgrading training for handling Help Desk customers.
   If not 5, please explain: _____

   _____

6. I receive training for all versions of tools and software.
   If not 5, please explain: _____

   _____

7. I receive training in new or upgraded software before it rolls out to customers.
   If not 5, please explain: _____

   _____

8. Our Help Desk tools are effective: they work well and make my job easier.
   If not 5, please explain: _____

   _____

9. I am confident that calls I pass on to other support areas for resolution will be resolved and closed satisfactorily.
   If not 5, please explain: _____

   _____

10. The work I do is interesting and important.
   If not 5, please explain: _____

   _____

In this staff evaluation, you're looking to make sure that workloads are reasonable, calls are legitimate, staff are getting the training they need when they need it, and staff have the tools they need to provide effective support. You also want to get their perception of customer satisfaction—they are close to the customers and sometimes hear things that no one else hears. This evaluation is also looking for activities that staff feel are unimportant (these could be candidates for automation or outsourcing) and for indications of job satisfaction or dissatisfaction.

The staff evaluation in Table 7.5 shows several areas for improvement:

- A customer satisfaction (or perception) problem in the Marketing department ("Marketing customers don't think much of us") needs to be addressed.

- Customers are wasting their own and Help Desk time on WordPerfect questions; some WordPerfect courses need to be brought in.

- There is an indication that the workload may not be reasonable. Call management statistics, specifically trends, need to be checked.

- Help Desk staff are not receiving the training they need in customer support, new software, and tools. The whole training area seems to be neglected. Training requirements must be gathered and the ap-

Table 7.5 Help Desk Staff Evaluation Results

	1	2	3	4	5	Staff Comments	Help Desk Manager Observations
Customers pleasant		2	3	1		Marketing customers don't think much of us.	*Backlash from last quarter's outage on the Marketing LAN. Needs to be addressed.*
Feedback positive			2	3	1		
Customers have legitimate calls			6			We're getting too many simple WordPerfect questions!	*Arrange for courses next quarter.*
Workload is reasonable			6				*Check traffic statistics.*
Receive training for handling customers	6						*Oops. Check to see what's available next quarter.*
Receive training for tools		4	2			Could make better use of them if we had training.	*Get staff to recommend courses.*
Receive training for software before it is rolled out		6				It's embarrassing not to know a package when the customers do.	*Check into why this is happening.*
Help Desk tools effective			4	2		They could be more effective if we knew how to use them.	
Calls passed on will be resolved		2	4			Problem with application support.	*Same as last quarter; need to address this.*
Work I do is interesting and important			4	2		Am tired of fixing config files.	*Can we automate this?*

propriate training administered. A process needs to be put into place to ensure that staff continue to get the required training.

- External support areas—specifically the Technical support group—are not providing an adequate level of support. Perhaps procedures need to be revisited with that group.
- There is also some frustration with the monotonous task of fixing configuration files. Automation could be indicated.

Help Desk Function

Quantitative measures of day-to-day Help Desk function include the following:

- Number of calls.
  Here you are looking for trends. Are calls increasing at a rate that will become unmanageable if left unchecked?
- Numbers (or percentages) of specific types of calls.
  Is any type of call taking up too many resources? What are the trends in types of calls? Is any one type showing signs of continuing growth?
- Number of calls resolved at point of call.
  The higher the number is, the better.
- Average problem resolution time.
  Is this increasing or decreasing? Do you need tools or automation to help?
- Average problem resolution time for calls passed to other areas (could be by area).
  Is this acceptable? Is it consistent?
- Number of problems that were not resolved correctly the first time.
  Is this number growing? Is it too high?
- Numbers of PCs (or number of customers) supported.
  Here, again, you are looking for trends. How quickly is this number growing? Will the Help Desk need help to be able to support it?

Consider a sample Help Desk. Figure 7.3 shows that the number of calls is steadily increasing. If this continues, the workload could become unmanageable. Further investigation needs to be undertaken to determine what can be done to either reduce or handle the call load.

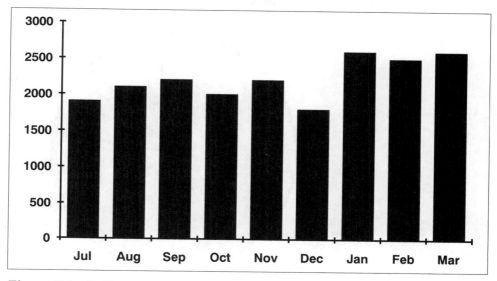

Figure 7.3 Calls coming into the Help Desk for the last nine months.

Figures 7.4 and 7.5 show two trends, one good and one bad. The number of abandoned calls has gone down—that's good. This indicates that people are getting through to the Help Desk more easily. Training-type calls have doubled—that's probably bad. It means that people are calling the Help Desk (to the tune of 30 percent of all calls) with problems and questions that could be resolved by training. Something needs to be done to get this type of call down.

Figure 7.6 shows that calls resolved at point of call have increased, which is positive. Probably you've implemented a change, and it seems to be working. (In the objectives in Table 7.1, this was a remote diagnostic tool and your target was 80 percent of calls resolved at first call, so there is still room for improvement.)

In your measures you're looking for resolution times to be less or the same, if you're happy with them. Figures 7.7 and 7.8 show that resolution times have gone down slightly, so you are headed in the right direction. You need to go to your customers to find out whether these times are adequate, if you haven't done so already.

In Figure 7.9, you can see that the number of PCs grew substantially this quarter. You will want to investigate whether this is an anomaly or the start of a trend. You might need to consider getting some third-party help to get you through this period of growth without service degradation.

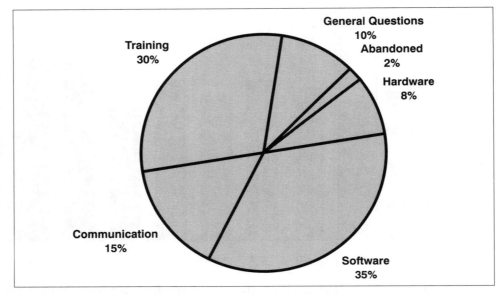

Figure 7.4 Calls (by type) coming into the Help Desk for this quarter.

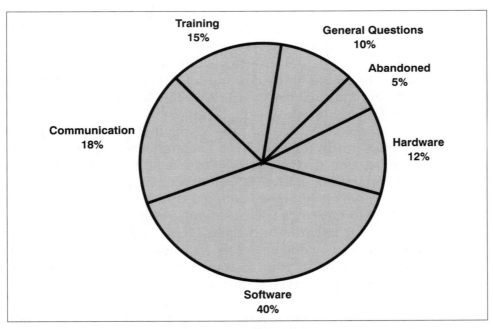

Figure 7.5 Calls (by type) coming into the Help Desk for the previous quarter.

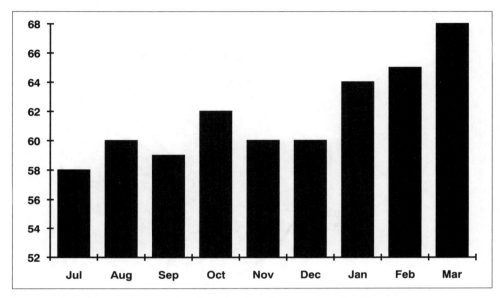

Figure 7.6   Percentage of calls resolved at point of call.

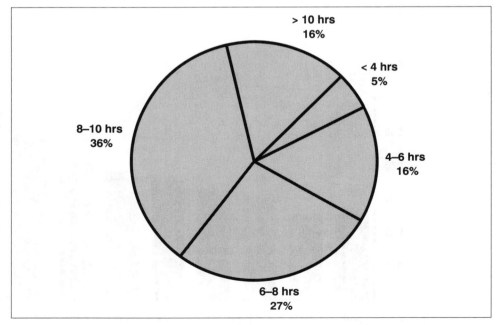

Figure 7.7   Resolution times for calls not resolved at point of call this quarter.

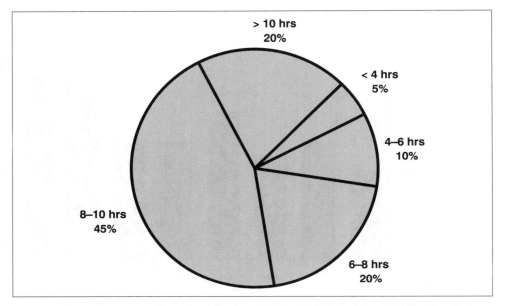

Figure 7.8   Resolution times for calls not resolved at point of call last quarter.

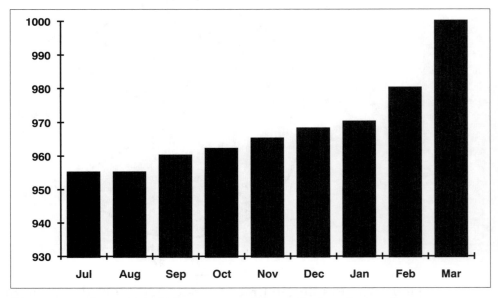

Figure 7.9   Growth in PCs supported over the last 9 months.

Help Desk Manager Evaluation

In putting together an evaluation of the Help Desk, a Help Desk manager must gather performance information from:

- Objectives
- Budget
- Any service-level agreements
- Customer evaluations
- Staff evaluations
- Help Desk function

How often should this happen? Evaluation should be an ongoing process, with constant adjustment, as trends are noticed. A more major performance review should occur quarterly, along with all of the other planning and budgeting functions. This is probably when management will want to see everything as well.

In doing an evaluation, the Help Desk manager must:

- Gather and summarize the data.
- Interpret it, drawing conclusions about performance and identifying areas needing improvement and trends that may affect future performance.
- Make recommendations for changes in Help Desk operation, and courses of action for improvement and problem prevention.
- Put together a summary for management.

Table 7.6 shows a sample summary of identified areas of improvement and recommendations for each.

Table 7.6 Recommendations

Area for improvement	Immediate recommendation	Longer-term recommendation
Help Desk does not communicate adequately with customers.	Need to do marketing to customers about remote diagnostics. Put temporary procedures in place for communication of call status and system problems.	Ensure that a communication plan is part of each change affecting customers. Set up procedures for communicating to customers about status of their calls and status of the system.

(continues)

Table 7.6 Recommendations (*continued*)

Area for improvement	Immediate recommendation	Longer-term recommendation
Objectives were not reasonable in the area of PC upgrades.	Make a note of how long PC upgrades take so that we can estimate more accurately next time.	
Vendor for monitors is not honoring warranty.	Have a meeting with vendor to review warranties and procedures for product replacement.	Find a new vendor.
Customers bypassing formal problem reporting.	Meet with customer management.	Increase marketing efforts to let customers know what this is costing other customers and how it is increasing their resolution times.
Customers not taking required training.	Same as above.	As above. Must show customers what their unwillingness to get trained is costing in terms of Help Desk support and mistakes they may be making.
Staff not getting required training.	Meet with staff to find out who needs what training and get it administered as soon as possible.	Review training requirements quarterly with staff. Have temporary staff fill in as needed.
There may be some peaks in traffic that are not staffed for adequately.	Review detailed call reports to find these peaks.	Adjust staffing to handle the understaffed peaks.
Fixing configuration files is repetitive and monotonous and frequent.	Check into why the configuration files are getting corrupted. If this is a customer issue, do some immediate communication about the consequences of changing these files.	Check into the possibility of automating this task.
Calls increasing and number of PCs increasing.	Ensure that enough training programs are being offered and that the Help Desk can handle the increased setup and support. If not, perhaps temporary help can be brought in.	Look into ways of decreasing calls through automation, training, etc.

The performance data that you have so painstakingly collected and interpreted has netted you several valuable suggestions for improvement and shown you trends that you can address now, rather than finding out about them after there is a problem.

The Ideal

What kind of performance are you working toward?

- All objectives are met.
- Best use is made of Help Desk budget, and Help Desk support cost per PC is lower than that of the competition.
- Service-level agreements are met: quantitative measures are positive, response times are being met, and both Help Desk staff and customers have positive feedback.
- Customer evaluation is positive. Help Desk staff are regarded as effective, and service and communication are considered good. Services provided are considered worthwhile.
- Help Desk staff evaluation is positive. Staff have the tools and training to do the job, they are motivated, and the workload is adequate.
- Good Help Desk function. Number of calls is remaining almost steady. Automation seems to be holding them at bay. The PC environment is growing, but response times are remaining at a fairly steady (good) level, and interfaces with other support areas are working well. Problems not resolved correctly the first time are very rare.

You may not be quite there yet, but every performance evaluation you do will give you the data you need to move closer.

Put Together a Summary for Management

Management will make its own evaluation of Help Desk performance based on the information it receives from you, the Help Desk manager. You need to ensure that the information is accurate, so that any misconceptions that they may have picked up elsewhere are cleared up and that you have recommendations for resolving each problem identified. Don't try to hide poor performance. You won't be able to do it for long. Focus your efforts on recommending good solutions for any problems that you do have. Even departments that are functioning well will have problems—but they will make sure that the problems are resolved quickly and permanently. Using the data you gather to identify problems and trends, reporting them honestly, and recommending well thought out solutions will help gain you and your Help Desk the respect and support of management.

The way you present information is important, in that it could determine whether the information even gets read. Be clear and concise. You can always have more detail ready should anyone require it—or you can present it as an appendix. Graphs can communicate a lot of information in a relatively small space.

Management will want to know:

- What the Help Desk achieved that was of business value. Whether objectives were met and, if not, what was accomplished instead.

- How much the Help Desk is costing the company. Management may have a specific preference for the way this is presented. You can try presenting the financial data in various ways to see which is of most value to them. They may just tell you.

- Whether service-level agreements were met.

- Whether customers are satisfied with Help Desk performance.

- The volume of work that is going through the Help Desk.

- How the supported environment is changing.

- Significant trends.

This will vary from company to company. It may take a few iterations to get it right, to give management exactly what they want. When you present to management, always ask for feedback so that you can improve for next time.

Following a sample of a performance report that the Help Desk might give to management for evaluation.

Help Desk Performance Report

Period: Jan 1 through March 31

Current Environment

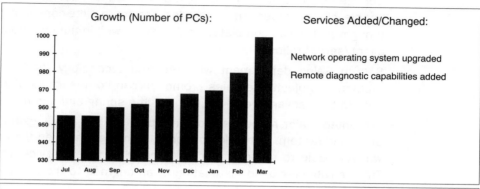

Growth (Number of PCs):

Services Added/Changed:

Network operating system upgraded

Remote diagnostic capabilities added

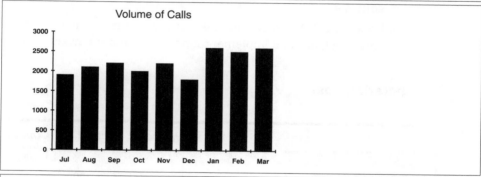

Volume of Calls

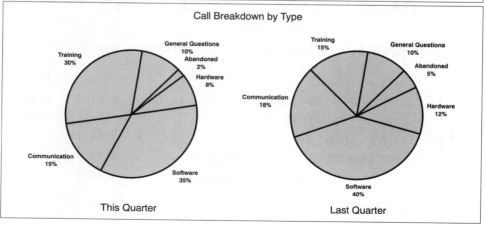

Call Breakdown by Type

Major Accomplishments

- Increased resolution of problems at point of call from 60 percent to 68 percent using remote diagnostics. This percentage will be increased to 80 percent as customers' concerns over privacy issues are addressed.

- Completed three-quarters of upgrades necessary for the environment to handle client/server. The upgrades are more time-consuming than first thought and will be completed next quarter, well in time to support the first client/server rollout.

- Set up Sales department with required technology for the new sales promotion project. The sales promotion can go ahead, as planned and in time to take advantage of the high-volume spring and summer season.

- Prevented major response problems by installing new version of network operating system. Network monitoring software identified the problem and we were able to respond quickly, preventing major service interruptions. This activity precluded installation of an upgrade to the standard desktop software.

- Handled a 22 percent increase in the number of calls to the Help Desk. This precluded the implementation of automated inventory management.

Operating Cost

		Projected	Actual	Comment
EXPENSE:	Salaries	$58,000	$58,000	
	General Office	$20,000	$20,000	
CAPITAL:	Help Desk Software	$12,000	$8,000	Waiting for component. Will defer to next quarter.
	Network operating system upgrade	$70,000	$70,000	Instead of desktop upgrade.
TOTAL COST:		$160,000	**$156,000**	
COST PER PC:	**This Quarter:**		**$156**	
	Over last 4 quarters:		**$680**	

Service-Level Agreement

Overall performance of the Help Desk against service agreement and customer evaluation survey was good. Two concerns were identified:

- Customers are not taking the training they require. Training calls have doubled, putting a strain on Help Desk resources.

- The Help Desk is not communicating system status and individual call status to customers. This is causing a lot of needless calls to the Help Desk and an inability of customers to plan workload around any down time.

Summary/Recommendations

Although use of PCs has been growing steadily for the last year, this quarter saw an unusually large increase in the number of PCs being supported by the Help Desk. The number grew by 51, to 1,000. This, together with lack of customer training and inadequate Help Desk communication, has been responsible for a 22 percent increase in Help Desk calls. The number of calls must be reduced and contained so that support costs do not increase needlessly. This quarter, the increased support load prevented the Help Desk from implementing automated asset management. Recommendations to achieve a decrease in calls are as follows:

- Bring training course in-house for customers and enforce attendance so that they can meet the conditions of the service-level agreement. Calls of a training nature doubled this quarter, making up 30 percent of all calls received.

- Institute more effective procedures for communicating call status and system status to customers so that they don't have to call the Help Desk. Put together a communication plan as part of introduction of each new tool (such as remote diagnostics).

- Investigate reasons for calls in more detail to see whether they can be either eliminated or automated.

Communicating Performance

You've gone to a lot of trouble to evaluate your performance. Who needs to know how you are performing? Your customers, your staff, and management.

Customers

In evaluating Help Desk performance, you received input from your customers. You need to summarize the results of this information and feed it back to them, along with any changes that you plan to make to address any of the problem areas that were identified. This will show your customers that their input does make a difference and that you are serious about improving. They also need to see results from any service agreement evaluations so that they know how they have been rated as customers.

You also want your customers to see call volumes, breakdowns by type, and growth in the environment so that they understand something of the environment you have to support and the challenges you face in doing so. If training calls are 30 percent of your call load and this is preventing the Help Desk from making improvements, they should know this. Their refusal to get the proper training is expensive.

By educating your customers in this way, you can give them the tools and encouragement to use the Help Desk more effectively.

Survey results should be fed back to customers as soon after they happen as possible. They can be fed back in a summarized version as report cards. Information about call volumes and growth can be published monthly. You could do something as simple as printing out graphs (call volumes over nine months; calls broken down by type; response times; growth in number of PCs) on a poster and putting them up for customers to see.

Help Desk Staff

Communicate everything to staff: information that is going to management, information that is going to the customers, and your own (Help Desk manager) evaluation. The more Help Desk staff know about their environment, the more informed will be any decisions they have to make. The more feedback they get, the more they can improve. It is also useful for Help Desk staff to see call and growth information on a monthly basis. They can see for themselves how they are performing or where any problem areas are. Posting this information will reward positive performance and encourage improvement of less than positive performance.

Tell your staff what you plan to do based on their feedback specifically (staff evaluations), and on the feedback of the service-level agreements, customers, objectives, and budget. They will know that you take their input seriously and value their opinions. It is, after all, Help Desk performance that you are evaluating, and they are the Help Desk.

Management

There is a lot of valuable information in the performance report that you have created for management. Rather than just sending it out, if you could meet with managers and make a presentation, so much the better. You could answer questions and concerns as they came up and provide more details as they were asked for. If you have to send the report, follow up a week later to see if each recipient has read it and if there is any feedback.

You can and should communicate performance to management less formally at more frequent intervals than quarterly. Information such as call volumes, volumes by type, response times, and environment growth will be of interest to them, as will be any specific accomplishments that demonstrate the business value you provide. The information doesn't necessarily have to be sent directly to them, although you may find that they request it. You can put performance information on posters and in newsletters—places where they are likely to see it. If they do request monthly updates, or if you feel it is appropriate, put together the same information in report format and send it out at each month's end.

Measuring the performance of your Help Desk thoroughly and regularly will give you more control over the success of your Help Desk. You will have the information necessary to make improvements, address problem areas before they get out of control, and plan accurately for the future. You will know what the business needs and will be in a good position to provide it. Your Help Desk will be difficult to compete with.

Summary

Measuring Help Desk performance will give you not only an indication of the success of your Help Desk, but also information on ways to improve your Help Desk, trends that need attention, and information to help you plan for the future.

In order to get the total picture of how your Help Desk is performing, it is necessary to get the perspective of customers, Help Desk staff, the Help Desk manager, and management. Without all of these, you will not understand how your Help Desk is really performing.

From a customer perspective, the Help Desk that is successful has knowledgeable staff, resolves problems quickly and accurately, and keeps staff informed of status of calls and status of the system. Customers want as little down time as possible. Customers also measure Help Desk performance against any service-level agreements that they might have.

Help Desk staff look at Help Desk performance somewhat differently. Customer satisfaction and confidence in staff ability is important to them, but they also consider the Help Desk tools that are available to them, their workload, the interest level of the work, the support they are getting from other areas, and the training they are getting to help them be more effective on the Help Desk.

Help Desk managers consider both staff and customer input when evaluating Help Desk performance, as well as performance against objectives, budgets and service-level agreements, and the internal workings of the Help Desk. These include call volumes, procedures, priorities, and resolution rates. Help Desk managers also look at growth in the environment. What the Help Desk is handling well now it may not be able to handle tomorrow, if the environment is growing quickly and the Help Desk is not preparing for it.

Management have the broadest perspective on Help Desk performance, taking all others into account. They are looking for business value. They want to know if objectives are being met, if spending is within budget and allocated as planned, if customers are satisfied, and if the Help Desk is offering value to the business. They will be comparing the Help Desk to its external competition in terms of business value delivered vs. cost.

In order to get all of these perspectives when you are measuring the performance of your Help Desk, you need to measure it in terms of performance against objectives, budget, service-level agreements, customer evaluations, staff evaluations, Help Desk function, and Help Desk manager evaluation.

Once you have gathered all of this performance data, you need to summarize it, interpret it to find any areas needing attention, recommend improvements or resolutions to problems, and then develop a summary for management so that they will have an accurate view of Help Desk performance to base their evaluation on.

Measurement by objectives involves looking at the business value of what the Help Desk said it would achieve compared to the value of what it actually achieved. The Help Desk must be responsive to the business, and if something came up that was more important than a planned objective, the best business decision would be to address the new issue rather than the planned activity.

As with objectives, performance against budget is determined by the value of what was purchased. It goes without saying that overspending is not acceptable. If Help Desk actual spending varies from planned spending in terms of allocation of funds, then it is still considered successful if the actual purchase had a greater business value than the planned purchase.

Service-level agreements not only define a Help Desk performance measurement, but also clarify both customer and Help Desk responsibilities and expectations. A service-level agreement contains information on Help Desk services, responsibilities, and hours of operation, as well as customer responsibilities. It details out priorities and resolution times, systems and components supported and which of those is critical, and additional services and fees. Both Help Desk and customers are measured against the agreement. Performance against agreement is evaluated by customer and staff surveys and by call management statistics.

A customer evaluation is a report card of Help Desk performance and deals with such measures as quality of Help Desk staff, speed, accuracy and quality of service, and quality of communication.

A Help Desk staff evaluation is also a report card of Help Desk performance, but with a somewhat different focus. It looks at feedback from and attitude of customers, legitimacy of customer calls, reasonableness of workload, training received, tools used, and value of work performed.

Evaluating Help Desk function involves looking at quantitative measures of day-to-day Help Desk function—such as number of calls resolved at point of call, average problem resolution times, and so on—and identifying any trends that need addressing.

A Help Desk manager's evaluation of Help Desk performance involves gathering information from all other evaluations, and then using this information to draw conclusions about performance and identify trends and areas needing improvement. The Help Desk manager also makes recommendations based on the evaluation and puts together a summary for management.

A summary report of Help Desk performance for management is what management will use to make its own evaluation of the Help Desk. The Help Desk manager needs to ensure that the information is accurate and that all problems identified are accompanied by recommendations for their resolution. A management summary report for Help Desk performance should include what the Help Desk accomplished that was of business value, how much the Help Desk is costing, whether service-level agreements were met, whether customers are satisfied with Help Desk performance, the volume of work that is going through the Help Desk, and how the support environment is changing.

Performance needs to be communicated to staff, customers, and management. Staff should be fed back any survey results, as well as information about call volumes and growth. Customers should know what the Help Desk intends to do with the feedback it received from them and how they as customers could be using the Help Desk more effectively. Staff should receive all evaluation information. The more they know about their environment, the more informed will be any decisions they have to make. Management will generally appreciate receiving quarterly evaluations of Help Desk performance as well as ongoing performance updates.

Thorough and accurate performance measurement will give you more control over the success of your Help Desk. You can prevent problems from getting out of hand, plan accurately for the future, and give the business what it needs. You will be tough competition.

CHAPTER EIGHT

Marketing

Your Help Desk is a business. You have products and services to sell, and you have customers to sell them to. Customers aren't going to buy from you just because you're there. Management isn't going to fund you or support you just because you're there, either. You need to show customers and management what the Help Desk offers, what it can do for them, and what it can do for the business.

You also need to show your customers how to use what you're selling (witness the legendary vacuum cleaner salesperson). If you sell a person a vacuum cleaner and don't take the time to explain what it does or demonstrate how to use it, it might not be long before that person is back telling you that he can't use it to brush his guinea pigs because it keeps sucking them up. Your customers probably have access to some expensive technology, and if they don't know what to use it for or how to use it, they could not only fail to realize its benefits, they could cause problems for themselves or the business. You need to market—to tell people what you're selling, why it's important, and how to use it.

Marketing will also help you stand up against the competition. Whether you realize it or not, you are competing. You may be an established internal Help Desk, but that is no longer a guarantee that you will get the company's business. Outsourcing is almost always an option, and one that is becoming more popular as organizations are forced to cut costs. If you want to continue to do business, you must market your value and your accomplishments. It may be the case that you offer better service and better value than a third-party service provider, but if your customers and management don't know this, or aren't reminded of it on a regular basis, then you might lose out to your competitors, who aren't afraid to market their value. You need to pull out your suitcase of samples and start pounding the pavement.

Marketing is important to Help Desk success, but it will not replace or hide poor Help Desk performance—at least, not for very long. Your marketing can be only as effective as your Help Desk is. It should be considered a showcase for your services and your performance, not a substitute. If you are performing well, your marketing can spotlight the value you are adding to the business. If you are performing poorly, any marketing efforts will be greeted with cynicism and ridicule, and people's already poor perception of you will get poorer. Don't try to market something that you don't have.

What Marketing Can Do for You

Consider the Help Desk that does no marketing whatsoever:

- Customers don't know that the Help Desk is there, or what it offers. They might waste time struggling with a problem on their own, or they might go to a colleague for help, wasting the colleague's time as well as their own. Two people who should have been focusing on their jobs and contributing to the business have instead gone into another time-consuming business: support.

- Customers aren't aware of any policies or standards that are in place. They may introduce nonstandard products, which will increase the complexity of support, and they may inadvertently breach security, perhaps allowing a virus into the system.

- Customers base their opinion of the Help Desk on an occasional, poorly written communication that they might happen to see. This may cause them to avoid using the Help Desk, and even to pass their own unfavorable opinions on to their colleagues. They are passing on a negative Help Desk image, even though they may never have used the Help Desk themselves.

- Help Desk successes go unnoticed and unrecognized, so that customers and management only remember problems. If cost cutting or outsourcing comes up, the Help Desk will be on the "endangered department" list.

On a more positive note, consider the Help Desk that creates and executes a marketing plan:

- Customers are kept up to date on the range of services that the Help Desk offers.

- Customers know how to use the Help Desk.

- Customers are encouraged to use the Help Desk.

- Customers use technology effectively.

- Customers are aware of all policies and procedures and updates to them.

- There is excellent two-way communication between the customers and the Help Desk. The Help Desk knows what's going on in the customers' world and vice versa.

- Customers and management are kept abreast of Help Desk performance and understand the business value that it is delivering.

- The Help Desk has a professional, service-oriented image.

A good marketing plan can bring all of these benefits to your Help Desk (see Figure 8.1) and doesn't require a huge or expensive effort. As

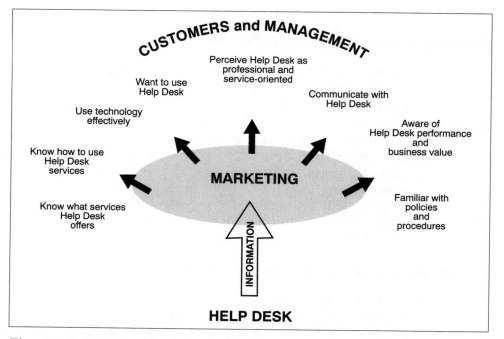

Figure 8.1 What marketing can do for you.

a Help Desk manager, you have a lot of options when putting a plan together and a good variety of communication vehicles to choose from. The first thing that you have to do in putting a plan together is to decide what you want to accomplish through your marketing plan. Following are some suggestions.

Keep Customers Up to Date on Your Range of Services

Keeping customers informed of your range of services will help manage their expectations. If you are a "delivery within 30 minutes" pizza restaurant, you want your potential customers to think of you in that way. You will be prepared to meet their expectations of pizza in 30 minutes. If you are a pizza restaurant that does not offer guaranteed delivery, you certainly don't want your customers to expect pizza in 30 minutes. This would only lead to annoyed customers, frustrated employees, and a loss in business.

If customers understand what services your Help Desk offers, they will have realistic expectations when they call. They won't be calling you for services you don't offer. On the other hand, they will know where to go for the services you offer, should the need arise.

Teach Customers How to Use Your Services

Customers will make make more effective use of the Help Desk if they know what information they need to have when they call and how they should go about requesting service. They should know how to access and use any automated Help Desk functions.

Customers also need to be aware of what not to use the Help Desk for. Misuse of the Help Desk can be very expensive. If customers are too lazy to look up a simple command in a manual, or are too busy or disinterested to take training, then they shouldn't look to the Help Desk for a solution. Marketing will help make customers aware of the costs associated with misuse, such as additional Help Desk staff, or other customers with important problems who must wait for service.

Encourage Customers to Use Your Services

You don't want customers misusing the Help Desk, but you also don't want them to go too far the other way and simply go elsewhere for help when they have a legitimate request or problem. Successfully encouraging customers to use Help Desk services will reduce the problem of customers wasting their own time, or that of their colleagues, in trying to figure out something that the Help Desk already knows and could help them with. Customers could focus on their own jobs, rather than on trouble-shooting. Marketing can show what this kind of unofficial support is costing the company. Marketing can also show the services and benefits to the company that the Help Desk offers.

Help Customers Make More Effective Use of Their Technology

Through marketing, your Help Desk can give its customers the information they need to use their technology more effectively. You can publish hints and tips to make using technology easier, along with solutions to common problems, and you can make customers aware of recommended courses and seminars so that they know where to go for training. Customers will make better use of the technology, and fewer costly errors, if they are properly trained.

Disseminate Information Such as Policies, Strategies, Procedures

You can make customers aware of any policies that are in place for security, PC purchase, PC use, and so on. This will not only help ensure compliance, but will also help ensure that there are no surprises when customers go to do something and find that they are constrained by a policy.

Improve Two-Way Communication with Customers

A good marketing initiative can encourage input from customers, showing them that their feedback is valuable to the Help Desk. It can make customers less afraid of making suggestions or giving comments, which will provide the Help Desk with valuable feedback and ideas for improvement.

Communicate Help Desk Performance and Business Value

Communicating Help Desk performance will make customers aware of what the Help Desk is accomplishing, the workload it deals with, and the challenges of growth it is facing. It also provides a vehicle for feeding back results from customer surveys and service-level agreements (see Chapter 7).

In the current corporate environment of cutbacks and cost cutting, it is more important than ever for management to be aware of the value your Help Desk provides to the business. If management does not understand this, it may make cost cutting or outsourcing decisions that might not be the best for the business, and that will most likely not be the best for your Help Desk. If you can show what the Help Desk is contributing to the business, you have a better chance of getting the funding and management support you need to continue operating and to undertake improvement initiatives such as automation.

Enhance the Image of the Help Desk

Each example of Help Desk communication that a customer comes into contact with affects that customer's perception of the Help Desk. For example, if a written communication coming from the Help Desk is haphazard, poorly written, and hard to understand, a customer who reads it may decide that the Help Desk is disorganized and unprofessional. That customer may write off the Help Desk without even having tried its services. A good marketing plan will ensure that Help Desk communication consistently reflects the image that the Help Desk wants to portray. If that image is one of professionalism and efficiency, then communication will be businesslike, concise, and clear.

Enhancing Help Desk image can involve creating a specific look for Help Desk communication that will distinguish it from other communication, making it easily identifiable. People will know, at a glance, that a communication is from the Help Desk.

You may want to accomplish some or all of these in your marketing plan. Perhaps you have a specific problem area that you want to focus on for now. Once you've decided what it is you want to accomplish, you're ready to put the rest of your plan together. A plan should describe what you want to market, to whom, how you are going to market it, and how frequently. It will help ensure that your marketing is consistent, that you market everything you need to, and that it actually gets done. Your next steps are:

- Decide what information you need, whom it should go to, and how often it needs to be communicated.
- Decide what image you want to communicate.
- Select the communication vehicles for your marketing.

Information You Need to Market

The information you need to get across in your Help Desk marketing efforts will vary, depending on your audience and what you want your marketing to accomplish.

Keep Customers Up to Date on Your Range of Services

To keep customers up to date on your range of services, you will need to provide them with a list of your services, information on Help Desk hours, off-hours support, and any guaranteed response times. You will need to provide information on updates to your services before and after they are actually implemented.

Examples

Hours:

- Help Desk hours are 7 A.M. to 7 P.M.
- Off-hours support will be provided by Operations and appropriate staff will be notified by pager.

Response times:

- All level-one severity calls are guaranteed a response time of one hour or less.
- Time from order to installation of PC is based on demand, but is generally within two weeks of receiving an authorized purchase order.

Services provided:

- Resolution to all PC hardware and software problems.
- Answers to PC software questions.
- Fax back of PC policies and standards.
- Terminal resets.
- Ordering of PC hardware and software.

Updates:

- Our fax-back service has been enhanced to include a "hints and tips" information sheet to help you use your standard desktop.

- We will no longer be providing loaner equipment. You may call TLC Computer Leasing at 444-9876.

Audience

- All customers.

Frequency

- Updates should be communicated before they occur, so that people can prepare for them, and then again as soon as they occur.
- Help Desk services can be distributed to everyone once (and then on request) and to new customers as they come on board; refreshers or reminders can be published every six months or so. You might have a specific place (document, information phone line) that customers can go to get service information any time.

Vehicles to Consider

- Pamphlets, newsletters, meetings, an information phone line, information printed on inventory stickers or mouse pads.

Teach Customers How to Use Services

The information you will need to pass on to customers to show them how to use your services includes all phone numbers, fax numbers, and electronic mail IDs that you want customers to use to access your services; standard information or identification that customers will be asked to supply; and instructions on how to use any automated features. You may also want to communicate priorities and any information that is required for special services such as ordering PCs, and any information about misuse, if that is a problem in your environment.

Examples

Contacting the Help Desk:

- Use of any of the following methods:
  - Call the Help Desk at 222-4567.
  - Fax the Help Desk at 222-3333.
  - Send electronic mail to the Help Desk at HELPD.
- Don't forget to include your user ID in all communication.

Using automation:

- To use the automated voice response unit, simply select option 2 when calling into the Help Desk, then follow the instructions. You need a touch-tone phone with touch-tone service to use the voice response unit. If you need help at any time, press 0.

Priorities:

Your call will be assigned a priority according to the following definitions when you call the Help Desk. Critical systems and components are as defined in the Corporate Security Manual:

- 1: Critical system or component down. Immediate response.
- 2: Critical system or component degraded. Response within 15 minutes.
- 3: Noncritical system or component down. Response within four hours.
- 4: Noncritical system or component degraded. Response within eight hours.
- 5: General question. Response within one day.

Misuse:

- Calls to the Help Desk that could have been resolved by training doubled last quarter. Of all Help Desk calls, 30 percent were training related. They clogged up the Help Desk, making it difficult for other customers with more serious business problems to get through. We can't afford to keep adding staff. Take the training you need, and let the real problems get through.

Audience

- All customers.

Frequency

- Information on how to access the Help Desk and on Help Desk priorities can be communicated along with services (see above, "Keep Customers Up to Date on Your Range of Services"). It can also be stored with service information for access any time by customers.

- Any changes (e.g., automation of some functions, changed priorities, or changed phone numbers) should be communicated before they occur so that people can prepare for them, and then again as soon as they occur.

- Information on the effects of Help Desk misuse should be communicated only when there is a problem, and only for a specific length of time—say, one month. After that time, if the marketing is successful and the misuse decreases, market the success. If the problem has not gone away, you need to try something else.

Vehicles to Consider

- Meetings, newsletters, pamphlets, posters, an information phone line, and a priority list for customers to keep by their phones.

Encourage Customers to Use Your Services

To encourage customers to use your services, you will need to have information on how the Help Desk helps both customers and business, and how not using it can hurt the business. You will want to pass on information about new Help Desk services and what they offer to customers.

You will also need to find out which customers do not use the Help Desk, so that you can find out why, and perhaps rectify the situation.

Examples

Hurting the business:

- The next time you're tempted to ask the person at the next desk for help with your PC, stop and think: how much will what you're about do cost the business? Add up the time you spend going to people for help, or having people come to you for help. Just ten hours a month, for two people, adds up to 30 working days a year. That's more than a month. Call the Help Desk—it's a lot cheaper, and we've seen it all before.

New Services:

- Remote control help from the Help Desk! We can fix most of your PC problems while you're still on the phone! Try us out! 222-4567.

Audience

- All customers.

Frequency

- Information on new features that will attract customers should be communicated continuously before the new features are actually put into place. People will be curious about them. Once the features are actually in place and usable, the information should be communicated again.

- Other information can be communicated as required. For example, if you wanted to communicate reminders that were not time-dependent, then putting the information in a monthly or bimonthly newsletter would suffice. If you wanted to address a specific problem, then you would communicate immediately and frequently until the situation improved. Then you could go back to your less frequent but ongoing reminders.

Vehicles to Consider

- Meetings, newsletters, an Open House, an information phone line, posters, and seminars.

Help Customers Use Technology More Effectively

To increase the effectiveness of customers' use of technology, you can communicate suggestions from power users, tips on how to solve or prevent common problems logged by the Help Desk, and consequences of misuse of technology (if your environment has a problem in that area). You could also include tips and suggestions from vendors, magazines, and from users that have called in. Customers will also need information on new releases of software being installed and the features they offer.

Your tracking data will help identify common and recurring problems and questions. It will also identify customers who may need training so that you can market directly to them.

Examples

Hints and tips:

- A new electronic mail function is now available for quick notes. Simply press PF5 to get into edit.

- Lost your mouse pointer? If you lose track of your mouse pointer on your laptop, go into the Control Panel, select the Mouse option, and then select the Mouse Trails option. "Mouse trails" will cause a trail of pointers to follow the mouse pointer so that it will be easier to see.

- If you frequently edit lengthy documents, press Shift+PF5 to return to where you were editing when you last saved and left the document.

Warnings:

- Thirsty? Then have a drink—but not anywhere near your PC. Last year, PCs that had been "drinking" cost the company $10,000 in repairs and employee time. Help us eliminate this unnecessary expense.

Training:

- *You are invited* to a seminar on "Downloading data from the mainframe," given by the Help Desk. Invest 30 minutes and you'll never have to rekey your mainframe data again!

Audience:

- All customers. Some customers, such as those needing training, can be targeted specifically.

Frequency:

- Tips can be gathered and communicated every month or so. You don't want to communicate tips too often, because people will lose track of them or miss some. You can put tips in the same place all the time (e.g., newsletters, posters, or documents) so that people know where to look and will start expecting them. You can keep a document of all of the tips published to date so that customers can go and browse through them any time.

- Cautions can be communicated immediately and frequently until the situation improves. Then you can go to less frequent but ongoing reminders.

- Information on training should be communicated continuously, and well before it occurs so that people can make time. A training schedule might be sent out or put somewhere that customers have access to, and then updates and reminders issued every two months or so.

Vehicles to consider:

- Newsletters, on-line documentation, posters, training, and seminars. Also, postcards that contain an invitation to a software upgrade seminar on one side and a quick reference for the software upgrade on the other.

Disseminate Information Such as Policies, Strategies, Procedures

To distribute information from documents such as policies or strategies, you will need to have those documents somewhere where everyone can access them. You want to avoid dealing with sending out copies of documents so that you don't have a maintenance nightmare on your hands when changes come along. You will have to let customers know where documents are, and then communicate updates as they occur.

Example

Policy:

- Please note that no external software is allowed on your PCs. All installed software must be on the approved software list, and must be supplied by the Help Desk. Violation of this policy makes the corporation vulnerable to prosecution for software theft. For further PC policies, check the Help Desk menu.

Audience

- All customers.

Frequency

- Updates to policies and procedures should be communicated continuously before they are put in place so that people will be prepared for them, and then again as soon as they take effect.

- Policies and procedures should be in a place accessible to all customers; refreshers or reminders can published every two months or so. You might just pick specific points to highlight depending on problems or trends you have noticed. Location of policies and procedures can be included in the Help Desk list of services. (See "Keep Customers Up to Date on the Range of Services," above.)

Vehicles to Consider

- On-line documents for the actual policy and procedure documents; newsletters, fax back documents, posters, or electronic mail for the reminders and updates.

Improve Two-Way Communication with Customers

To encourage communication from customers, you need to let them know how they can give input, and that you welcome it. You might want to communicate feedback from customers that the Help Desk actually used to make changes, so that customers know you are really listening.

You can send out surveys to get feedback on areas such as performance (see Chapter 7). The results can be summarized and sent back out to customers, along with a description of any actions you plan to take based on survey results.

Example

Suggestion:

- Have feedback or suggestions for the Help Desk? Call 222-4567 and select the suggestion option. And guess what? The suggestion line was a suggestion!

Audience

- All customers.

Frequency

- Reminders could be published every two months; updates could be published as required.

Vehicles to Consider

- An Open House, a question-and-answer column in a newsletter, a suggestion line, calls to customers, surveys in report card format for evaluating Help Desk performance, and results of surveys, also in report card format (see Chapter 7).

Communicate Help Desk Performance and Business Value

Communicating Help Desk Performance

To communicate Help Desk performance to customers and management, you will need the results of any performance surveys you may have conducted, as well as feedback from Help Desk staff and statistics from your call tracking system. You will also want to communicate performance against objectives and any service-level agreements. You can communicate the information formally, as part of regular (quarterly) performance evaluations (see Chapter 7), and less formally, as performance updates. Updates should contain performance information that is important to your customers (for example, response times). They will be most effective as short, graphical items, sprinkled through newsletters or highlighted on posters.

Examples

Updates:

- Did you know that the Help Desk handled 2,600 calls last month? And it resolved 80 percent of them in four hours or less! Call 222-4567 and we can do the same for you.
- You've grown from 968 to 1,000 PCs in just 3 months! Yet the Help Desk still resolved 80 percent of your calls in less than four hours!

Graphs:

Figures 8.2 and 8.3 show examples of using graphs to communicate Help Desk performance.

Poor Help Desk Performance

If you have been experiencing problems with your performance, be very careful of what you communicate. Trying to justify poor performance can make you the object of ridicule. For example, if you are responsible for local area network performance and the LAN has been down regularly in the last while, communicating that "The industry standard for LAN up time is 87 percent and we're up 95 percent of the time!" means nothing to your customers. It will probably annoy them. They don't care what the industry standard is or that the LAN was up 95 percent of the time. They care about the 5 percent of the time that it wasn't up. What's important to them is the cost to the business of the LAN being down, not the length

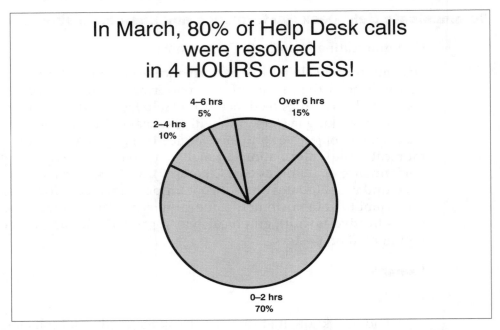

Figure 8.2 Using graphs to communicate performance in resolution times.

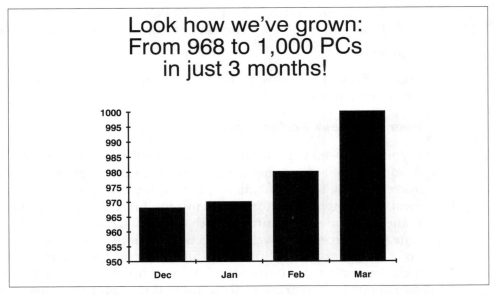

Figure 8.3 Using graphs to communicate growth in environment supported.

of time it is down. In this situation, it is best to be honest and let them know what happened and what you are doing about it. For example, you could say, "We apologize for the poor LAN performance. We do not yet understand the reasons for the problem and have called in technicians from LAN, Inc. to help us out. We will keep you informed of our progress." You can communicate more information as you get it. Customers will appreciate knowing that something is being done.

When the problems you are experiencing are actually affecting the performance of the business, you have to go somewhat farther. Your communication to the customer should include not only a description of the problem and its severity, but the actions you are planning to take to ensure resolution and prevent recurrence. Customers will understand the severity of the situation and will be able to make the appropriate adjustments to their schedules and work. They will also be less likely to phone the Help Desk, because you have given them a clear understanding of what is happening, and they can see that you are doing everything possible to resolve the situation.

Your Help Desk may be experiencing poor performance in handling requests. Perhaps problems aren't getting resolved quickly enough. They are logged and then sit in the queue for a few days before Help Desk staff have a chance to get to them. You should communicate to your customers that you recognize the problem and that you are addressing it. (Hopefully, you are addressing it—if not, don't bother communicating anything.) As you select and implement a solution to the problem, you can let customers know what you are doing and when it will be in effect. For example: "We have been experiencing problems with our call handling. Your calls are not being handled as quickly as they should be. We are investigating the problem and will be putting temporary measures in place to improve service in the meantime." Then, "In order to improve service to our customers while we address our call handling problem, we have temporarily increased the number of people resolving calls. You should notice a marked improvement in response time for your problems."

Bad news is best communicated in an electronic mail message or in person. It needs to be communicated quickly (it can't wait for the next issue of a newsletter), and updates need to be communicated often. You might want to give people a number to call to ask questions or to inquire about the status of the problem. Delivering the message in person allows people to get their questions addressed on the spot. If bad news becomes a regular occurrence, then you have a more severe problem that needs focused attention and possibly management involvement.

Once the problem you have been addressing has been resolved, you need to communicate the good news to get your customers back and to let them know that service has improved. But be sure that the problem really is fixed before you embark on any kind of marketing campaign. You can communicate the good news the same way that you communicated the bad news—via electronic mail or in person. Once you see that things are working well, you can communicate a little more strongly. For example, if you have improved your call handling by upgrading your Help Desk software (perhaps you didn't have any before), you can advertise this in newsletters or on posters.

Example

- "We've improved! Our new call handling system will allow us to serve you *faster*. Try us out!"

Audience

- All customers and management.

Frequency

- Communicate formal performance information every quarter, or more often if specifically requested by customers or management.
- Communicate performance updates more often—every month. Use several media. If you have an exceptional performance situation that you want to communicate, do it right away.
- For bad news (poor performance), communicate continuously until the problem is resolved. Let the customers know that you are working on the problem. Once the problem has been resolved and you are sure everything is working, communicate the good news.

Vehicles to Consider

- For good news: reports, posters, newsletters, presentations. For bad news: electronic mail, meetings.

Communicating Business Value

Business value is really a part of Help Desk performance, but it is not always obvious from standard performance information. Management is very interested in understanding the business value that the Help Desk is providing. Therefore, it is worth taking the time to make your performance communication reflect business value, or to create a separate communication that focuses on it. Management wants to know that the company's investment in the Help Desk is paying off. Information that you can use to show this includes Help Desk performance against objectives, budget, and service-level agreements, as well as any customer evaluations, staff evaluations, call tracking statistics, and growth statistics that you have. You will want to include information on specific instances in which you saved the company time or money or made an important project possible. You can market this information formally in quarterly performance evaluations (see Chapter 7 for a detailed example), and less formally on an ongoing basis, the same way as you would communicate regular performance updates.

If you are just putting a Help Desk together and want to market its value to management so that you get the funding you need, you should be using a cost/benefit analysis. Chapter 9 gives a detailed example of such an analysis.

Information that communicates business value, and that you would want to include in your business value communications, includes the following:

- Specific accomplishments, such as installation of automation. You could show before-and-after call distribution graphs and explain the value in terms of faster service and staff freed up.

- Specific problems that were prevented or resolved that could have cost the company significant dollars or business were they allowed to happen or continue.

- Work that was done to make the environment able to handle systems required by the business. For example, upgrading memory on PCs so that new client/server applications could be rolled out.

- Money saved through volume licensing agreements, maintenance contracts, and so on.

- Any processes that are in place that help ensure data security—for example, virus scanning and security procedures.

- Time that the Help Desk saves employees by getting them up and running as quickly as possible.

- Time saved by eliminating informal support. Customers call the Help Desk directly, rather than trying to figure out a problem on their own or with a colleague.

- Anything that was done to make employees more productive: training or new or upgraded products. For example, if everyone is upgraded to the same version of the same software, information sharing and communication becomes easier. If people are trained on the use of the network, they can use it more effectively and take advantage of all of its functions.

Some Examples

Updates:

- Network monitoring software alerted the Help Desk to a cabling malfunction on the Advertising LAN. The situation was fixed quickly before it could affect LAN performance, and Advertising was able to handle its morning rush. Had the Help Desk not noticed the problem, Advertising would have experienced at least 30 minutes of down time during the busiest part of the morning, which amounts to 100 ads and revenue of $80,000!
- We're ready for the new sales application! The Help Desk upgraded 200 PCs from 4 megabytes of memory to 8 megabytes of memory, in just three weeks!

Graphs:

Figures 8.4 and 8.5 show examples of using graphs to communicate business value.

Audience

- Management.

Frequency

- Communicate business value along with formal performance information every quarter, or more often if specifically requested by management.
- Communicate business value updates more often—every month. Use several media. If you have an exceptional example of business value that you want to communicate, do it right away.

Vehicles to Consider

- Reports, newsletters, presentations, posters.

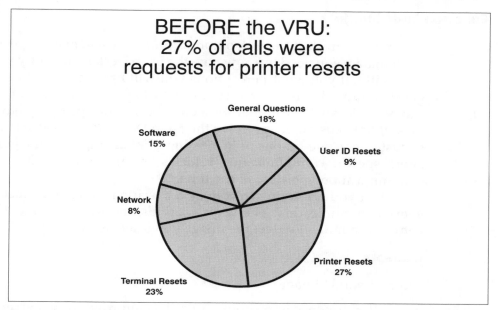

Figure 8.4   Using graphs to communicate the "before."

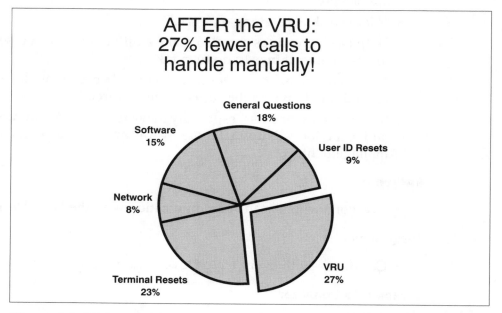

Figure 8.5   Using graphs to communicate the "after": the business value.

Enhance Your Image

Before you can start to work on projecting a consistent and specific Help Desk image, you need to know how the Help Desk is currently perceived. This will tell you what perceptions you will have to overcome. You can get this through customer surveys (see Chapter 7) and from Help Desk staff who deal with customers on a daily basis. They probably have a good idea of how customers perceive the Help Desk. You can also simply talk to customers, one-on-one or in meetings. Enhancing your image isn't just about specific communication vehicles or specific times, it is about all communication vehicles, all the time.

When you are trying to convey a specific image, you must do so in every communication. The way it sounds, the way it looks, the tone it conveys should all reflect the image you select for your Help Desk.

Example

"Not-so-good" image:

- "Performance in response times has improvd by 60 percent."

  Simple things like spelling mistakes make a difference in how you are perceived.

- "Help Desk here. Hang on a sec."

  Help Desk greetings can also make a difference. This person seems to have better things to do than take your call.

- "We were unable to meet our objectives because the development team did not give us the support we required."

  Blaming someone else, especially in writing, is very unprofessional, and isn't looked upon favorably by anyone—especially not by management.

Audience

- Everyone who has any communication with the Help Desk.

Frequency

- Constant—with every Help Desk communication.

Vehicles to Consider

- All vehicles must be considered.

Communicating an Image

Image is your outward appearance—how you look to your customers. It determines how, and even whether, your customers will interact with you. Your image can bring on reactions such as "Oh no. It looks like I've got a problem, but I sure don't want to talk to the Help Desk. Maybe I'll just go over and ask Tom. He'll know how to fix this." Or, more positively, "Uh-oh. Looks like I have a problem. I'd better call the Help Desk."

Image is built by your performance, but it is affected by every interaction—oral or written—that you have with your customers. Each communication represents the Help Desk to the customer who is receiving it. If it is of poor quality, then the customer will perceive the Help Desk as delivering poor quality. In order to help ensure that this doesn't happen, you want to be as consistent as possible in communicating the image that you want people to have of your Help Desk—for example, professionalism and service excellence. You want to be consistently sending the "professionalism and service excellence" message to your customers, whenever you interact with them.

Help Desk staff and manager should work together on the image they want to convey. All need to support it and to be aware of it always. Something as simple as a sloppy, poorly written communication of some kind can give a customer a poor opinion of the Help Desk, even if that customer has never actually called the Help Desk. Worse still, that customer might share that negative opinion with other customers.

A major challenge in communicating a consistent image is that Help Desk staff (and managers) will have varying degrees of communication ability. What one person might be horrified by (for example, "We've fixed the LAN problem, so don't call us any more"), another might find perfectly acceptable. Chances are that the company is not going to put a full-time marketing representative at your disposal, so you have to find other ways to ensure that your communication consistently reflects the image you want. Some things you can do are:

- Get your staff (and yourself) trained. There are numerous customer service courses available that deal with effective communication.

- Set standards for Help Desk greetings and voice messaging. Have standard Help Desk greetings for Help Desk staff to use. For example, "Corporate Help Desk, Paula speaking. How can I help you?" rather than "Paula here."

Make sure voice messages in all parts of your Help Desk systems are consistent. Find a good voice and use it everywhere. (One company surveyed their Operations and Communications Support staff to see who had the best voice. The woman selected now creates the voice messages, which have received very positive responses from clients.) Keep your messages clear and concise. Credit your customers with some intelligence. Don't have the voices speaking too slowly and repeating things.

- Automate and standardize written communication wherever possible. This will discourage creative writing that might violate your image. Have standard templates for as many types of written communication as possible, and have the system generate memos to clients wherever possible (for example, once a problem request has been completed). If you have a logo, make it a standard part of your written communication.

- Establish some form of quality control procedure for all communication. Perhaps you could have each communication checked by a person other than the one who created it before it goes out. Or it could be checked by a specific person—either yourself, as Help Desk manager, or someone on the Help Desk who is good at written communication.

- Encourage staff to give dry runs of any presentations they have to do. Have other staff critique them and ensure that they are prepared.

Communicating an image isn't something separate from communicating information. The way the information is presented reflects the image. In fact, if you do this successfully, customers will be able to identify a document as yours just by the writing style or the look.

A major step toward communicating a positive image consistently is being constantly aware of it. Once you achieve this, ensuring that the chosen image is reflected in any communication you send out will become almost automatic.

Communication Vehicles

In deciding how you are going to get information to your customers, you can choose from a wide variety of communication vehicles—everything from a memo to an open house. Regardless of the vehicle you choose, you will have the challenge of communicating to people who are deluged with information and who are very busy. In order to help ensure that your communication gets through to them, whatever vehicle you choose, you need to do the following:

1. Cater to your audience.

   Know who your audience is, and design the communication specifically for them. If your audience is your customers, go back to the customer profile you created when you were getting your Help Desk focused, back in Chapter 1. This will tell you who you need to market to, where they are, how technology-literate and technology-friendly they are, what technology they use, and what they use it for. You need to make sure you send information to your customers in a way that they will receive it. If they have access to and use electronic mail, then electronic mail is available to you as a marketing medium. If they use voice mail, then voice mail is also available to you. If you have pockets of customers who are not (yet) technology-literate, use other media, such as posters or newsletters, to get your information to them.

   Be aware of any company-wide initiatives that will affect your communication, such as paper conservation. If you are putting out reams of paper when the rest of the company is trying to conserve, you will annoy a lot of people, and they probably won't get the information you're sending.

2. Be concise.

   No one has time to read long missives or listen to long, repetitive messages. Make your communication short and to the point. Even meetings and seminars can be tightened up so that you use only the time you need to get what you want accomplished.

3. Think image.

   Make sure that your communication reflects your image. The more consistent you are about this, the more customers will start to notice, and perhaps think more positively about your department.

The communication vehicles you use in your marketing efforts will depend on your audience and what you are marketing. You have a wide range to choose from, and will probably end up using a mix. Following are various media that you might consider using, and how you might use them. They are broken down into five categories:

- Paper-based
- Electronic
- Voice
- In-person
- Specialty

Paper-Based Communication Vehicles

Advantages of paper are that it is portable and concrete. You can read a newsletter on public transportation, for example, or you can hang a priority list on your wall. A disadvantage is that there is just too much of it around, and paper communication could get lost in the crowd. Conservation-minded customers could be put off if you use too much paper.

Company Newsletter

Company newsletters can be used to communicate Help Desk updates of any kind, including performance and business value. They reach a wide audience, and you might be able to get a regular space.

Information in company newsletters could include:

- Hints and tips for making better use of technology.
- News about product upgrades.
- New Help Desk tools and services, such as remote diagnostics or automation.
- Help Desk accomplishments—these could serve to communicate business value to management.
- Performance information.

Fax-Back Items

One way to give remote users (who don't have access to the main network) information on demand is by setting up an automated function that will allow them to request documents—such as Help Desk news, policy updates, and so on—to be faxed back to them. If you have a VRU, have already implemented fax-back for other functions, and have enough remote customers to justify this, then this might be a good way for customers to get the information they need without having to call anyone.

Items to be faxed back could include:

- News of upcoming Help Desk events.
- Policies.
- Updates to software or to Help Desk services.

Help Desk Newsletter

A Help Desk newsletter can serve as a central source for all Help Desk updates and information. Copies can sent to all customers and to management. The newsletter can contain separate sections or columns of "specific interest" topics so that people can quickly pick out what they wanted to read. Frequency depends on how dynamic your environment is. A one-page, two-sided bimonthly newsletter is a good starting point.
Newsletters could include:

- Hints and tips for making better use of technology.
- A question-and-answer column to present answers to common questions or problems, and to encourage communication with customers.
- News about product upgrades.
- New Help Desk tools and services, such as remote control diagnostics or automation.
- Help Desk accomplishments—these could serve to communicate business value to management.
- Performance information.

To help you get started, you can have someone create a template that you can use each issue to fill in with Help Desk news, or use a template that comes with the software you use (if one is provided). Keep everything very simple to minimize the amount of work involved.

Laminated Priority List

In order to ensure that their customers used and understood agreed-upon priorities, one company had the priority list printed on fluorescent paper (8.5 x 11), laminated, and then sent to all customers. This proved to be a very effective marketing tool. Customers keep the lists posted on their walls near their phones, and can assign the priorities themselves when they call in to report a problem or ask a question.

Pamphlets

Pamphlets are useful for delivering a fair amount of information that customers might want to save. Pamphlets could be used for:

- An introduction to the Help Desk.
- A list of Help Desk services.
- Information on how to access and use the Help Desk.
- Response time promises.
- Priorities.
- Any other information pertinent to a Help Desk customer.

Postcards

Standard-sized postcards can be used to deliver short clips of information. Postcards are fairly sturdy and people won't like throwing them out, so they should be used in a way that will encourage them to be saved for reference or reused in some way. For example, on one side print an invitation to a Word 6.0 update seminar, and on the other side a quick reference card for Word 6.0.

Cards could be used for:

- Invitations.
- Advertising for new services or software:
  Tips for using the new service or software could be printed on the back.
- Surveys:
  Customers could fill the surveys out anonymously and send them back to the Help Desk.
- Report cards:
  The Help Desk could create a report card for itself, based on the result of surveys or of performance against service-level agreements. These cards, in a report card format, could be sent to customers.

Posters

Posters are good for quick reminders or short advertising clips. They can be set out in customer areas—in halls, near elevators, in work spaces—and are easily distributed in greater numbers in areas where a denser distribution is desired. Posters can be printed very cheaply on colored, standard-sized paper. If you want them to appear larger, you can add a backing of larger paper, such as bristle board. A few posters can reach a large audience.

Posters could be used to:

- Announce Help Desk events, such as seminars or an open house: "A Help Desk Open House!"
- Announce product upgrades: "Word 6.0 will be here August 5th. To find out more, attend a Word Update seminar."
- Display graphs and short updates for Help Desk performance and activity: "Help Desk Activity for January"
- Increase awareness of the Help Desk, especially in areas of low use: "Got a PC problem? We can help. Quickly. Call 222-4567."

Reports

Reports that are generated at regular intervals to management and/or customers can be used to communicate:

- Performance against service-level agreements.
- Overall Help Desk performance (to management).
- Help Desk activity.
- Justification of Help Desk improvements (to management).

Surveys

Surveys that measure your performance from your customer's point of view let your customers know that you care what they think—especially if you feed back the results to them. Surveys can take several forms. One suggestion is to send them out on postcards, and to return the results as report cards (still printed on postcards).

Electronic Communication Vehicles

Advantages of electronic communication are that everyone gets instant, personal delivery, and that there's no paper involved. Disadvantages are that it is difficult to read long documents on-line, and that electronic mail has become so well used in many companies that junk mail has become a problem.

Electronic Newsletters

The content for on-line newsletters could be the same as for paper-based newsletters. You could use electronic mail (if your software allowed it) to send the newsletter document to all customers and management, or you could simply put it in a central place for read-only and print-only access. In the former case, the newsletter would go to the customer; in the latter case, the customer would have to go to the newsletter, which might mean that it wouldn't be read.

The success of this kind of newsletter would depend largely on how technology-literate and technology-friendly your customers and management are. This might have greater appeal in an environment where paper use was an issue.

Electronic Mail

Electronic mail is a good medium for short, important messages that apply to all recipients, or for notes to specific customers. It is easy to get sloppy when sending electronic messages—try to use templates wherever possible. Be careful not to overuse electronic mail for sending global messages. People could start looking upon your messages as junk mail.

You could use electronic mail for:

- Announcements and descriptions of service changes (for example, an announcement for a new VRU and instructions on how to use it).
- Notes to individual customers.
- Invitations to individual customers—seminars, education, and so on.
- Notification of service degradation of some kind, and explanations of what is being done to resolve the problem.

Electronic Surveys

These are the same as paper-based surveys. You may want to allow for anonymity, which could be difficult.

On-line Documents

Larger documents such as procedures, policies, and so on are best stored on-line for easy updating and easy reference. Software packages designed for building and reading on-line documents make documents easy to read and easy to search. You could have a whole on-line library of the most-referenced documents.

You could use on-line documents for:

- Policies for security and standards.
- Any customer-created documentation for in-house applications.

Voice Communication Vehicles

Use of voice communication in marketing includes talking to customers on the phone to market various aspects of the Help Desk, and using voice messaging to allow customers to retrieve Help Desk information on their own, or to leave messages.

Phone

The phone is an excellent marketing tool for the Help Desk, because it is used by almost all customers to access the Help Desk. Help Desk staff can offer customers, at the end of calls, information about new products or services, such as product upgrades or automation. If calls are for services that have been automated, staff can walk customers through the auto-mated procedure and encourage them to try it.

Voice Messaging

Using voice messaging as a marketing tool is a good idea if your custom-ers are comfortable with and use voice mail.

Voice messages can be used:

- For general Help Desk information. This could be an option on the Help Desk phone menu that offered customers information such as services, hours of operation, and service guarantees.
- For feedback. You could set up an option on your Help Desk phone menu on which customers could record their comments or sugges-tions on Help Desk service.

In-person Marketing Vehicles

Sometimes the best way to market is face-to-face. You can demonstrate new products, gauge reactions, and handle questions and concerns as they arise.

Demonstrations

Demonstrations can be used to showcase what technology can do for the customer. Help Desk staff, customers, or vendors could demonstrate how customers can get the most out of their existing technology, what new technology offers, and what upgrades offer.

Your Help Desk could offer regular demonstrations during lunch hours, offering a different product or set of products each time.

Seminars

If your Help Desk call statistics indicate a need for training on some kind of internal procedures or processes, a seminar might be a good way to handle this. A seminar would also be good for addressing recurring questions, or for explaining the new features of an upgrade and how to use them.

Training

Even if training is outsourced, take the time to make sure that the outsourcers are providing your customers with the training they require. Make sure they conform to your Help Desk image and that content is appropriate to your environment. If training is in-house, it can be used to market Help Desk services. In fact, using the Help Desk can be incorporated into the training sessions. (This can probably be arranged with outsourced training, as well.)

Meetings

Help Desk staff can attend customer departmental meetings to sell services, answer questions, gather suggestions, and get feedback. Customers will appreciate the fact that Help Desk staff take the time to explain and to listen. Attending these meetings is also useful for areas that are getting specific technology for the first time, to help prepare them for what is coming and to handle concerns as they come up.

Presentations

Presentations are good marketing vehicles for presenting cost justifications or plans to management. You have a variety of audio-visual tools at your disposal and an audience whose questions and concerns you can address immediately.

Focus Groups

Focus groups are a good marketing tool for introducing new products or upgrades. The customers in the group will do a lot of free advertising for the Help Desk. If the product is not appropriate and is discarded, it is good to find that out as early as possible, and the focus group will feel that you have really listened to their feedback. If the product is brought in, the group will already be familiar with it and will let others know about it. They will also have positive things to say about a Help Desk that takes their input so seriously.

Open House

An open house is an excellent way of introducing a new or improved Help Desk. The event could include demonstrations of software packages, seminars on topics of interest such as "what our network looks like," and demonstrations of physical equipment such as servers or communication equipment. Customers could be involved, and could host areas such as demonstrations or expert forums. Refreshments and prize drawings could be part of the event. Open houses tend to be very popular, and you may find customers traveling from remote sites to attend.

Specialty Communication

This category includes some simple but very effective marketing vehicles.

Help Desk Mouse Pads

If the technology you support is largely PC based, you can use mouse pads to market how to use the Help Desk. You can have mouse pads made up with Help Desk phone number, fax number, and/or electronic mail ID on them. Often, a PC vendor can be talked into making up these mouse pads for free or for a minimal charge. They will be a constant Help Desk reminder for customers.

Inventory Stickers for PCs

You probably have some kind of stickers on your PCs, terminals, and printers with asset information. When you get these stickers made up, you can have them made up a little larger and preprinted with information on how to access the Help Desk. Again, the stickers will be constant Help Desk reminders.

Table 8.1 offers a summary of which communication vehicles to use to achieve specific marketing objectives.

Table 8.1 Summary of Communication Vehicles

Goal	Information Required	Marketing Vehicles	Audience
Keep customers up to date on the range of services.	Services, hours of support, response times	Inventory Stickers, Meetings, Mouse pads, Newsletters, Pamphlets, Information line	All customers, focus on new customers
Teach customers how to use your services.	How to access and use Help Desk, how to use automation, priorities	Meetings, Newsletters, Pamphlets, Phone, Posters, Priority List, Information line	All customers, focus on new customers
Encourage customers to use your services.	New services and features, how using the Help Desk can help, consequences of not using Help Desk	Meetings, Newsletters, Open House, Information line, Posters, Seminars	All customers
Help customers use technology more effectively.	Call statistics to identify customers needing training, tips, suggestions, solutions to common problems, how to perform specific tasks that seem to be a problem	Newsletters, On-line documents, Postcards, Posters, Seminars, Training	All customers, focus on those needing training
Disseminate information such as policies, strategies, and procedures (and updates to these).	Location of policies and procedures; all updates to them	Electronic mail, Fax-back documents, On-line documents, Posters, Newsletters	All customers
Improve two-way communication with customers.	Feedback from customers, how customers can give Help Desk suggestions and information	Open house, Phone, Post cards (for report cards to feed back customer evaluation), Q&A in newsletter, Suggestion line	All customers

Table 8.1 (*continued*)

Goal	Information Required	Marketing Vehicles	Audience
Communicate Help Desk performance and business value.	For formal quarterly reporting: Performance against objectives, budget, and service-level agreements; employee evaluation; staff evaluation; call statistics; growth statistics	Presentations, Reports	Management and customers
	For updates: Call statistics, growth statistics, money and time saved.	Electronic mail (for bad news), Meetings Reports, Newsletters, Posters, Presentations	Management and customers
Enhance Help Desk image.		All vehicles, but specifically templates for communication	

Your Marketing Plan

You now need to put everything together to create a plan for your marketing efforts. Your marketing plan will consist of:

1. What you want to accomplish through marketing—your marketing objectives.
2. What information you want to communicate.
3. Communication vehicles that you want to use, who your audience is for each, and what the frequency is for each.
4. The image you want to communicate.

Your plan will need to be updated about every quarter, when you do your budget and performance updates. The value in a marketing plan is that it will help ensure that you actually do marketing, which often gets tossed aside when things get busy. You want customers and management to know what you're doing and what you've accomplished. If you leave this up to them, they will get the information but it may be incorrect, incomplete, or they may not understand all of the factors involved. The more control you have over this information, the more positive use you can make of it. The following is an example of a marketing plan.

Marketing Objectives:

- Communicate monthly performance update to customers and to management.

  Want to show call volume and distribution, changes in calls over 6 months, and changes in the number of PCs being supported. Growth has been pretty phenomenal the last couple of months. Also want to communicate business value to management; they've started asking. Customers don't like getting reports, so we'll use posters for them. We can use reports for management.

- Keep customers up to date on our range of services and teach them how to use our services.

  We have a lot of new customers, so it would be a good time to get something together explaining who we are and what we do. We could also include some information about what kinds of policies exist for their technology. We could put reminders about our services in the company newsletter, too.

- Increase the effective use of technology.

  We've noticed that there are a few areas that are really misusing the spreadsheet package. We need to get some training together to address that. People are still having problems with using the network, so we should have a seminar to address that. This would be good for all of the new customers we have, as well. We could do a few sessions. We'll put some hints and tips for network use in the company newsletter.

Image:

We want a very professional, service-oriented image. We're pretty good on the phones, but we need some help with our writing. Two staff will go to an Effective Communications course, one this month and one next month.

We also need to create some templates for answering customers' questions on electronic mail. I've noticed some pretty rough answers going out.

Table 8.2 Marketing Plan

Marketing Objectives	Information Required	Communication Vehicles	Audience	Frequency
Communicate performance update	Call statistics and growth statistics	Posters with graphs	Customers	Monthly
		Reports with graphs	Management	Monthly
Communicate business value updates	Accomplishments; instances of Help Desk saving time or money	Reports (same as for performance —add business value material)	Management	Monthly
		Company newsletter	All	Bimonthly
Keep customers up to date on range of services; teach them to use services	Services and usage information	Pamphlet	Initially, all; then, new users	Update yearly
		Company newsletter for updates	All customers	Bimonthly
Increase effectiveness of technology use	Call statistics to see who needs training and to see what things customers have problems with; hints and tips	Posters to advertise training and tips	All customers	Two (one for tips and one for training) each month
		Seminars on network use	All customers	One each month
		Training for Excel	Available to all; targeted at those who stats say need it	Two courses this quarter
		Company newsletter for tips, training dates	All customers	Bimonthly

(continues)

Table 8.2 Marketing Plan (*continued*)

Marketing Objectives	Information Required	Communication Vehicles	Audience	Frequency
Enhance professional, service-oriented image	Need a communications course	Effective communications course for staff	Two staff	Once, refreshers as required
	Need to clarify the components that go into answering a customer query	Reply template for staff	All staff	Once, update as required

Summary

Your Help Desk won't be successful just because it exists. You have to let customers know that it exists and what services it offers. You also have to let management and customers know what value it is bringing to the business and how well it is performing. Your Help Desk faces constant competition from outsourcing, so you have to ensure that management knows what you offer in terms of business value and cost-effectiveness.

Marketing will help you do all of this, but it won't replace or hide poor performance. You cannot market something you don't have—at least, not for very long.

Some of the things that marketing can do for you are:

- Keep customers up to date on your range of services:
  Customers will know what you do and will have realistic expectations of your service.

- Teach customers how to use your services:
  Customers will know how to use the Help Desk and what is expected of them when they call.

- Encourage customers to use your services:
  You can market Help Desk benefits and services so that customers won't be tempted to take the very expensive route of informal support.

- Help customers use technology more effectively:
  Show customers how they could make better use of their technology so that they can increase their productivity and their contribution to the business.

- Disseminate information such as policies, strategies, procedures:
  This will help ensure that customers understand and abide by any required procedures or restrictions.

- Improve two-way communication with customers:
  Customers can offer the Help Desk valuable feedback and suggestions, and this input needs to be encouraged.

- Communicate Help Desk performance and business value:
  This is absolutely essential for the continued health and funding of the Help Desk. It is also important for facing up to the competition.

- Enhance the image of the Help Desk:
  Each Help Desk communication affects a customer's perception of the Help Desk. Making sure that these consistently reflect the image your Help Desk wants to portray will help ensure that it achieves that image.

In order to ensure that your marketing is consistent, that you market everything you need to, and that the marketing gets done, you need to have a marketing plan. To put one together, you need to decide what you want your marketing to accomplish, what information you need to do this, to whom it should go (and how often), what image you want to communicate, and what vehicles you want to use for your marketing.

Information that you need to achieve your marketing objectives is as follows:

- To *update* customers on your range of services: Help Desk hours, list of services, off-hours support, guaranteed response times, and any updates to service.

- To *teach* customers how to use your services: phone and fax numbers, electronic mail IDs, what customers need to tell the Help Desk when they call, instructions on using priorities and any automated features.

- To *encourage* customers to use your services: new services, what value your Help Desk can add to customers' work, what the cost is of not using the Help Desk.

- To *increase* the effectiveness of customer's use of technology: call statistics to indicate who needs training, hints and tips from Help Desk staff, power users and vendors, solutions to common problems, features of software upgrades, what technology can do for the customer.

- To *disseminate* information such as policies, strategies, procedures: policies, procedures, strategies, and any updates to them. Also, why these need to be followed (i.e., the cost of not following them).

- To *improve* two-way communication with customers: how customers can pass suggestions to the Help Desk. Also, results of any customer surveys or suggestions, to feed back to customers.

- To *communicate* Help Desk Performance and business value: Help Desk performance against objectives, budget, and service-level agreements. Also, call management statistics, growth statistics, customer evaluation, and staff evaluation.

- To *enhance* the image of the Help Desk: how the Help Desk is currently perceived, and how you want the Help Desk to be perceived. You also need to be aware of the communication abilities of your Help Desk staff.

Help Desk staff and manager should work together to define and support the Help Desk image. It needs to be reflected in every interaction they have with their customers and every communication they produce. A challenge will be to communicate this image consistently with staff who have varying levels of communication skills. Some suggestions to address this are training, setting up standards for voice messages, setting up templates for written messages, automating wherever possible to ensure consistency, establishing some quality control procedures for any communication leaving the Help Desk, and having staff critique each other in dry runs of any presentations they have to give.

When you are doing any kind of Help Desk marketing, you have numerous communication vehicles to choose from. People are flooded with communication and don't have a lot of time, so regardless of the vehicle you choose, you should make sure that you cater to your audience (know who your audience is and how to reach everyone in it), be concise, and make sure that your communication reflects your image.

Some communication vehicles that you have to choose from are:

- Paper-based: a spot in company newsletters, fax-back of information, a Help Desk newsletter, a laminated priority list, pamphlets, postcards, posters, reports, and surveys.
- Electronic: electronic newsletter, electronic mail, electronic surveys, and on-line documents.
- Voice: the telephone and voice messaging.
- In-person: demonstrations, seminars, training, attending customer meetings, presentations, focus groups, and an open house.
- Specialty: mouse pads and hardware inventory stickers printed with Help Desk information on them.

Putting all of this information together, you can create your marketing plan: your marketing objectives; the information you want to communicate; communication vehicles you want to use, including audience and frequency; and image. Your plan can be updated quarterly. It will give you control over the information you market, so that you can make more positive use of it.

CHAPTER NINE

Cost/Benefit Analysis

Whether you're just starting a Help Desk, or whether you have an established Help Desk and are trying to make improvements, you're going to have to go through the process of justifying the cost of what you are proposing. You might see the value in what you're trying to do very clearly and wonder how anyone could doubt the worth of a Help Desk or improvement, but management might not see it quite like that. They have to make sure you're spending the company's money on something that will bring value to the business. They need to understand the business value of what you're trying to do. The purpose of the cost/benefit analysis you prepare will be to demonstrate that value.

Business Value

Demonstrating business value might not be as much of a challenge if you were in the business of producing widgets. You could calculate the cost of producing, marketing, and selling each widget versus the price you got for it. On the Help Desk, you aren't producing anything. Instead, you are enabling other people to produce, sell, and distribute things, be they widgets or information. This makes it difficult to put a value on the Help Desk function.

In order to show the business value of a Help Desk, it is necessary to look at the situation from a different perspective: what would the environment be like without a Help Desk? What would it be costing the business, in terms of extra time users would have to spend solving problems, figuring out where to go to get problems resolved, performing any activity associated with support? What would it be costing the business not to have a technology environment that was stable enough to support critical production applications? The difference between this environment and the same environment with a Help Desk added is the business value of your Help Desk. This is what you have to try to estimate when you're putting your cost/benefit analysis together.

The same applies to doing a justification for an improvement, such as installing a voice response unit. Consider what it is costing the business not to have a voice response unit, in terms of customer time, support staff time, and strategic direction. Then consider the same environment with a VRU: the costs may have disappeared and extra benefits been realized. This is the business value. In the case of a VRU, you will have data from your call tracking statistics to help you estimate business value. When you're setting up a Help Desk for the first time, you don't have those statistics.

Creating Measures

In order to put a value on the difference between the existing situation (that is, no Help Desk) and the one you are proposing (Help Desk), you need to create some kind of measure. You may not have any real data for the current situation, but you do have information that you can gather from users and support staff. For example, users might be taking much longer than required to accomplish their work because they are doing things inefficiently: they don't know how to pass data along the network, so are putting their work on diskettes and sending them to people via internal mail; they don't know how to download from the mainframe, so are rekeying data; their PCs are incorrectly configured, which is slowing them down. You estimate that half of all users (there are 1,000 users in total) experience situations like these, and that this is costing each user on average six hours each month. This means that in any given month, 500 users are spending 6 hours that they shouldn't have to. Over a year, this is 36,000, hours or 4,500 eight-hour days. Broken down by user, this means that on average, users are spending 4.5 days per year, or 2.4 percent of their time (assuming 188 available days per year), on unproductive tasks that would not be necessary were they in a supported environment. You could break this number into minutes or hours per day or week if it were more relevant. You now have a business cost associated with the unsupported environment. You also have a business benefit for the supported environment: you are freeing up 2.4 percent of user time. Add any other benefits that your supported environment brings, and you have your measure.

You need to be careful when dealing with these kinds of measures. They are very rough estimates meant to show trends and magnitudes, not exact figures. It would be almost impossible to get this kind of information accurately. When you talk in terms of user time spent or saved over a period of time, you have to remember that you can't simply add it up and present it as a cost or savings in terms of people. First of all, it is a very rough estimate. Second, what you are adding is bits of time from many users. You can't take all of this time, put it together, and talk about staff savings—you are putting bits of people together, not whole people. For example, say you have 500 users and you claim that you are saving them each 3 days per year. This is 1,500 user days. You cannot say that this is equivalent to 8 people (at 188 days per year). This would imply that you could get rid of 8 people, and this isn't true—you are giving 500 people 3 days each a year to spend on something of greater business value, which is quite a different story. Management will be very quick to pick up on any hint of staff savings, so be careful of making inadvertent promises in this direction. Keep any time measures to per-user units— such as 3 days per user per year, or 1.5 percent of users' time.

Preparing Data for the Analysis

In order to put your cost/benefit analysis together, you are going to have to:

- Describe the current situation in terms of cost to the business.
- Describe the proposed situation or improvement in terms of eliminating some or all of that cost and adding more value.

Describe the Current Situation

You need to determine what the problems are with the current situation and what each is costing the business in terms of person time, money, or strategic growth. If you are trying to cost-justify a Help Desk and you don't have any historical data to work with, you will have to interview customers and support staff to get an idea of the problems they face and the time it costs them. Don't worry too much about being 100 percent accurate. You're trying to get indications, magnitudes, and trends, not 100 percent accuracy. Give consideration also to other, tangible costs: equipment that has to be maintained, or any extra help that has to be hired.

If you are trying to cost-justify improvements to the Help Desk and you have historical data, you can use this along with user and support staff interviews (if they are necessary) to get the data you need. For example, support traffic might be so high that a customer spends ten minutes trying to get through to the Help Desk to get a terminal reset. That ten minutes could be a combination of trying, hanging up, and trying again, or it could be just staying on the line for ten minutes, waiting for a free support person. If it were the former, you'd have to actually talk to that customer to find out that total time wasted was ten minutes.

As well as costs for individual problems, you need to consider costs to the business as a whole, now and in the future. For example, if a company has no PC Help Desk, development of critical business functions using client/server might be impaired, because there would be no support for them.

Describe the Proposed Situation

Here you need to describe your proposal and what it would mean to the business. Would all of the problems disappear? Would the business realize other value? What would this mean in terms of the company's future? The improvement could be stated in terms of time saved, money or staff saved, and opportunities for the business. For example, your proposal of putting in a Help Desk might mean that each technology user can free up 3 percent of the time spent struggling with technology to focus on the business. It could also mean the very real savings associated with centralized software purchase. The local area network environment would be more stable so that the business could use client/server for critical production applications.

Building a Proposal

As well as a cost/benefit analysis for what you are proposing, it would be wise to have the support of your customers, or potential customers. Talk to the customer managers, show them drafts of your proposal, and ask for their feedback. The more support you have, the easier it will be to get what you are asking for. If possible, go to senior managers who are willing to advise you as to how to put the proposal together—try to get their support. It would be frustrating and embarrassing, to say the least, to put the whole proposal together, just to have the customers tell senior management, "We're okay as we are. We don't need a Help Desk." Going through this whole justification exercise and talking to various managers should indicate, very early on, whether you have a case for putting a Help Desk together.

The level of detail required in a cost/benefit analysis will vary depending on your own environment, the dollar amount you're trying to justify spending, and whether you need expense or capital. Some organizations have standard forms for cost/benefit analyses. If your management believes in what you're trying to justify, or you have a champion somewhere higher up, you may require a much less detailed document. Expensive initiatives need more detailed analyses than less expensive ones, and something that can be written off as an expense usually requires less detail (if any at all) than a capital outlay.

A cost/benefit analysis can be divided up into five sections:

1. A brief description of the current situation and what you are proposing.

2. Problems with the current situation and their impact on the business.

3. A description of what you are proposing and the benefits it will bring to the business.

4. Implementation options and cost.

5. Recommendation.

If your proposal is longer than a few pages, you will want to preface it with a management summary containing all of this information in a very summarized form. Your proposal may require a discussion of risks involved in the proposed undertaking, such as when outsourcing is being considered. This can be added to the section containing what is being proposed and the benefits to the business.

The focus should always be on business value. As much as you can, describe problems in terms of how they affect the business.

Presenting Your Case

Once you have put your proposal together, you need to present it to some level of senior management. Hopefully, you have shown enough evidence and offered enough solutions that management will realize the value of your proposal and accept it. The way you present your case is important. Sending off a report in the mail isn't usually the best way. You want to make sure your report is looked at by the right people and given enough attention. If possible, present your case in person and hand the reports out at the presentation. You will be able to handle comments and concerns as they come up. Ideally, one or more of the managers at the presentation will have helped you put the proposal together.

In the sections following, three examples of cost/benefit analyses are presented. The first is a justification of a Help Desk. Although the example is set up for a Help Desk, much of the material in the section can be used to justify other business initiatives, including improvements to the Help Desk. The second example deals with justifying a voice response unit. The third example deals with outsourcing. It is a cost/benefit analysis to justify outsourcing the training function of the Help Desk. A management summary is presented at the end of each of the three analyses. Normally, and especially for proposals presented to management, the management summary is included at the very front of the document. For the purposes of this book, however, it is placed at the end to show the natural progression of data collection, analysis, and summary.

Example 1: Justifying a Help Desk

The following example is a cost/benefit analysis for a Help Desk. The environment currently has no Help Desk. Its 2,000 users generate approximately 1,000 support requests each month. The actual number is probably much larger—1,500 or 2,000. The 1,000 estimate was made by the staff from network support, software support, and hardware maintenance, who provide some PC support as a sideline to their real jobs. Users get a lot of help on their own, either by going to vendors directly or by asking their colleagues for help. No one is responsible for customer support, and no calls are logged. When users need help, they phone around until they get a network support person, a hardware maintenance person, a software maintenance person, a vendor, or a colleague who knows something about computers. There is no coordination between support staff. They often work on the same problem without knowing it. Peole in management who introduced PCs (and who are no longer there) felt that the technology wouldn't require any support, and that users could be self-sufficient. Training was left up to individual users, and generally wasn't taken. A lot of time is being wasted by people who don't really understand how to use the technology and who are constantly running into trouble. A lot of the equipment that was purchased initially is now slow and has incompatibility problems with some of the newer equipment. PCs are purchased centrally, but no standards exist—all users just purchase what they want.

The Help Desk being proposed draws all support areas together and adds three front-line staff, an ACD, and Help Desk software.

A management summary is presented at the end.

1. Current Situation and Proposed Solution

Currently, there is much confusion among technology users about whom to call when they experience a problem with any of their PC technology, or want to ask a question about using it. Users are getting support for their PCs, monitors, and printers by going to the technical staff who install and maintain the PCs, going to a colleague who can help, or by calling a vendor directly. There are 2,000 PC users who generate an estimated 1,000 support requests per month. The number is probably actually much larger, but support requests are not logged and users often get their own support. These users are spending a significant amount of their time trying to get the support they need for their technology, which is time they could be spending contributing to the business. They are also not making as effective use of the technology as they could—the return on the company's PC investment is not nearly at the level that it could be. No one is fully dedicated to providing support for PC users, and many aspects of the purchase, installation, and use of PC technology remain nonstandardized, uncoordinated, and unplanned. Support staff who install and maintain PC technology are the main source of support. This support load, in addition to their other responsibilities, is such that they are unable to perform functions that would make the technology environment more stable and lessen the number of problems that users are experiencing.

A Help Desk would offer a central point of contact for problems, questions, and requests for users of PC technology. It would bring all PC support staff and functions under one roof and give them tools to do their jobs more effectively. Users would know where to call when they had problems, would have their technology set up for maximum effectiveness, and could take advantage of organized training to learn how to use it to its full capabilities. Technology standardization efforts could be started, equipment could be kept up to date, and problems could be logged and tracked to identify negative trends for resolution and to help manage the support load. Users could get their focus back on the business, and off of the tools that support it.

2. Problems with Current Situation and Impact on Business

Five support staff and 40 (out of 2,000) users were interviewed to get the data in the tables following. Working days are assumed to be eight hours. The problems can be summarized as:

- Lack of centralized and coordinated support for PCs
- Untrained technology users
- Lack of upgrade strategy for equipment
- Lack of standards and strategies
- Lack of planning

These problems are shown in Tables 9.1 and 9.2.

TABLE 9.1 Problems from Users

Problem	Effect	Est. Yrly cost (in 8-hour days)
Don't know whom to call when they have a problem.	Time away from business trying to call various people to find some support.	125 days
	Estimate: 50% of callers don't know whom to call; Take approximately 10 minutes to find out. (Yearly Cost: 500 * 10 * 12 / 60 / 8 days)	
Don't know when support will come or how long fix will take.	Time not fully productive while waiting for support; difficult to plan alternatives because don't know how long fix will take.	270 days
	Estimate: Time waiting is, on average, only 70% productive; 10% of calls have average wait time 6 or more hours. (Yearly Cost: 100 * 6 * 30% * 12 / 8 days)	

TABLE 9.1 (*continued*)

Problem	Effect	Est. Yrly cost (in 8-hour days)
Often go to colleagues for help.	Users who can help others have to take time away from their jobs to so. **Estimate**: Approximately 5% of all 2,000 users help others; Average help time is 10 hours per month. (Yearly Cost: 100 * 10 * 12 / 8 days)	1,500 days
Individual users some- times hire consultants off the street to help.	Consultants don't know environment; some of their work has to be redone. **Estimate**: 2 incidents per month; one day each to recover. (Yearly Cost: 2 * 12 days)	24 days plus any data loss
Often have to redo work because of incorrect use of technology.	Time and work lost through errors that could have been avoided by getting help or training. **Estimate**: For three examples: a) Files not saved often enough; data lost; rekeying necessary. b) Bought wrong software; wasted time trying to get it to fit the application. c) Incorrect use of formulas in spreadsheet. (Could cause misinformed business decisions.) For these three examples: Approximately 10% of all 2,000 users; Average of 2 hours lost per month. (Yearly Cost: 200 * 2 * 12 / 8 days)	600 days plus cost of any data lost or misin- formed business decisions
Subtotal for problems from users		2,519 days plus cost of any data loss and misin- formed business decisions

Table 9.2 Problems from Staff Doing Support

Problem	Effect	Est. Yrly cost (in 8-hour days)
Users are doing things inefficiently, due to lack of knowledge and availability of standard setup.	Tasks take longer to accomplish. **Estimate**: For three examples: a) Users don't know how to pass data along network; instead, they copy to diskettes and deliver or mail. b) Users are rekeying rather than downloading data from mainframe. c) Incorrectly configured files are slowing individual workstations down. Approximately 35% of all 2,000 users are doing at least one of these; Taking approximately 6 hours each month. (Yearly Cost: 700 * 6 * 12 / 8 days)	6,300 days
There is a lack of coordination. Users are down longer than necessary because a support person working on a problem would not know if another person had already worked on it and resolved it.	Time wasted in duplication of effort; customers are down longer than necessary. **Estimate**: Happens almost daily; Approximately 20 hours per month; (Yearly Cost: 20 * 12 / 8 days)	30 days for user 30 days for support staff
There are no firm hardware or software standards, so compatibility and communication between users can be difficult and time-consuming.	Customers waste time reformatting data in efforts to interface with each other. **Estimate**: For this example: Have three different word processors (Word Perfect, Word for Windows, and Ami Pro) and the mainframe text editor; Documents need to be imported and reformatted when being shared; True of approximately 10% of all 2,000 users;	800 days

Table 9.2 *(continued)*

Problem	Effect	Est. Yrly cost (in 8-hour days)
	Takes approximately 20 minutes per document; Happens 8 times per month per user. (Yearly Cost: 200 * 20 * 8 *12 / 60 / 8 days)	
Old, obsolete equipment is still in use and making the users very inefficient. No standards or upgrade strategies are in place.	Time is lost through inefficient and slower processing. Also, the cost of maintaining old equipment is high, and time to get new software working on it is high. **Estimate**: For users: Users on 200 old PCs are approximately 10% less productive in a given day than users with newer models, due to a much slower processing speed and higher maintenance time; Average user time spent on a PC is 3 hours per day; Loss of productivity is approximately 6 hours per month. (Yearly Cost: 200 * 6 * 12 / 8 days for users) For support staff: 10% of the 200 machines require approximately 4 hours of extra support in a month, just to keep them running. (Yearly Cost: 20 * 4 * 12 / 8 days)	1,800 days of user time 120 days of support time
Planning for any aspect of PC technology is very difficult. Support staff work in reactive mode to solve continuous crises (e.g., viruses, lack of backups, software upgrade requirements).	Time is spent cleaning up and fixing problems rather than preventing them. There is also a very real cost associated with virus damage, loss of backups, etc. **Estimate**: For these examples: Virus damage: 2-hour recreate time per 10 users per month; Lost data (no backups): 3-hour recreate time per 10 users per month. (Yearly Cost: 5 * 10 * 12 / 8 days)	75 days of user time 75 days of support time (at least) Cost of data lost or destroyed Cost of inability to provide secure environment for mission-critical applications

(continues)

Table 9.2 Problems from Staff Doing Support *(continued)*

Problem	Effect	Est. Yrly cost (in 8-hour days)
Subtotal for problems from support staff		9,005 user days 225 days for support staff plus cost of any data loss and business cost of inability to provide secure environment for mission-critical appplications
TOTAL		**11,524** user days (*6 days per user per year = 15 minutes per day = 3.2% of user time*) **225** support staff days PLUS cost of data loss, misinformed business decisions, and inability to provide secure environment for mission-critical applications

Impact on the Business

Lack of centralized support is causing technology users to spend significant time trying to get help on their own. This is time away from the core business, away from their jobs. This time is also making projects take longer and making employees less productive. Employees cannot use the technology as effectively as they might, because they do not receive the training they need, and the nonstandard environment often makes information sharing difficult. Support staff do not have the organization or the tools required to identify and solve recurring problems, to handle problems efficiently, to put standards into place.

Using the examples from the tables above, which are representative but by no means comprehensive, employees using technology are spending slightly more than 3 percent of their time, or 15 minutes each day, struggling with some aspect of technology while returning nothing to the business. On top of this is the cost to the business of any data that has been lost, and of not being able to provide a stable production environment for future business applications. The technology environment cannot safely support any client/server applications until some kind of centralized support is in place.

3. Proposed Help Desk and Benefits

A solution to the current situation needs to address:

- Lack of training of technology users.
- Lack of upgrade strategy for equipment.
- Lack of standards and strategies.
- Lack of planning.
- Lack of centralized and coordinated support for PCs.

A Help Desk Solution

A Help Desk would provide a single number to call for all PC problems, questions, and requests. Services offered would be as follows:

- One number to call for support, 6 A.M. to 6 P.M.; pager support after-hours.
- Hardware maintenance.
- Local area network maintenance.
- Customer support for PC hardware and software.
- Management of hardware and software inventory, including upgrades.
- Testing and installation of software upgrades.
- Source and purchase of hardware and software.
- Organization of training.
- Coordination of planning for the PC environment.
- Coordination of PC standards and security.

Benefits

Technology users could spend more time on the business:

- They would not need to waste time looking for help or dealing with external resources whenever they had a problem. The Help Desk would take care of all aspects of support.

- Informal support networks would no longer be necessary, and those employees who had been providing informal support could once again focus on their own jobs.

- Problems would be responded to more quickly. Users would know the status of their problems and could plan around any anticipated down times.

Users could make more effective use of the technology in supporting the business:

- Training needs would be tracked, and organized training made available, so that users could learn to use technology correctly and avoid costly errors.

Technology use would be more cost-effective:

- Standards would be in place so that economies of scale could be realized in hardware and software purchase and licensing.

- Obsolete equipment could be either upgraded or replaced so that users could make use of more current software, and spend less time waiting for response. Maintenance and support costs for the equipment would be lessened.

The technologcial environment would be more stable:

- Problems would be tracked so that recurring errors and duplication of effort could be stopped.

- Creation of standards would be coordinated and promoted so that technology between departments was compatible. Sharing documents and data would be easier.

- Support staff would be able to do preventive maintenance and planning to decrease instances of down time and last-minute emergencies. They could install virus and security software, monitor hardware and software use so that licensing and upgrades could be accomplished before any limits were reached, and set up proper backups.

- Client/server development initiatives would have much greater chance of success.

Impact on the Business

Technology users would no longer have to be in the business of support. They could make more productive use of the technology because it would be more stable, and because they would have a better understanding of how to use it. Technology down time would be lessened because support would be faster and more effective: calls would be logged, tracked, and handled on a priority basis. The more stable technology environment could handle mission-critical applications.

As technology is added, these benefits would be compounded—greater gain could be realized through greater stability of the technology and more effective use. Current spending on PC technology is approximately $4,000,000 annually. The business cannot hope to see a return on this investment without a support organization to ensure that it is working properly and being used effectively.

4. Implementation Options and Cost

The Help Desk would incorporate and enhance several areas that are currently in existence, and would require three additional staff to provide a first line of support for logging and resolving problems. Existing areas that would be incorporated into the Help Desk are:

- Hardware maintenance.
- Local area network support.
- Management of hardware and software inventory.
- Testing and installation of software upgrades.
- Source and purchase of hardware and software.

Functions that would be added:

- Management of hardware upgrades.
- Organization of training.
- Coordination of planning for the PC environment.
- Coordination of PC standards and security

Setting up the Help Desk would take one internal support staff member approximately eight weeks.

Table 9.3 shows Option 1, an internally staffed Help Desk.

Table 9.4 shows Option 2, which is to outsource the three new positions as part of an existing maintenance contract.

Table 9.3   Internally Staffed Help Desk

Component	One-Time Cost	Yearly Cost	Other Consideration
Three new internal staff (could be new hires)	Possible finder's fee if hiring from outside	$150,000 (including benefits)	Need increase of 3 head count
Training cost		$6,000	
Replacement staff for training, vacation, illness (6 weeks each)		$36,000 (18 weeks @ $2,000)	
Help Desk software	$20,000	$1,000	
ACD	$50,000	$5,000	
Help Desk setup	8 weeks, 1 staff member: $8,000		
Total	$78,000 plus any finder's fee	$198,000	

Table 9.4   Outsource the Three New Positions as Part of an Existing Maintenance Contract

Component	One-Time Cost	Yearly Cost	Other Consideration
Three contract staff; added to hadware maintenance contract. Located on-site.		$180,000	No head count increase; no vacation/ sickness/etc. issues. Two staff will always be there. Save by using same contract as hard- ware maintenance.
Help Desk software	$20,000	$1,000	
ACD	$50,000	$5,000	
Help Desk setup	8 weeks, 1 staff member: $8,000		
Total	$78,000	$186,000	

5. Recommendation

The recommendation is Option 2. Information Services is very satisfied with the service being provided as part of the hardware maintenance contract. The firm providing the service is also in the business of providing Help Desk staff, and is willing to expand the existing contract to include three such people at an advantageous price. The Help Desk would be relieved of the responsibility of training the three staff, staffing during sickness and vacation, and adding head count. This option has a one-time cost of $78,000 and an annual cost of $186,000.

6. Management Summary

Background

The PC environment has grown to its present count of 2,000 over the course of only a few years. Hardware and software are sourced and purchased centrally, but no one is concerned with standards, so there is a mix of technology. There are several different groups involved in working with some aspect of support for PCs. Hardware maintenance has been outsourced and is looked after by three on-site third-party staff. LANs are looked after by an internal group, as are testing and installation of upgrades. There is no group for customer support. Every time customers run into a problem, they have to figure out whom to call and then try to chase that person down. Support staff are very busy trying to maintain a growing environment and don't have time for supporting customers. There is no coordination between them, so they are often working on the same problem without knowing it.

Customers often spend time struggling with problems on their own or going to colleagues for help—a very expensive network of informal support has been created. There is no organized education. Older equipment is now out of date and slow, and is not always compatible with other technology. The company has started work on client/server, but the current environment does not provide the stability that such an environment would require.

Proposal

A PC Help Desk: a central support group to provide front-line support for PCs and local area networks, and to coordinate the efforts of all support groups. The group would take on additional functions of coordination of planning and policies, organization of training, and upgrading of hardware.

Cost of Not Having a Help Desk

- The 2,000 employees are spending, on average, 15 minutes each day (just over 3 percent of their work time) struggling with some aspect of technology. Employees are not trained, so they often misuse the technology; this results in lost data and misinformed business decisions.
- Support staff have no coordination, and often find themselves spending time working on the same problems as other support staff.
- The company does not have the stable microcomputer environment required to support future business applications.

Help Desk Benefits

- Employees would have at least 3 percent more time to spend on their own part of the business. Supporting the technology they use would become someone else's (the Help Desk's) business.
- Employees would make more effective use of technology in supporting the business. There is a $4,000,000 annual investment in technology for which return cannot begin to be realized until the technology is performing at some level of stability and people understand how to use it.
- A more stable technology environment. The business could implement fully supported client/server.
- More cost-effective use of technology through standardization.

Cost of Implementing a Help Desk

- Many components of the Help Desk exist currently as separate entities, but must be organized and consolidated into one group. Three additional (outsourced) staff and Help Desk software are required.
- Initial setup cost would be $78,000. Cost required annually, over and above the cost of the existing Help Desk components, would be $186,000.

Example 2: Justifying a Voice Response Unit

When you are justifying a Help Desk tool, or some other form of improvement, you can use statistics from your call tracking data to strengthen your case. In the case of automation—for example, a voice response unit —these statistics are often how opportunities for improvement and solutions to problems are identified.

In this example, we will be putting together a cost/benefit analysis for a voice response unit (VRU). The situation is as follows:

The Help Desk requesting the VRU supports both PC and mainframe users. The front line is staffed by four people, and an automatic call distributor is used to distribute calls and gather statistics. Help Desk software also gathers statistics. The current volume of calls is 3,600 per month: 60 percent for PC issues and 40 percent for mainframe issues. There are currently about 1,000 PCs and 2,000 terminals being supported. Terminals are decreasing in number, while PCs are exploding.

The support load has increased by about 50 percent in the last nine months, and support staff are having a hard time keeping up. Customers are having a hard time getting through to the Help Desk—it is taking them longer. Some 38 percent of calls are for functions that could easily be automated. The Help Desk wants to use a VRU to automate all of these functions. The VRU could also be used by the automation project currently taking place in the data center. Following is the cost/benefit analysis for the proposal to introduce the VRU. A management summary is given at the end.

1. Summary of Current Situation and Proposed Solution

Support calls to our Help Desk have increased by 50 percent in the last nine months (see Figure 9.1), due to the ongoing introduction of newer and more complex technology, specifically in the PC area. PCs have been increasing at a very strong rate, as shown in Figure 9.2. The Help Desk now supports 1,000 PCs as well as 2,000 terminals. The trends of increasing calls and PC growth show no sign of slowing down. The support staff cannot handle the current support load effectively; customers are forced to spend a longer time getting through to the Help Desk, and then waiting for service.

The mainframe environment has been fairly stable and accounts for 40 percent of all calls to the Help Desk (see Figure 9.3). Of mainframe-based calls, 65 percent are repetitive requests for routine tasks such as printer resets, terminal resets, and password resets (see Figure 9.4). These requests, which make up 26 percent of total calls to the Help Desk, place a significant demand on support time. A further 12 percent of total calls

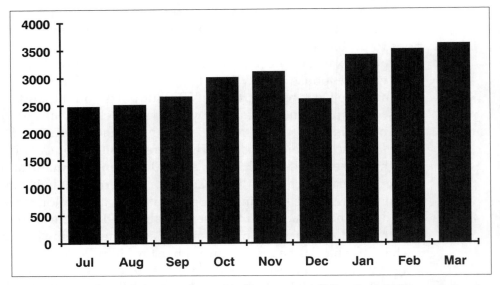

Figure 9.1 Growth in number of calls per month has been 50 percent over the last nine months.

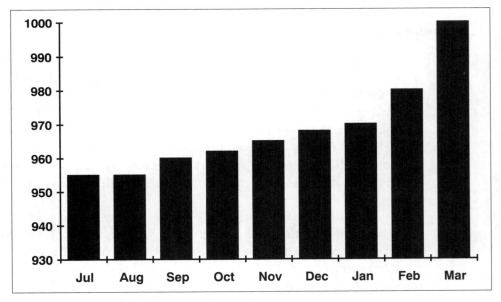

Figure 9.2 Growth in number of PCs.

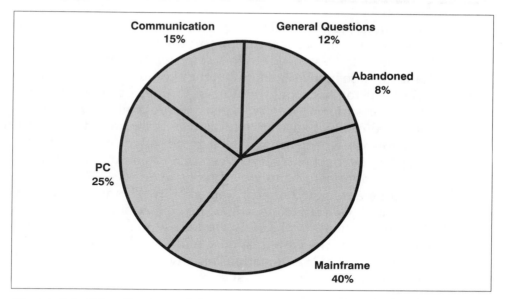

Figure 9.3 Distribution of the 3,600 calls received in a month.

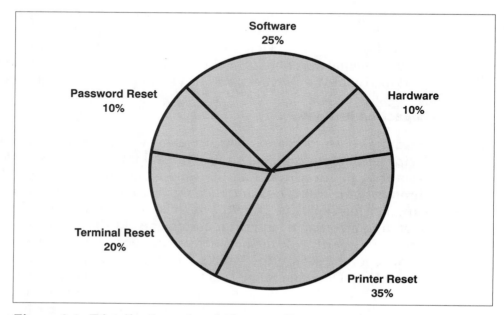

Figure 9.4 Distribution of mainframe calls.

are general questions. These questions are also repetitive, have routine answers, and are a drain on support time.

The Help Desk needs to find some way of containing the increases in calls. If these increases continue, they could degrade service to the point where customers would be forced to develop their own informal networks of support—a very expensive proposition. At the same time, it needs to channel support efforts away from mundane, repetitive tasks and toward work that will add more value to the business—such as preparation for client/server. A voice response unit would allow the Help Desk to automate handling of repetitive tasks—38 percent of all calls could be automated almost immediately. This would improve support levels and free staff to investigate further automation; call levels could be kept down to allow the Help Desk to support the coming client/server environment. The voice response unit would also be a valuable addition to the data center automation initiative that is taking place. It could be used for various functions, such as remote support.

2. Problems with Current Situation and Impact on Business

Routine, repetitive tasks are draining time away from the Help Desk and preventing it from providing the levels of service required by the rapidly expanding technological environment. Table 9.5 provides details of the time being spent by the Help Desk on repetitive, administrative tasks and the detrimental effect this is having on service. The table also shows how workload could be alleviated and service improved through automation.

Impact on Business

Help Desk customers are facing increasing wait times for service from the Help Desk. Routine, repetitive tasks are taking up significant Help Desk resources, in effect doubling the time a customer must spend getting through to the Help Desk and then waiting for service. PC technology is experiencing explosive growth, which has been accompanied by a corresponding increase in support requirements. PC-based client/server applications, which will further increase support requirements, are being planned for the near future. Unless something is done to alleviate the load on the Help Desk and allow it to focus on what is most important to the business, it will not be able to adequately support the growing PC environment. This lack of support will endanger the integrity of any PC-based applications that are developed.

Table 9.5 Details of Help Desk Time Allocation and Effect on Service

Tasks or Problems	Effect on the Help Desk and on Service	Estimated Monthly Cost without VRU	Estimated Monthly Cost with VRU
Terminal resets, password resets, printer resets	Mainframe calls = 40% of 3600 = 1440 Terminal, password, printer resets = 65% of 1440 = 936	20 days customer	2 days customer (with 1 minute per call)
	Average customer time to get through to Help Desk and get terminal reset is 10 minutes; Average support time is 5 minutes **Estimate**: 936 calls 10 minutes per user per call = 20 days 5 minutes support per call = 10 days	10 days support	0 days support
General questions	General questions make up 12% of calls. 12% of 3,600 = 432	5 days customer	1 day customer (1 minute per call)
	Average customer time to get through to Help Desk and get information is 6 minutes. Average support time is 2.5 minutes. **Estimate**: 432 calls 6 minutes per user per call = 5 days 2.5 minutes support per call = 2 days	2 days support	0 days support
Increased wait time	3,600 calls Average customer wait time to get through now has increased by 3 minutes. 3600 * 3 / 60 / 8 = 23 days	23 days customers	0 days
	30% of Help Desk calls (1,080) cannot be resoved at point of call. Average resolution time for these calls is 8 hours (up from an average of 4 hours over the last 9 months). Estimated average productivity loss during wait time is 30%. 30% of 8 hours is 2.4 hours 1080 * 2.4 / 8 = 324	324 days customer	Resolution time would go back at least to previous levels: 162 days

(continues)

Table 9.5 Details of Help Desk Time Allocation and Effect on Service (*continued*)

Tasks or Problems	Effect on the Help Desk and on Service	Estimated Monthly Cost without VRU	Estimated Monthly Cost with VRU
Totals		372 customer	165 customer
		12 support	0 support
Notes on totals	Calls that can be automated include the 936 mainframe resets and 432 general questions. This is 1,368, which is 38% of the total calls. (1368 * 100/3600 = 38%)		With automation, save 207 customer days. This is a decrease of 56%. With automation, save 12 days of support per month = over half of a support person's time.

3. Proposed Solution and Benefits

A VRU would automate the handling of approximately 38 percent of Help Desk calls—those dealing with terminal, printer, and password resets, and general questions. All manual handling of these would be eliminated, improving service to customers and freeing Help Desk staff for more important work. The VRU would also provide a basis for future growth. As repetitive, recurring processes were identified, they could be automated.

Benefits

- Each user would typically see a 56 percent decrease in time spent dealing with and waiting for the Help Desk.
- Help Desk staff could focus on work more important to the business, continuing with automation and problem elimination to make sure that the Help Desk could handle the support requirements of the growing PC environment. This is especially important since critical applications are being developed for client/server.

- The data center automation project could make use of the VRU in areas such as remote problem handling.
- The VRU could handle most of the mainframe calls so that Help Desk staff could focus on the PC environment.

4. Implementation Options and Cost

Two options are presented. The first involves internal staff doing the work while outsourced staff temporarily look after calls, and is shown in Table 9.6. The second option, shown in Table 9.7, involves outsourced staff doing the work.

5. Recommendation

The recommendation is Option 1. Having some in-house expertise in VRU will allow the Help Desk to plan and use the VRU in other ways. These could include improving the effectiveness of the Help Desk and the up time of customers, and consulting with other areas of the company that might be contemplating VRUs.

Table 9.6   Option 1

Component	Description	Cost (One-Time)	Other Consideration
Staffing	1 internal staff to work on VRU project	Would be performed by current Help Desk staff; would require $2,000 in training	VRU expertise would stay in-house
	2 temporary staff to work on Help Desk to field calls at acceptable service levels	$80,000 for 6-month time period	
VRU		$100,000	$15,000 yearly maintenance
Total		$182,000	$15,000 yearly

Table 9.7 Option 2

Component	Description	Cost (One-Time)	Other Consideration
Staffing	VRU outsourced	$60,000 for 6 months	VRU expertise would be outside; would lose
	1 temporary staff to help work on Help Desk to field calls at acceptable service levels	$40,000 for 6 months	knowledge that could help us find other uses
VRU		$100,000	$15,000 yearly maintenance
Total		$200,000	$15,000 yearly

6. Management Summary

Background

Support calls to our Help Desk have increased by 50 percent in the last nine months, due to ongoing introduction of newer and more complex PC technology. The number of PCs has grown to 1,000 and continues to grow. Neither trend shows sign of slowing down. The business will soon be implementing client/server applications, which will further increase the support requirements. The mainframe environment is fairly stable, and 38 percent of calls to the Help Desk are requests for administrative functions that could easily be automated.

Proposal

A voice response unit would allow immediate automation of 38 percent of the calls coming into the Help Desk, improving support to customers and lessening the load on staff.

Cost of Not Having a VRU

- PCs are experiencing explosive growth, and client/server applications will soon be rolling out. Given the current growth of technology and support, the Help Desk will be unable to support these applications with current staffing levels.

- Approximately 56 percent of the time that customers spend each month getting through to the Help Desk and waiting for support is taken up by routine tasks and delays that could be eliminated through automation.

- Of all calls, 38 percent require a support person to perform repetitive, administrative functions, which could be automated. More than half of a support person's time is spent providing these functions.

- As the environment that is being supported grows, this situation will only worsen.

Benefits of a VRU

- Each user would see, on average, a 56 percent decrease in time spent dealing with and waiting for the Help Desk.

- Help Desk staff could focus on work more important to the business: eliminating problems and automating resolutions to ensure that the Help Desk can handle the support requirements of the growing PC environment.

- The data center automation project could make use of the VRU in areas such as remote problem handling.

Implementation Cost

Total initial cost of $182,000: $100,000 for the hardware and $182,000 to set the project up. Yearly maintenance costs would be $15,000.

Example 3: Justifying Outsourcing of the Training Function

In this example, we will be putting together a cost/benefit analysis for outsourcing the training function. The situation is as follows:

Providing training in PC software is currently a Help Desk responsibility. All aspects of training are provided by three trainers. The Help Desk currently supports 1,000 PCs and 1,000 terminals, but terminals are rapidly being replaced by PCs, and additional PCs are being added almost daily. Most customers are still fairly new to PCs, but a growing number are becoming more experienced and require more advanced training.

New versions of software come out so quickly that trainers are having trouble learning them and modifying courses before the new versions are introduced. They can't provide courses that customers are requesting for new software, because they have no time. Learning, course administration, and preparation are taking up all of their time outside of actual training. The whole training function has become very expensive for what it provides.

The solution being suggested is to outsource the training function and to bill customers directly for the training they take. Currently, cost of training (as part of the whole cost of the Help Desk) is charged back to departments at a very high level, in background transactions.

The cost/benefit for outsourcing follows. A management summary is included at the end.

1. Summary of Current Situation and Proposed Solution

The Help Desk currently offers PC training to all of the customers that it supports. Three trainers handle all aspects of training, from sign-up, scheduling, and administration, through course design, to course delivery. The supported environment consists of 1,000 PCs and 1,000 terminals, but this is changing rapidly as terminals are being replaced by PCs and additional PCs are added. A large proportion (approximately 65 percent) of customers are new to PCs and require extensive but very basic training, while a smaller percentage are quite experienced and are looking for more advanced training.

The trainers cannot keep up with the rate at which new versions of PC software are introduced and implemented. They seem to be consistently one version behind: by the time they modify their courses for a new version, the next is already waiting to be installed. The trainers also can't keep up with requests for new courses. As new software is purchased, customers request training, but the trainers cannot learn software and develop courses quickly enough to give customers what they need. Already, they are learning software just steps ahead of their students. Customer feedback indicates that this is affecting quality of training. Customers do not have confidence in the trainers' knowledge of the software being taught.

As a result of all of this, customers are not getting the training they need when they need it. They are wasting, on average, from 10 to 15 hours each month struggling to learn and use the software that they need to use. Some customers are going out to external vendors to get training at their own cost, but this often is not an ideal solution. Customers don't always know exactly what they need, and the whole training experience can be frustrating and time-wasting if they choose a course that is either too basic or too advanced.

The training function has become very expensive for what it provides. Maintaining three trainers on staff to handle only a small number of PC courses does not make financial sense. Trainers are spending 30 percent of their time on all of the administration that goes along with teaching—registration, changes, and schedules—which is an expensive use of their time. On top of this, the rate of no-shows and last-minute cancellations is 15 percent. Customers don't always take their training commitments seriously. They don't see the cost involved in their actions.

The existing training function is one that worked well in the mainframe world, where things did not change as quickly or as often, but in the PC world it just does not suffice. It is creating a bottleneck for people needing training, and forcing a certain level of inefficiency and productivity loss upon them.

Outsourcing the training function would give customers better access to a wider variety of training at a lower cost. Courses would be offered more frequently, at a greater variety of levels, and trainers would be more experienced. Training administration would no longer be a Help Desk responsibility, but would be looked after by the company providing the training. The training company would take responsibility for interaction with customers, scheduling, sign-ups, and billing. Customers could call the company directly (via an internal phone number) to arrange for training, and would be billed directly. Charging the customers directly for each course (currently, a high-level charge-back process goes on in the background) would give them a vested interest in showing up. No-shows would decrease. Training could be offered on-site in the existing training facility, or off-site in the third-party facilities.

Outsourcing the training function would mean redeploying or laying off the three training staff.

2. Problems with Current Situation and Impact on Business

Quality and Timeliness of Training

- PC training is not current. Trainers cannot keep up with how quickly PC software changes.

- PC training is limited to a few (five) standard software packages. Customers are forced to go elsewhere for training for other packages, and often find that training inappropriate because they did not understand what they were signing up for.

- Trainers are learning software just a few steps ahead of the classes they are teaching, and their lack of experience with the software shows in their training. Customers do not have confidence in the trainers' knowledge of what they are teaching.

Impact on the Business

- Customers are hampered in their efforts to make effective use of technology in their jobs. Customers who can't get the training they are looking for from the Help Desk (approximately 50 per month) estimate that they lose between 10 and 15 hours each month because they don't know or use the software properly. That's 50 customers each losing approximately 12.5 hours per month.

- These same customers need to spend time looking for alternate training. If the training turns out to be inappropriate, then further time is wasted. Averaged out, this cost is estimated to be approximately 30 minutes for each of the 50 customers per month.

- Inability to use technology properly can cause errors in data, which can lead to bad business decisions.

- Lack of training has become a bottleneck to effective technology use that will inhibit business improvements and advancements. This situation will only worsen as the PC environment expands.

- Cost of the training function is very high for the value it provides.

Cost of the Training Function

The cost of the Help Desk training function is shown in Table 9.8.

3. Proposed Solution, Benefits, and Risks

The proposed solution to the problems described above is to outsource the entire training function to a third-party training provider. The third party would take over all aspects of training, including:

- Registration
- Scheduling
- Advertising scheduled courses
- Training

Table 9.8   Cost of the Help Desk Training Function

Item	Annual Cost	Notes
Salaries	$140,000	For three trainers.
Training materials	$40,000	Manuals, notes, etc.
Cost of training room	$12,000	Part of office rental.
Miscellaneous office costs and supplies for trainers	$10,000	
Training equipment and maintenance	$20,000	
Training for trainers	$6,000	
Variety of training offered		Five different courses are taught: three at an introductory level, two at both introductory and advanced.
TOTAL:	**$228,000**	
Cost per training day:	**$1,583**	Using current average of 12 training days per month (=144 per year).
Cost per student per training day:	**$264**	Assuming a full class of six students.
Cost per student per training day, taking no-shows into account:	**$310**	No-show rate is 15%. This means an actual rate of 5.1 students per class.

- Measurement of training effectiveness
- Tracking of training statistics
- Billing

Business Benefits

- Customers would have access to training for a wider variety of courses at all levels, and courses would be offered more frequently. Trainers would be more experienced. Customers would receive the training they needed when they needed it, effectively reducing or eliminating the 13 hours currently being wasted each month by approximately 50 customers.
- The training bottleneck inhibiting business improvements and advancements would be removed, and occurrences of errors due to improper use of technology would be reduced.

Table 9.9   Cost of Outsourced Training

Item	Annual Cost	Notes
On-site training, at $1,000 per day	$180,000	Average of 15 days of training per month.
Cost of training room	$12,000	Part of office rental.
Training equipment and maintenance	$20,000	
Variety of training offered		15 different courses are taught, each having from one to three levels. A much wider variety of courses are available at the third-party site.
TOTAL:	**$212,000**	
Cost per training day:	**$1,178**	Will be training 15 days per month (=180 per year).
Cost per student per training day:	**$196**	Assuming a full class of six students.

- Customers would be billed directly for training and charged for no-shows and last-minute cancellations, which would almost eliminate the occurrences of these.
- The cost of training would be reduced from $310 to $196 per student per training day.

Cost of Outsourced Training

The cost of outsourced, on-site training is shown in Table 9.9.

Risks

- Outsourced training must still be managed and measured to ensure that it is meeting the requirements of the business. If this is not done and training fails to meet the needs of the business, the anticipated benefits will not be realized and the current problems will continue to grow.
- If training is outsourced, three current training staff will need to be laid off or redeployed elsewhere. Every effort needs to be made to redeploy these staff within the company. This process needs to be handled very carefully and fairly, with honest communication to all

Help Desk staff at timely and frequent intervals. Failure to do this could impact morale and performance of Help Desk staff.

4. Implementation Recommendations and Cost

Implementation recommendations are as follows:

- All training functions, from registration to billing, to be performed by a third-party training provider (yet to be selected).
- Third party to report to the Help Desk regularly.
- Customers will be billed directly for training.
- Courses to be offered on-site, except for more specialized courses, which are typically attended by fewer customers. These will be taken at the third-party site at discounted rates.
- Implementation, initial advertising, and so on, to be performed by the selected third party at no cost.
- Every effort must be made to redeploy the three training staff within the company. If redeployment is not possible, staff layoffs will be necessary.

Cost of On-site Training

Estimated at $1,178 per training day, or $196 per student per training day (assuming a full class of six students).

Cost of Off-site Training

Will range from $300 to $400 per student per day, depending on specific course.

5. Management Summary

Background

The PC environment is changing and growing so rapidly that the Help Desk training function is unable to keep up. Training is not current enough, is offered for a limited selection of software, and is offered by trainers who have little experience in the software itself. As a result, PC users are wasting time trying to learn software themselves or to find somewhere that teaches it, and they are not using it as effectively as they could. The training function has become very expensive for what it delivers.

Proposal

Outsource the training function to a third-party training provider. Continue to offer on-site training, through the third party.

Problems with the Current Situation

- Customers who can't get the training they are looking for from the Help Desk estimate that they lose an average of 13 hours each month because they don't know or use the software properly, and have to spend time looking for alternative training. That's 50 customers each losing approximately 13 hours per month.

- Inability to use technology properly can cause errors in data, which can lead to bad business decisions.

- Lack of training has become a bottleneck to effective technology use that will inhibit business improvements and advancements. This situation will only worsen as the PC environment expands.

- Cost of the training function is very high for the value it provides, on top of which there is a 15 percent no-show rate. Cost per student per training day is $310.

Benefits of Outsourcing

- Customers would have access to training for a wider variety of courses at all levels, and courses would be offered more frequently. Trainers would be more experienced. Customers would receive the training they needed when they needed it, effectively reducing or eliminating the 13 hours currently being wasted each month by approximately 50 customers.

- The training bottleneck inhibiting business improvements and advancements would be removed, and occurrences of errors due to improper use of technology would be reduced.

- Customers would be billed directly for training and charged for no-shows and last-minute cancellations, which would almost eliminate the occurrences of these.

- The cost of training would be reduced from $310 to $196 per student per training day.

Implementation and Cost

- Cost of on-site training would be $1,178 per training day, or $196 per student per training day.
- Cost of off-site training would be between $300 and $400 per student per training day.
- Implementation costs will be absorbed by third-party training provider.
- Management of the outsourced function would remain the responsibility of the Help Desk.

Risks

- Outsourced training must still be managed and measured to ensure that it is meeting the requirements of the business. If this is not done and training fails to meet the needs of the business, the anticipated benefits will not be realized and the current problems will continue to grow.
- If training is outsourced, three current training staff will need to be laid off or redeployed elsewhere. Every effort needs to be made to redeploy these staff within the company. This process needs to be handled very carefully and fairly, with honest communication to all Help Desk staff at timely and frequent intervals. Failure to do this could impact morale and performance of Help Desk staff.

Summary

A cost/benefit analysis illustrates the business value of what you are proposing. This is a challenge when you're dealing with all of the intangibles involved in Help Desk function. A Help Desk doesn't produce anything; it enables other people to do so. This makes it difficult to put a value on the Help Desk function.

The way to evaluate Help Desk function is to consider what it would cost the business not to have a Help Desk. This would include extra user time required to get problems resolved, money being spent on maintaining out-of-date equipment, and strategic considerations such as not having an environment stable enough to handle production applications. Then consider the difference between this environment and the same environment with a Help Desk. This is the business value. In order to put a measurable value on this, you need to estimate the costs based on data gathered from users and support staff. For example, you might find out that about half of the 500 users are spending six hours each month on inefficiencies due to lack of training. This works out to 4.5 days per user per year, or 2.4 percent of their time. This is a measure you can use, but you need to be careful not to misuse it. You cannot add bits of user time up and get whole users. It is not valid to say that you are saving the equivalent of 12 people per year based on adding up the six hours that 250 users save each month. This would imply that you could get rid of six people, and that is not true. Management will be very quick to pick up on any hint of staff savings, so unless you want to get rid of staff, don't misuse these measures.

In order to put your cost/benefit analysis together, you are going to have to describe the current situation in terms of cost to the business—what the problems are and what they cost—and describe the proposed situation or improvement in terms of eliminating some or all of that cost and adding more value. It's a good idea to get support from user management as you do this, to help ensure that your proposal gets accepted.

A cost/benefit analysis can be divided up into five sections:

1. A brief description of the current situation and what you are proposing.
2. Problems with the current situation and their impact on the business.
3. A description of what you are proposing and the benefits it will bring to the business (may include a discussion of risks involved).
4. Implementation options and cost.
5. Recommendation.

A management summary should be included at the front if the analysis is longer than a couple of pages.

Once you have put your proposal together, you need to present it to management. Try to present your case in person so that you can answer concerns directly and provide more detail as required.

CHAPTER TEN

Outsourcing

There are two extremes of thought about outsourcing:

1. It's a dirty word.
2. It's a panacea for all your ills.

The truth for you will depend on where you're sitting. If you're caught in the middle of a consolidation or takeover, or the outsourcing of the complete IS function, you'll probably lean toward thought number 1. If you have a problem area that you've just outsourced with a big sigh of relief, and the ink on the contract is still wet, and you think that that's the end of that, you'll probably be leaning toward thought number 2. If you're an executive who wants to impress the board with dramatic cost-cutting and outsourcing, you'll probably also be leaning toward number 2.

If you don't fall into any of these categories, then the truth for you is probably somewhere in between. Outsourcing doesn't have to be a dirty word. You can use it as a tool to add value to your Help Desk. Outsourcing certainly isn't any kind of panacea. You may have outsourced a part or all of your Help Desk, but someone, most likely you, will still be responsible for its successful performance. Things will not necessarily go smoothly simply because they have been outsourced. Outsourced work needs to be managed and measured. You still have customers and a business to keep satisfied. Something as simple as outsourcing a PC hardware and software inventory can become a nightmare if not managed. Data that is incorrect, incomplete, inconsistent, or in the wrong format can make what was supposed to be a no-brainer into an administrative headache. This kind of situation can and has happened, as many of us can attest to from painful personal experience.

When you think in terms of outsourcing, you should be thinking in terms of value to the business. Sometimes it just does not make business sense to do something in-house that could be done more cost-effectively by a third party. Unfortunately, you don't always have a say in what is considered good business value. A decision might have been made higher up in the organization, without your input or knowledge, to outsource the Help Desk—either on its own or with the rest of IS. On the other hand, sometimes you do have a choice. You can choose to make sure that your Help Desk is effective and adds value to the business, or you can choose to leave things as they are and run the risk of not being able to meet the company's strategic needs. Choosing the former may involve using outsourcing to allow your Help Desk to focus on the work most important to the business. Tasks such as telling customers how to put a border around a WordPerfect document can be given away. Outsourcing can free staff to work on projects such as automation, fixing causes of recurring problems, and eliminating reasons for customers calling the Help Desk—all activities that add business value. When your Help Desk is engaging in these kinds of activities, and marketing them so that management realizes what is being accomplished, it is in little danger of being outsourced for reasons of not offering business value. If a third party can do a job better and more cost-effectively than your Help Desk, without taking anything important away from the business, then you need to either give up and be gone, or change the way you're doing things, and that might include using outsourcing.

What Can Outsourcing Do for You?

If outsourcing is used as a tool, applied only where it is needed, and is managed and measured, it can bring tangible benefits:

- Reduction in costs.
- Improvement in productivity and performance.
- Increased flexibility, so that business requirements can be responded to more quickly.
- A wider range of services.
- Increased skill level.
- More control over the Help Desk function.
- Increased ability to focus on what really matters to the business.

Reduction in Costs

Third parties, who are focusing on servicing several customers, can realize economies of scale that your Help Desk could not possibly achieve. They can spread the cost of research, purchases, training, marketing, and consulting over many customers. They are motivated to stay on top of emerging technologies so that they can benefit their customers and nurture their business.

Third parties can afford to give their staff the ongoing training required to keep staff current and ensure their expertise in various products. You might not be able to. Staff who have been trained and are current on new technologies are less likely to make costly on-the-job decisions than those who do not completely understand the technology and alternatives.

Training isn't the only cost associated with keeping current. Shelf life of packaged software is estimated to be approximately nine months. This means that to keep up with current versions, you need not only to train staff, but to purchase, test, and install each new piece of software approximately once a year. That is an expensive proposition in terms of staff time. A third party may be able to do this more cost-effectively.

Some support skills, such as those required for networks, are particularly expensive to keep and maintain. Staff require significant (and expensive) training and are in great demand by the industry, and turnover is high. If you feel you need to keep these skills in-house, you can choose to outsource some network support positions and keep the rest in-house. This will allow you to stretch the staff that you do have without completely handing the skills away.

Third parties can also afford a higher quality and wider assortment of tools than you might be able to. For example, one outsourcing company specializing in banking applications has a state-of-the-art call center that offers specialized call management software, knowledge of all the standard banking software, automated call distribution, remote LAN management, established processes, and a guaranteed response time. Setting that kind of structure up from scratch would be an expensive and time-consuming proposition, involving significant management, learning, and pain. To buy into one that you know is working, especially when you don't want to be in the business of Help Desks, means that you can become operational quickly and have plenty of experience at your disposal without a large capital outlay or a big learning curve.

Improvement in Productivity and Performance

Staff who are completely focused on their jobs naturally produce more and perform better than staff who are constantly being interrupted and pulled off current work to do other things. Outsourced staff are allowed to be focused, while full-time staff are not always allowed or encouraged to be. Not only are they being pulled in several ways, they have to worry about company politics; about what the company is or is not planning; about their future. Outsourced staff worry about their performance. If they work for themselves, their whole reputation and future employment is based on it. It is easy for a company to get rid of contract staff who are not performing well. If they work for a third party, the third party will make sure that they are performing; again, their future business depends on it. Outsourced staff have a vested interest in performing well. Full-time staff can be more complacent about their stability. They don't necessarily have to worry quite as much about where their next paycheck is coming from, or about their reputation. If they miss a deadline by a day—what's a day? To outsourced staff, a deadline is part of the contract. Miss it and you're out.

One outsourcing company reports that it constantly gets the same feedback from its customers: after four to six weeks on the job, outsourced Help Desk staff are more productive than equivalent internal staff. Even Help Desk customers comment on how focused the staff are. A Help Desk manager reports similar findings. One person on the Help Desk was responsible for the mass production of cartridge tapes containing new releases of internally developed application software. The person was not doing a good job, and was constantly complaining about the monotony of the task. The Help Desk was forced to cut costs, and the Help Desk manager decided to outsource that position. At the suggestion of management, and against the Help Desk manager's better judgment, the function was outsourced to the person who had been doing it. The result was amazing: a 100 percent improvement in performance and innovation. Soon after the function was outsourced, the person was developing various efficiencies, including bar coding the cartridges. The Help Desk manager is now extremely pleased with that person's performance.

There are, of course, exceptions. Almost everyone has outsourcing disaster stories: maintenance staff who came in to fix a server and destroyed it in the process; network maintenance people who accidentally took a LAN down and then couldn't get it back up; network designers who designed and implemented a state-of-the-art network with several points of failure that quickly made their presence known; a consultant who came in to reconfigure some PCs, which then actually had to have hard drives replaced. The fact that you've outsourced a function is no guarantee that it's going to be performed well. It might take you several tries to find an outsourcing company and staff that work well in your environment.

If your Help Desk has well-defined tasks that you can outsource, you might find them being done faster and more effectively by outsourced staff. At the same time, internal staff could do the work that was more important to the business. They could be more focused because someone else would be there to handle the routine work and at least some of the interruptions.

Outsourcing could also help eliminate the problem of absences on the Help Desk, where a person taking a vacation or calling in sick leaves a big hole. If you've outsourced the position, the third party will have the responsibility of making sure that a qualified person is there every day, with good motivation: your business and your reference.

Increased Flexibility, So That Business Requirements Can Be Responded to More Quickly

On a Help Desk, especially on the front line, staffing requirements vary from one time period to the next. During the day, there are peaks and slow times for call traffic; over weeks, months, and the whole year, there might be peaks and slow times for all of the various tasks that your Help Desk performs. Outsourcing can help you meet the peaks without being over-staffed during the slower times. Outsourced staff can be used to handle daily traffic peaks, perhaps even from a remote location. They can be used to provide extra staffing to handle the increased call volume resulting from installation of a new software package or some other form of new technology. They need only be on the Help Desk for a period that covers the customers' learning curve. Some outsourcing contracts allow for increase or decrease in staff as required. Unusually large Help Desk requests, such as a big PC order that needs to be tested, configured, and installed, can be completely outsourced so that the workload of internal staff won't be disrupted. Outsourcing allows you to keep your Help Desk staffed for the straight line and let someone else worry about the blips.

A Wider Range of Services

If the business you support is demanding services that you don't have enough staff, budget, or skills to provide, you can use outsourcing to fill the gap. If your customers are using too many different software packages for you to support effectively with the resources you have, you could outsource support for those packages. You could even outsource some or all of the installation, testing, management, and training. A third party who is serving several other customers and has the skills required can probably do these more cost-effectively than your Help Desk.

Increased Skill Level

Outsourcing can provide the Help Desk with skills and experience in areas in which it is weak, or in which it simply has no skills. Third-party staff can often provide knowledge and experience in the various options that technology allows, and in the identification and resolution of problems that may crop up with the technology. They may be familiar with problems and methods that the Help Desk has not seen before. Using third-party staff may be a more cost-effective and quicker way of increasing skill level than hiring new staff.

More Control Over the Help Desk Function

Outsourcing can actually provide you with the tools or people you need to manage the Help Desk more effectively. If you don't have the staff or tools to do network monitoring, you might be able to outsource that function. A third party could dial into your network and monitor it remotely, providing you with accurate and timely reporting for traffic patterns, network performance, and situations needing immediate attention. This information would help you prevent, eliminate, or quickly resolve problems, making your environment more stable. A third party could also perform (or even set up) some or all of your Help Desk management functions in this way, providing you with problem management reporting and information on Help Desk performance. Having a third party do this, even for a limited time, would give you valuable feedback from which you could plan improvements.

Increased Ability to Focus on What Really Matters to the Business

When you're trying to focus your Help Desk on delivering business value, and you don't have an unlimited head count, it doesn't make much sense to be spending time and resources on nonstrategic activities that take away from your ability to do this. Ordering PCs, matching purchase orders to invoices, or explaining to someone how to use Word for Windows to rotate an address on an envelope don't add a lot to your business value, and you would not lose anything of value by outsourcing them. Help Desk staff would be able to focus on work that is more important to the business: automation, planning for upgrades to ensure the environment can handle new mission-critical software, giving customers tools to make them more self-sufficient, finding and eliminating the causes of recurring problems, and making the environment better able to support the business.

Figure 10.1 summarizes what outsourcing can do for you. What outsourcing will not do for you is free you from having to manage what

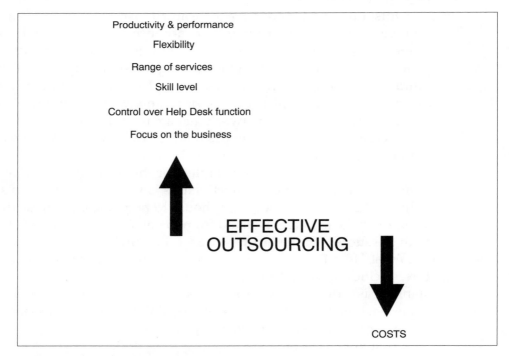

Figure 10.1   What outsourcing can do for you.

you've outsourced, or from being accountable to your customers. Functions are not guaranteed to run smoothly just because you've outsourced them. Regardless of whether you are performing the function or are paying someone else to do it, you need to make sure that objectives are met, customers are satisfied, and the business is being served effectively. You will need to set objectives and performance measurements with the outsourcing party, and communicate often to review these. Failure to do this can result in work that does not meet expectations, and in customers and a business that are not happy with your performance.

When to Use Outsourcing

Outsourcing as much as possible without stopping to consider the consequences makes just as little sense as stubbornly refusing to outsource anything without bothering to consider the potential benefits. It is a tool to be used selectively.

Outsourcing does not have to be an all-or-nothing proposition. It can involve a complementary blend of in-house and outsourced functions. There are as many combinations and choices in outsourcing as there are companies to provide them. Outsourcing can fill in gaps; it can stretch or build onto existing staff, skills, or services. It can be as simple as providing one person to handle peak call traffic remotely, or something as complex as taking over the whole network management function.

Deciding what to outsource is more complex than using the formula: a function should be outsourced if a third party can do it more cost-effectively. Environments are too complex for the decision to be that simple. Sometimes the loss in cost-effectiveness is worth something in strategic value, in having the expertise in-house to help make strategic decisions. Technology is no longer isolated from the business. It is often at the heart, with the success of the business depending on it.

What Help Desk functions you outsource will depend on many factors, including your technological environment (how large, complex, stable it is), the variety of services you provide, the growth you are experiencing, the staff you have (skills, ability, number), the demand you are experiencing, and the focus of your business.

Possibilities for outsourcing are almost endless. Some of the circumstances in which outsourcing might help you are as follows:

- Your customer base is experiencing rapid growth.
- Routine work seems to be taking over your resources.
- The Help Desk is drowning in support.
- You simply need more people.
- You really don't know how the Help Desk is performing.
- You're going through a transition.
- You're finding it difficult to support remote locations.
- You require expensive tools that you can't afford.
- You have a requirement for a skill that you use infrequently.
- You need one or more people with very expensive skills.
- You require skills that are specialized but not strategic.
- You're in a business you want to get out of.
- You need to support a wide variety of packaged software.
- The Help Desk is getting a lot of how-to questions for packaged software.

Customer Base Is Experiencing Rapid Growth

PCs are being rolled out at a rate that is making the environment unstable and making your support calls skyrocket. You can either outsource some of the support to help your staff handle the load, or you can outsource the whole support load for a specific time so that your staff have time to investigate why the environment is unstable and what the Help Desk could do to eliminate the problems being experienced. It would give you time to see just how much support the Help Desk will need to provide. Once the time was up, you could either staff permanently or leave some or all of the outsourced staff there so that your other staff could focus on more strategic activities.

Routine Work Seems to Be Taking Over Your Resources

If routine, repetitive work is consuming more and more Help Desk time and keeping you from doing other more important work, such as making improvements or becoming more proactive in managing the environment, you should consider either outsourcing or automation. If you can't automate, outsource—or outsource some of your support so you have time to automate.

The Help Desk Is Drowning in Support

There are so many problems that you just can't get ahead. You can barely keep up with the calls, and that's all you do. You don't have time to identify and solve recurring problems, or to look into what is required to reduce the number of calls. A solution would be to outsource part or all of support while your staff researched and implemented ways of reducing calls.

You Simply Need More People

You just don't have enough staff to provide your customers with what they need. You can't get an increase in head count, but you might be able to get money for outsourcing.

You Really Don't Know How the Help Desk Is Performing

You're too busy to do the work necessary to measure your performance, but you might be able to outsource that function. A third party could come in, put in place the reporting that you would like to see, and leave the rest for you. Alternatively, that same person (or persons) could do your performance measurements on a regular basis, even designing and distributing customer surveys. Having an outside person do this would serve as a good audit.

You're Going through a Transition

Perhaps you are moving all of your customers to a new hardware or software platform, and you need someone to support the old environment while you prepare for the new one. Several software companies have this same problem. They solve it by outsourcing customer support for their older products while in-house staff focus on learning and supporting the new products.

You're Finding It Difficult to Support Remote Locations

Supporting remote locations can be expensive, especially if you constantly have to send staff there. Outsourcers might be able to manage it remotely, or may be in a location to support it more cost-effectively than you.

You Require Expensive Tools That You Can't Afford

If you need to perform functions that would require a large investment in tools and skills, such as wide area network management, it might be wiser to outsource this function to a third party who has the tools, skills, and experience necessary to do the job. You would be saved the capital outlay.

You Have a Requirement for a Skill That You Use Infrequently

If you require a skill to perform a function that you need only occasionally, it doesn't make a lot of sense to support the cost of that skill. Outsourcing would probably be more cost-effective. An example is hardware installation in an environment that is experiencing almost no growth.

You Need One or More People with Very Expensive Skills

Some skills, such as LAN support (e.g., network engineers), are very expensive to maintain. The people with these skills require a lot of training, and if you don't pay them enough, they will leave, because they are in great demand. Turnover, which is very expensive, could be high. It might be more cost-effective for you to keep some of these skills in-house and outsource the rest. The knowledge would still be in-house to some extent, but could be stretched and made more efficient through use of the outsourced staff.

You Require Skills That Are Specialized but Not Strategic

An example of this is hardware maintenance. The skill is expensive to maintain because technology is changing so quickly. Maintenance technicians are portable from environment to environment—their skills are based on the tools, not on the company. It is not necessary for them to know anything about your business. Just as the photocopier repair person can go into any company, so can the PC maintenance person. Having your own maintenance staff would mean having not only staff costs, but the costs of stocking and replenishing parts. A third party could do this more cost-effectively by reason of economies of scale.

You're in a Business You Don't Want to Be In

If you're a Help Desk with internal training staff, you might be spending too much time and effort in a business that could be done more cost-effectively by someone whose business is training. To support your training business, you need to support the trainers while they learn software packages, and put together and prepare for courses. You also need to support all of the administration that goes along with training: scheduling, course sign-ups and cancellations, and perhaps even internal records and billing. A training company would have all of this set up, and would have enough trainers to cover all of the software packages you need training for. It could spread the expense of keeping all of this running over several customers, of which you could be one.

You Need to Support a Wide Variety of Packaged Software

One person can learn only so many software packages in the detail required to support them. Supporting a wide variety of packages means increased staffing requirements and increased training requirements. Shelf life of a software version is roughly nine months, so training requirements will be high. A third party will have the staff who know the software and who can learn the details of the customer's configuration and environment so that time is not wasted finding all of this out when a call comes in.

The Help Desk Is Getting a Lot of How-to Questions for Packaged Software

If your customers are demanding more software support than you have the staff to provide or want to provide, you can outsource support for standard packaged software. If funding or misuse was an issue, you could distribute the cost among the customers using the service.

Figures 10.2 through 10.5 show examples of when you might want to outsource.

When Not to Outsource

This is a well-debated topic. Some companies don't want to outsource any functions involving strategic decision making or planning; others refuse to outsource anything that is part of the core business; others won't outsource understanding and mastery of advanced technology; others will outsource anything that is cost-effective; and still others will outsource anything.

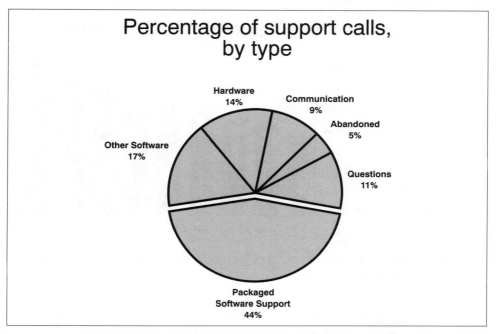

Figure 10.2 You may want to outsource if a large percentage of support is for packaged software.

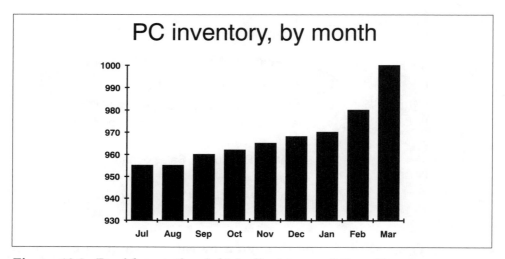

Figure 10.3 Rapid growth might indicate a good time to outsource.

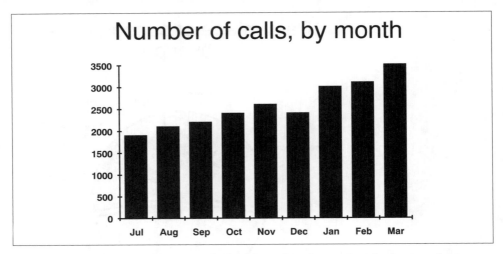

Figure 10.4 Outsourcing can help if you're drowning in increasing support levels.

If you are unsure whether or not to outsource, and money is not the issue, you will have to decide the costs, in terms of business value, of not having that function in-house. Then you'll have to decide how important that value is to the business and make your decision from there. Your

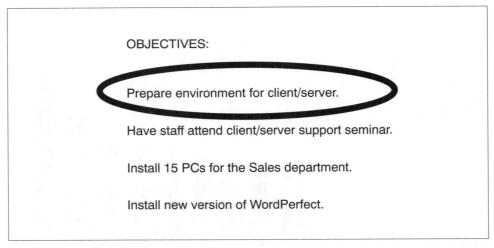

Figure 10.5 Going through a transition can often become easier with outsourced help.

outsourcing decision will be easier if you understand which Help Desk services are critical to the business and/or give it a strategic advantage in some way, and which services are simply a commodity. These will vary from business to business; what is strategic for one company could be a commodity for another. For example, a hardware retailer would probably not hesitate to outsource maintenance of telephone systems and voice networks, but a telephone company, or any other company dealing in voice communications, might not be as eager to do so.

One function that companies often hesitate to outsource is network management. Some won't outsource anything to do with the network: support, design, management. Reasons include:

- "We need to know everything about networks and how they work so that we understand the different ways we can use them to benefit the business."

- "Networks can get very complicated. If an outsourcing company makes a mistake in your network, it's a big deal. You might be stuck with a network that you don't know anything about, and a very expensive price tag to try to get it fixed. You won't understand your network, so how will you know if the company you hire to fix it will do any better?"

- "Networking requires knowledge and understanding of the business. Outsourced network engineers don't have this, and will find it hard to get it in the short time they have to design or reconfigure a network. They might overlook alternatives, or make critical mistakes that might limit the company's ability to compete in some way later on down the road."

You may require skills specific to your business in order to provide support to your customers. You might not want to or be able to outsource these. One Help Desk supporting a real-time retail environment found that in order for Help Desk staff to support the customers effectively, they needed to have store experience. That became one of the prerequisites to working on the Help Desk. A support person with store experience would understand what the customer was experiencing and would know the environment. That kind of knowledge and experience would be almost impossible to get from an outsourcer.

You also probably wouldn't want to outsource support of applications that are unique to your business. The more people you have understanding these applications, the better for the business. Outsourcing companies might not be able to support these applications any more cost-effectively than you, since they could not share the cost across any customers other than your company. They would also have the overhead of learning the application and your environment.

Another environment that would not be cost-effective to outsource would be a nonstandardized environment that included a wide variety of technology. A newspaper company with just such an environment was investigating the possibility of outsourcing the LAN support area, and the potential outsourcer reached the following conclusion: "LAN support consists of seven staff. The workload analysis shows that their responsibilities are diverse and varied over many different platforms and require very unique skill sets. Each individual has a specialized area of expertise and must be capable of supporting other platforms as well. Also, the selection of the router environment is a software solution as opposed to a hardware choice, making it impossible to monitor the environment remotely. Because of the diversity and requirement for on-site support, the only option in this scenario would be to hire the seven support staff to maintain this environment. However, this option makes the business case prohibitive in terms of cost savings."

Outsourcing Options

When you are outsourcing, you can mix and match between what you need and what third parties can offer. They want your business, so are usually more than willing to accommodate any special requirements you might have.

Following are some of the most commonly outsourced Help Desk functions. Each can be partially outsourced and combined with other functions, giving you several options for the kinds of outsourced services that are available to your Help Desk:

- Hardware maintenance
- Network support
- Software management
- Customer support
- Training
- Transitional work

Hardware Maintenance

Outsourcing maintenance for mainframe equipment has long been a given. The costs and skills involved in doing this in-house are prohibitive. Maintenance is typically outsourced either to the vendor or to one or more third-party service providers. Some service providers specialize in specific products, such as mainframe printers.

Maintenance of PC/LAN technology is also something that many companies are deciding to outsource. Service providers abound for PC/LAN hardware maintenance. Some provide maintenance for both types of environments—mainframe and PC. This discussion will focus on PC/LAN hardware maintenance.

Description

Outsourcing hardware maintenance for PC/LANs involves having a third party look after the maintenance and repair of all of your PCs, printers, servers, monitors, and all associated hardware (network cards, modems, CD-ROM, etc.). How this is actually implemented will vary widely from company to company. Some options are:

- Third-party staff on-site full-time.
  One or more technicians from the third-party service provider are actually on-site full-time. They do preventive maintenance on all equipment, and service or replace equipment that needs repair. They become part of the Help Desk team and are dispatched to customers to investigate potential hardware problems. They use the Help Desk call tracking system to track problems. The technicians maintain a spare parts inventory, and often take on the responsibility of maintaining hardware inventory. In fact, they often perform tasks other than maintenance, such as setting up and configuring new PCs for Help Desk customers. Because these staff are on-site, they become very familiar with the environment and the Help Desk customers.

- Third-party staff on-site half days.
  This option is identical to the one above, except that the technician is only at the customer's site for half of each day.

- Third-party staff on an on-call basis.
  Another option for hardware maintenance is to have the third-party staff visit your site only for specific problem instances. If a problem

occurs, you call the service provider and a service technician is dispatched within an agreed-upon response time.

- Carry-in service.
  This option involves taking the equipment directly to the service provider for repair.

Which of these options you choose depends on how large your customer base is. If you have enough PCs to justify a full-time service technician, then that option is preferable. Response time is best and you have control over that person's time.

Some companies choose a mix of options: a full-time technician at their main site, and on-call service for remote sites.

If you choose the option of having a technician on-site, you will most likely be getting services other than simply hardware support and proactive maintenance. Other services often incorporated into maintenance contracts are:

- Maintenance of hardware inventory
- Asset tagging
- Setup, testing, and installation of hardware
- Hardware relocation
- Hardware upgrade

The customer organization can specify how technicians are to report on services performed and parts used.

Other service maintenance options have to do with response time to calls. (If you have an on-site technician, this is taken care of.) You can pretty much set up whatever kind of response you want, if you are willing to pay for it. Some standard offerings are:

- Four-hour, eight-hour, same day, or next-day response:
  A technician will be on-site, looking at the problem within the time specified. Or—and this is usually reserved for critical hardware— replacement equipment will have been put into place within that time.

- Once-a-week visit:
  Another option is to have one or more service technicians visit your site at a specific interval—say, weekly—to perform all required maintenance.

Choosing among these options will depend on how important your hardware is to your business (how much down time you can afford) and how much redundancy you have. If you are supporting a mission-critical application on your PC technology, then service once a week is not going to suffice. You need not limit your response time specifications to one option. You can have several alternatives for hardware at different levels of critical-ity. For example, you might have four-hour service for your production and testing applications and next-day service for any other applications.

Another option to consider is business hours. You can specify that hardware support is to be provided during regular business hours, or up to 24-hour support if you need it. Cost of support will increase as response time decreases, and as after-hours coverage increases.

The hardware maintenance contract is usually set out for a year, and is typically a flat rate; services performed above and beyond those speci-fied in the contract are charged back on an hourly basis. The following is an example of a hardware maintenance agreement.

Hardware Maintenance Agreement

The Support Program:

- The third party proposes to provide three on-site engineers to the customer. At the direction and discretion of the customer, the engineers will perform tasks as defined in schedule A.

- The hours of the engineers will be staggered at the discretion of the customer to include coverage from 7:00 A.M. to 7:00 P.M.

- The third party promises to provide and maintain spare parts inventories at designated customer locations.

- The third party proposes to provide hardware maintenance on all customer equipment outlined in schedule B at an annual investment as follows:

Three field engineers:	$195,000
Refundable parts retainers:	$48,240
Total:	$243,240

- Please note: the parts retainer is capped so that the customer will not be charged for any parts in excess of the $48,240 figure, so the maximum charge for this program is $243,240. Any unused balance of the retainer is 100 percent refundable to the customer, so the actual amount paid may very well be less than the maximum price indicated, as illustrated in Table 10.1.

Table 10.1 Program Cost

Failure Rate	Failures	Average Parts Cost	Total Parts Cost	Annual Total
10%	134	$120	$16,080	$211,080
20%	268	$120	$32,160	$227,160
30%	402	$120	$48,240	$243,240

Hiring of Existing Staff

- The third party agrees to make every fair and reasonable effort to hire the existing support engineer at customer site, and agrees that an offer of employment will be extended to this individual (signed by third-party company president).

Schedule A: On-Site Engineer Duties and Capabilities

Software support:

Third-party on-site field engineers will perform software support and installations as directed by the customer. Based on our understanding of the customer's environment, the third party will provide field engineers trained in the Microsoft suite of products and other software packages deemed appropriate by the customer.

Service Call Tracking

Service call tracking will be performed by the third party as specified by the customer. For example:

- Department, location, and contact name.
- Make and model of equipment requiring repair.
- Date and time the service call was requested.
- Date and time the service call was completed.
- The repair description.

Asset Tagging

Asset tagging procedures will be performed by the third party as specified by the customer.

Hardware Maintenance and Support

- All personal computers and printers in standalone and LAN environments.
- Advanced diagnostics.
- Installation of parts.
- End user support.

Hardware Installations

- Set-up
- Testing
- Relocating equipment
- Equipment upgrades
  - Disk drives (transfer data, partitioning)
  - Video cards
  - LAN cards
  - RAM
  - Monitors
  - Batteries

Proactive Support

Proactive support helps eliminate equipment failure and leads to increased performance and longevity. At the discretion of the customers, each personal computer and printer will be supported proactively.

Proactive support for personal computers involves:

- Virus scanning
- Disk defragmentation
- An external cleaning
- An internal vacuuming and lubrication

Proactive support for laser printers involves:

- An external cleaning
- An internal vacuuming and lubrication
- Corona wires cleaned
- Fuser assembly inspected for wear
- Photo drum inspected for scarring

Physical Inventory and Audit

The third party will maintain a complete microcomputer inventory and generate inventory documents on request. This valuable physical asset listing will contain standalone and network-specified information for all physical components and resources. At the discretion of the customer, the types of information collected may include the following:

- Model of computer
- CPU type and speed
- Floppy drive size and capacity
- Hard drive capacity and type
- Disk controller type
- RAM conventional and extended
- Serial and parallel port number and configurations
- Network interface card
- Node address
- Disk co-processor board model
- Video board type
- ROM BIOS version
- Other internal hardware (modem, mouse, etc.)
- Software in use
- Warranty tracking, with the objective of eliminating any cost incurred for parts of equipment under warranty

The serial numbers of the major hardware and software components are included as part of the physical inventory and audit.

Schedule B. Equipment List (Summary Only)

Personal computers:	938
Printers:	
Laser printers:	123
Dot matrix printers:	261
Other printers:	14
Total units:	1,336

Note: In this contract, nothing is said about growth of the environment. Because growth is low and coverage was considered more than sufficient, management did not consider this an issue. Other environments might want to specify how much growth was allowed before the contract had to be renegotiated or a premium charged.

Network Support

Many companies refuse to outsource network support, claiming that it is critical to the business and therefore knowledge of it should remain in-house. But outsourcing offers many smaller options. If you are short of network staff, you can supplement your own staff with outsourced staff. You will have access to more staff, and you will retain the network skills and knowledge.

Description

Network support involves any or all aspects of network maintenance, monitoring, management, repair, and customer support. Some of the options third-party service providers offer are:

- Full management service to companies that don't have or want the skills and technology necessary to manage networks themselves.
- Filling in gaps in expertise or in number of staff:
  Third-party staff can provide skills in-house staff may not have yet, and can provide any extra personnel power required.
- Reconfiguring networks that have expanded and/or changed and are no longer able to handle the load, or need to be able to handle a different load:
  Third parties may be better informed and have more experience in modifying networks than internal staff. They may have processes in place that they can simply execute—they wouldn't have to reinvent the wheel.
- Tuning:
  Third-party service providers whose business is networks often know about and are using the latest techniques and tools to optimize performance.
- Performing upgrades to network operating system:
  Third parties may have done this dozens of times. Your Help Desk has probably never done it. Third parties may have standards and

procedures set up and know of potential pitfalls. They could save you a lot of pain.

- Performing diagnostics:
  This includes network monitoring, problem detection and resolution, network restoration, performance measurement, and performance reporting.

- Customer support:
  Taking and resolving calls from network users.

- Remote support after-hours:
  If you are only staffed to cover support during business hours, a third-party service provider may be able to provide support coverage after-hours by remotely monitoring your LAN. You could use this service to expand your support coverage to 24 hours a day, seven days a week.

- Remote support options:
  - The service provider can establish a permanent remote network connection to the customer site and take responsibility for resetting passwords, setting user access rights, performing file server diagnostics, and providing Help Desk and applications support.
  - The service provider can provide full remote services and dispatch staff to the remote site when something has to be fixed, or the remote services can remain in-house with only the visit to the remote site outsourced.

Your options in outsourcing parts of your network activities may be limited by the equipment or software you have. Remote monitoring may not be possible without some investment in hardware and/or software.

You may choose to have something outsourced for one time only, on an occasional or regular basis, or full-time. Outsourcing may be temporary until you either build up the skills that you're short on or purchase the tools that you need.

Contracts are as variable as the options are. If you specify what you want, the third party will probably accommodate you, if by doing so they can still make a reasonable profit.

Software Management

Keeping up to date with releases of packaged software is expensive and time-consuming. Software must be purchased, installed, and tested; Help

Desk staff and customers trained; and the product rolled out. The more standard packaged software packages you have to maintain, the more time-consuming this is. Outsourcing the whole or part of this process is an option.

Description

Software management involves responsibility for keeping software up to date and working smoothly. Tasks that you can outsource include:

- Maintenance of licensing:
  Keeping software licensing up to date is an arduous task, especially when you have a mix of standalone and networked PCs. Third-party service providers are willing to do this for you. They will make sure that you have adequate licensing at all times, that licenses are reused when someone no longer needs one, and that software upgrades are properly licensed.
- Testing and installation of software:
  Service providers can test and install packaged software or software upgrades, across the network or on individual PCs.
- Training:
  Service providers can train Help Desk staff and customers in upgrades.
- Complete management:
  The third-party service provider can take over all of the software functions. Even customer support can be outsourced.

Customer Support

Many organizations are outsourcing their customer support for packaged applications. They cannot afford to spend the necessary people and time to train for and support the calls.

Description

A third party provides support for Help Desk customers. Service can vary from answering software questions remotely to fixing all problems on-site. Some of the options include:

- Third-party staff on-site, as part of Help Desk team:
  The third party provides staff to either take over support on your Help Desk or add to the staff that you have. Staff would become part

of the Help Desk team. This is a good way of expanding the skills you offer customers, staffing for peaks and transitions, and lessening the support load so that in-house Help Desk staff can focus on improvement projects.

- Use of third-party call center:
  Customers call the third party directly when they have a problem. You could set up your phones so that this happens automatically when customers call a Help Desk number and select the support option.

- Outsource only support for packaged software:
  Support that is most easily outsourced is for standard packaged software. Some third parties specialize in certain applications, such as banking, so companies using those applications could also outsource fairly easily. For a third party to take on the support of your in-house applications, the cost to you would have to be very high. The expense of learning and supporting your application could not be shared over any other of the third party's customers.

- First-line support provided by third party, second-line by customer:
  For this option, the third party would take all of the calls and try to resolve them. Any calls that could not be resolved over the phone would be passed to the customer's second-level support area. Third parties report being able to handle approximately 80 percent of the calls without having to go to second-level support. (This depends very much on the environment, of course).

- Support for off-hours or specific times during the day:
  One way of extending your service to seven days a week, 24 hours a day, is to outsource any after-hours service. You can have the phones automatically switch over to the third party phone center as soon as your business hours are over. If the problem can't be handled over the phone, your staff can be paged to take care of it. This may also be a good way of handling your peak times; you can switch one or more lines to the third party for specific times during the day.

When you choose to outsource to a remote call center, you need to do some work up front to make sure that the staff at the call center are familiar with your environment so that customers don't have to spend time explaining the environment to them. Third-party staff can serve your internal customers more effectively if they have an understanding of the environment and standard configurations.

Outsourcing partial customer support to third parties is a popular solution for reducing support load on staff. Software development companies use it extensively: Borland International, Inc. in Scotts Valley, California, and WordPerfect in Orem, Utah outsourced support of older products and versions so that they can focus on new products. Software Publishing Corporation (Harvard Graphics, Professional Write) also outsourced support for its older products, but is keeping support for its new, strategic products in-house. Novell outsourced part of its support (the overflow from the Help Desk) for older Netware versions, and the internal Novell team will handle support for the new version. Novell is also formalizing relationships with third parties to be able to offer a more consistent level of customer support via Novell authorized service centers.

Training

Training is outsourced by companies that don't want to be in the business of providing training. They don't want to take on the cost or management associated with keeping training staff up to date on all packages for which training is required, supporting the trainers while they develop courses, and supporting administrative functions such as registration. Third parties make much more cost-effective use of their trainers and are able to offer courses more frequently and of greater variety. Each trainer can provide training for several clients. Their economies of scale are passed on to customers to make this an attractive outsourcing option.

Description

The third party is responsible for providing training to customer employees. Some of the options are:

- Training at customer site in facilities provided and maintained by customer:
  The customer maintains a training facility which the third party uses to provide on-site training. This option is attractive to those customers who already have some kind of training facility.
- Customer employees attend training at third-party site:
  Customer employees attend either the third party's regular course offerings, or course offerings that have been set up specifically for the customer.

- Outsource training only for standard packaged applications:
  Training for company-specific applications is not as cost-effective as training for the software that the third party already provides training for. Training for the customer-specific applications can be kept in-house.
- Have third party handle all aspects from registration to billing:
  Third parties providing training have all of these functions set up already, and can provide them to customers at an attractive rate.
- Customize training to customers' environment:
  Training, even at the third-party site, can be customized so that it reflects the environment of your internal customers. How to access software, information about common libraries, how to use the network, even how to call the Help Desk or to access security and standards documents can be included—everything particular to your organization.

You may want to offer your customers a few options: attending training on-site or—if the times are more suitable—attending a regular course offering at the third-party site. If your Help Desk supports some packages that have fewer users, training for those packages can be left at the third-party site. If you are charging your clients directly for the training, the training company can also take care of that for you. They can provide promotional material, such as training schedules, and take care of registration, scheduling, and billing.

A side benefit to outsourcing training is that sometimes internal staff don't take in-house trainers as seriously as external trainers, even though the skills may be equal. They might have more respect for, and be more satisfied with, third-party trainers who have more experience. Also, having the third party charge customers directly may cut down on no-shows and last-minute cancellations.

Transitional Work

Outsourcing can help during times of transition. If you need to focus your resources on new products, outsourcing support for the old ones can make sense. Software development companies often do this. You can also outsource part of the work for the new product, especially if it is something you will probably only be doing once or very infrequently.

Some examples of outsourcing transitional work:

- Outsource support so that staff can focus on upgrading the environment for client/server.
- Outsource the installation and initial setup of a voice response unit.
- Outsource the extra support that is required in the early stages of introduction of a new product or environment.

The Outsourcing Process

When you're considering outsourcing, you need to know who might be able to provide the services you need. Chances are that as a Help Desk manager, you're already getting endless calls from vendors about every service imaginable. It is sometimes difficult to make time for vendors, but by not listening, you can miss some valuable ideas. If you don't have time to talk to all of the vendors when they knock on your door, at least keep a file of cards and services so that you can go back to them when you need something.

Request for Proposal

Unless what you're doing is very small, you'll want to put together a request for proposal (RFP) to distribute to prospective service providers to explain what you need. The RFP should set out the details of the service(s) you are looking for.

Know the Third Party

Once you have a short list of potential service providers, you should do some serious investigation into the service organizations themselves, if you have not done so already:

- Check into the financial stability of the organization:
  Annual reports can provide valuable information on a company's financial health, as can any industry news or gossip. Taking a contract with someone who goes into receivership soon thereafter is something you want to avoid.
- Visit the head office:
  Make sure there is something solid behind the salesperson.

- Meet the staff who will be working at your organization:
  If you are not confident that they can do the job, then maybe you should go elsewhere.

- Check into their quality control:
  What measures does the service provider take to ensure that you are getting the service you require?

- Find out how they plan to communicate progress and performance to you:
  They should have reporting and procedures already in place for this.

- Check all references:
  This is an absolute imperative. Don't make any final decisions without talking to other customers of the company.

- Take your time:
  Don't rush into a decision if you're not sure about the outsourcing firm. You're going to have to live with the decision for a while, so take your time. You want to do everything possible to avoid making an expensive and time-consuming mistake.

A Clear Agreement

When you are ready to create an agreement with the third party of your choice, you need to make sure that each of you understands exactly what is expected of the other:

- Make sure the vendor understands what your objectives are and is ready to meet them:
  You have objectives to meet, and by outsourcing you are attempting to meet them through the third party. If the third party does not meet them, you will be held accountable.

- Define responsibilities for each party clearly, with nothing left to chance:
  Regardless of any "that goes without saying" promises, make sure that *everything* you expect from the third party is clearly documented. In the same way, what is expected of you must also be clearly stated.

- Build performance measures:
  You're going to have to have some way of measuring whether the outsourcing is working. Building these measures up front will not only make it easier to understand whether the contract is successful,

but will also help clarify performance expectations, ensuring that they get met.

- Put it all in writing:
  If it isn't in writing, it isn't in the contract and the vendor cannot be held to it.

Making It Work

Once the agreement is signed and the work has started, your responsibility is still not over. You have to monitor the contract, make sure that it is working. You will have to set up some form of communication with the company—face-to-face meetings are probably best—at which you review performance from both sides to see how successful the contract is. Start off by meeting frequently to make any adjustments required, and then settle into a schedule of perhaps every month or so.

An Example

One third-party service provider meets with each of its customers monthly to review performance. Customers rate each of its services on a scale of 0 to 7. Customers also evaluate:

- Performance against the service-level agreement—for example, speed of resolution.
- Quality of the front-line staff—skill level and call handling.
- Call statistics: wait time, response time, resolution time, abandoned calls.

Evaluation can sometimes be fairly subjective, and the service provider finds that often success depends largely on how customer employees get along with third-party support staff. Individual personalities make a difference.

The Human Factor

Don't expect your outsourcing suggestion to be greeted with open arms by your staff. Even if they are stressed and overworked, and you are providing relief in some form of outsourcing, they may not see it as help, but rather as a threat.

There is no such thing as overcommunication when it comes to letting staff know that you're considering, or have decided on, outsourcing. Staff will start to worry as soon as you mention the word. They'll be concerned about:

- Losing their jobs.
- A change in working conditions: "What will be expected of me? Will I be able to do it? Will they train me?"
- Their careers: "Will I lose my seniority? If they keep outsourcing, there won't be anywhere left for me to go."

They may feel as if they've been betrayed. A way to help combat all of these worries and feelings of betrayal is to make your staff aware of what is going on as early in the process as possible:

- Get them involved in making the outsourcing decision. Explain what you're trying to achieve and how outsourcing will help you achieve it within the constraints of your budget or any cost-cutting measures the company has put into place.
- Provide opportunities for them to ask questions and express their concerns. Be honest.
- Let them help form the agreement, getting them involved in setting up performance measurements.
- Make them part of the third-party review and selection process.
- Include staff in your regular performance meetings with the third-party service provider.

Your staff will feel a part of the process, and will be much more likely to give the outsourcing their support. Trying to make the outsourcing work without the support of your staff will be very difficult, especially in cases where an outsourced employee has to work with your staff. Table 10.2 shows some concerns you might hear from your staff and possible responses you might give.

When People Lose Their Jobs

Sometimes an outsourcing decision involves laying people off. You should be honest with staff from the beginning if there is a possibility of this. How you handle the situation will be very closely watched by other staff. If they feel you are hiding things or not telling the whole truth, you

Table 10.2 Concerns You Might Hear from Your Staff, and Responses to Them

Functions to Be Outsourced	*Concerns about Outsourcing*	*Concerns Addressed*
Software support	"If we outsource software support, the support analysts won't know our environment."	Third-party service providers can provide their support staff with all of the details and idiosyncrasies of your environment, including standards and security policies.
	"Outsourced support staff are too removed from our environment. They won't understand us."	Staff can be on-site. They get to know you and vice versa.
Mundane, simple tasks such as taking a hardware inventory.	"Can't we do that simple thing ourselves?"	Yes, we can, but at what cost? Consider the important work that is not being done because your qualified Help Desk staff are out counting PCs.
Training	"Third-party training is too generic. I won't know how to use the software in this environment."	Third parties are usually quite willing to customize training to your environment, and can even offer it on-site.
Network support	"The network is key to the company. We shouldn't outsource any part of it."	You can use outsourced network staff to supplement your own staff. You can keep the knowledge and expertise in-house, and outsource the workload that you can't handle. You don't have to add expensive head count.

are less likely to get their buy-in. They might worry that you are planning to outsource everything.

Don't write off the staff you are laying off. Make every effort to find different positions for them. Sometimes the outsourcing firm will hire the people whose positions you are outsourcing. They will train them, and often place them back with you. The advantage to the outsourcers is that they have someone who is familiar with your environment.

This seems like an ideal solution, but what can and has happened is that the outsourcing firm lays those same people off awhile later. The people have no seniority and get very limited severance. This solution is very cost-effective for the company that handed them over to the outsourcing firm, but very severe and financially damaging for the employees, who would have been much better off had the original company simply laid them off.

It is the original employer's responsibility to make sure that staff who are laid off get help in finding employment and the severance that is due them. If staff do go to the outsourcing firm, the original company can specify a guaranteed length of employment for them as part of the outsourcing contract, but the company should not force the outsourcing firm to take on employees that they don't need. That is not fair to either the outsourcing firm or the employees. If a company cannot find a place for its employees internally, and if the outsourcing firm has no place for them, the fairest thing to do is to lay them off with proper severance.

This is more than just a matter of moral responsibility. Staff who think they have been treated unfairly can do more than moan and groan. They can sue.

Both Kodak and Digital Equipment Corporation (DEC) faced a lawsuit when Kodak moved to implement an outsourcing contract with DEC. Former Kodak employees who went to DEC as part of the contract felt that they had not been treated fairly in the areas of job opportunities and benefits packages.

Blue Cross and Blue Shield of Massachusetts also faced a lawsuit when the company began outsourcing its computer operations and software development to EDS Corporation. Employees who were forced to either join EDS Corporation or resign were unhappy with how things had been handled. Issues at hand included amount of warning received and provision of proper severance packages.

Never underestimate the importance of the support of your in-house staff in any kind of outsourcing endeavor. Treat your staff fairly, especially when you have to let them go.

Summary

Outsourcing is neither a dirty word nor a panacea for all your ills. It is a tool that can add value to your Help Desk. How you use outsourcing will play a large part in your success with it. Outsourcing indiscriminately will get you into trouble—you might not realize the value or savings you promised, or you may outsource something that your business can't do without. Expecting outsourcing to work on its own will also get you into trouble. Regardless of the fact that you have outsourced a function, you are still accountable to your customers. You need to ensure that objectives are met, customers are satisfied, and the business is being served effectively.

Using outsourcing as a tool, applied where necessary, will bring tangible benefits:

- Reduction in costs:
  Third-party service providers can spread the cost of training, tools, purchases, marketing, research, and consulting over all of their customers. They can provide expertise, experience, and technology that you can't afford.

- Improvement in productivity and performance:
  Outsourced staff are more focused than in-house staff. They do not have the constant interruptions, new work, and politics that in-house staff do. Their tasks are usually well defined. They are allowed to produce more and perform better than in-house staff. The work they take on frees up in-house staff for work that is more important to the business.

- Increased flexibility, so that business requirements can be responded to more quickly:
  Outsourcing can provide the flexibility in staffing that will allow you to staff for peaks or handle special requests.

- A wider range of services:
  If customers are demanding a service that you don't have, you may be able to outsource it more cost-effectively than providing in-house staff to do it.

- Increased skill level:
  You can use outsourcing to fill skill gaps and add knowledge and experience in areas that the Help Desk may be unfamiliar with.

- More control over the Help Desk function:
  If you don't have the staff or tools to monitor your environment and create the reporting that you need, a third party may be able to do it for you.

- Increased ability to focus on what really matters to the business:
  Outsourcing can help you focus on the functions that add the most business value. You can outsource the nonstrategic activities and spend your time on more important work.

Deciding what functions to outsource isn't simply a matter of dollars and cents. Sometimes a loss in cost-effectiveness is worth something in strategic value. Technology is often at the heart of a business, so losing control of it in any way must be weighed carefully before any commitments are made. What you can outsource will depend on the complexity of your environment, the services you provide, the level of skills your staff have, and the demands and focus of your business. Some of the circumstances that might indicate outsourcing are as follows:

- Your customer base is experiencing rapid growth, and you need support relief while you try to deal with it and catch the environment up to it.

- Routine work seems to be taking over your resources, and you are unable to get to the work that adds business value. Routine work can be outsourced.

- The Help Desk is drowning in support, and you could use someone to handle the support while your staff implements improvements to reduce the volume of calls.

- You simply need more people to handle everything that needs to be done. You are understaffed, and outsourcing can let you add staff without adding head count.

- You really don't know how the Help Desk is performing, and no one has the time to measure performance. A third party could come in and set up the functions and reporting that would allow you to monitor and manage the environment more effectively.

- You're going through a transition, and you need help to look after the old while you go to the new. Outsourcing can do this.

- You're finding it difficult to support remote locations. It's expensive to send staff out there. A third party might be able to monitor your location remotely and send in local third-party staff to perform any required on-site repairs or maintenance.

- You require expensive tools that you can't afford, but that a third-party service provider has. A third party can spread the cost of tools over several customers. By outsourcing, you will have access to the tools (and the required skills) without a huge capital outlay.

- You have a requirement for a skill that you use infrequently, and bringing in a third party to provide these skills when required might be the perfect solution.

- You need people with very expensive skills, and you can't afford as many as you need. By outsourcing some of them, you can increase your skill complement and still keep expertise in-house.

- You require skills that are specialized but not strategic. You don't particularly want to acquire these skills, so you outsource them.

- You're in a business (e.g., training) you want to get out of because it takes your focus away from the business you're supporting. You can outsource it.

- You need to support a wide variety of packaged software and you can't afford the skills or the head count to do it, so you outsource the support.

- The Help Desk is getting a lot of how-to questions for packaged software, and this is not a high business value use of the Help Desk. You outsource support for packaged software.

Companies each have their own opinions of what should and should not be outsourced. You have to consider the costs, in terms of business value, of no longer having a specific function in-house. You'll have to decide how important that value is to the business and use that to make your decision about outsourcing that function.

Functions that you may not want to outsource are:

- Complete network management and control. A network is often considered too strategic to outsource in its entirety.

- Skills specific to the business. A third party wouldn't be able to provide these without coming into the business to learn and get experience. Cost would be prohibitive.

- Support of in-house applications that are critical to the business. Because they were developed in-house so there is no industry knowledge of them, and because they are critical, you want to retain as much expertise in these applications as possible.

- Support of an environment with few standards and a wide variety of technology, including in-house applications. Third parties could not support this cost-effectively without converting it into some semblance of order.

Outsourcing options and combinations of options are almost endless. Third-party service providers will be willing to give you just about anything you ask for as long as it is cost-effective for them. Some of the most common functions that Help Desks outsource are:

- Hardware maintenance, which might include inventory management and hardware installation.
- Network support. This could include some or all of network maintenance, monitoring, management, repair, and customer support.
- Software management. A third party can take on responsibility for software testing, installation, training, licensing, and management, or any subset of these.
- Customer support. Third parties can provide anything from full on-site support for the complete customer environment to first-line phone support from a remote location. Support can even be purchased for specific times to handle peaks and off-hours support.
- Training. The complete training function can be outsourced and training provided at the customer site and/or at the third-party site.
- Transitional work. Outsourcing can be a useful tool for taking the Help Desk through periods of transition such as changes in technology. Third parties could focus on the old environment while the Help Desk prepared for the new one.

When it's time to select a third party to provide the functions you want to outsource, you need to take the time to make sure that the party you select is the best choice. You need to:

- Check into the financial stability of the organization.
- Visit the head office to make sure there is something solid behind the salesperson.
- Meet the staff who will be working at your organization.
- Check into their quality control.
- Find out how they plan to communicate progress and performance to you.
- Check all references.

Once you have selected a vendor, you need to put together a clear agreement, making sure that responsibilities and expectations of each party are written down. Performance measurements should be agreed upon and documented, and a schedule of meetings set up between both parties for monitoring performance.

Never underestimate the importance of having the support of your internal staff for any outsourcing you are planning. You need it for your outsourcing efforts to succeed. In order to help ensure that your internal staff are supportive, you should get them involved in making the out-sourcing decision. Provide opportunities for them to ask questions and express their concerns and be honest in your responses. Involve them in all aspects of third-party selection and management.

Sometimes an outsourcing decision involves laying people off. Com-panies need to be honest with staff from the beginning, make every effort to find employment within the company, and pay full severance if noth-ing can be found. Sometimes staff are employed by the outsourcing firm, but this should only be done if the firm needs the staff and if the staff want to go. It should not be forced upon the third party as part of the outsourcing contract. This could result in staff being laid off from the third party later on, without the benefits they would have received had they just been let go by the original company. Treating staff fairly is more than a matter of moral responsibility. Staff who think they have been treated unfairly can and do sue, as several major companies can attest.

CHAPTER ELEVEN

Help Desk Case #1: Setup

In this example, a PC support group is set up amid incredible growth and support requirements.

Current Technology Environment

- Some 1,000 PC and local area network users are spread over several remote locations. Users access the mainframe via the local area network and wide area network.

- Hardware and software standards exist, and most users access a standard set of desktop applications from the LAN.

- Client/server applications are just starting to be developed, but no critical applications run on the LAN yet. Several performance and stability issues must be addressed before this happens.

Current Help Desk

- Staff consists of three front-line staff, one of whom is a student. Hardware maintenance is outsourced and performed by two on-site third-party staff. Two people look after PC ordering and invoicing. Five staff look after the local area networks.

- Most (but not all) calls are logged via a Help Desk package called Quetzal.
- The call volume is 80 to 100 calls per day
- There is no call distribution system. Calls into the Help Desk are fronted by a phone menu.
- Training is administered by an outsourcing firm, which takes care of everything from sign-up to billing.
- Support is from 7 A.M. to 6 P.M., and the hours are covered by staggered shifts.

History

This company came into PCs in 1990, very late in the game. Previous to this time, PCs had not been allowed into the company for a number of reasons, one of which was that PCs were considered a security risk. Along with a change in management came a change in policy. PCs were allowed in, and in they came—in droves. Everyone wanted one. Unfortunately, because none had been allowed in to date, there was no expertise in the area. Very few people in the company knew anything about PCs. The mainframe technical support group was given responsibility for PCs. A standard configuration was hastily put together and an ordering process set up. The technical support group could not handle the volumes of requests that came in. The PCs were set up with terminal emulation cards to enable communication to the mainframe. The first attempts at networking were fairly disastrous, as was the first network operating system selected. Neither the LAN operating software nor the PC operating system (OS/2) was very stable in the new environment, and neither was accepted by the users. People begged to be taken off the network, and went out and bought themselves Windows software. PC support was hit and miss. There just weren't enough technical support staff, and those who were there were just learning PCs.

In 1991, the first of many corporate reorganizations happened, and a proposal was put forward for a PC support group. Interestingly enough, management had a hard time accepting it, even with all the problems, because PCs were being touted as tools that made users completely self-sufficient. Eventually, the proposal was accepted and a PC group was put together. The team was designed and job descriptions were created for the participants.

Unfortunately, when it came time to staff the group up, the makeup of the group was largely determined by the reorganization and consolidation that had just taken place. Some functions didn't seem to have a home in the organization, so they were put into the PC group—for example, administration of electronic mail and an entire training function. The group was staffed from inside the company with people transferring or people who had lost their jobs through consolidation. Only two people on the team had PC experience: one of the technical support staff, and a person from another division who had very extensive experience and knowledge.

The team that was formed consisted of a manager, five staff to support PCs and LANs, two staff to administer the mainframe electronic mail system, three trainers, a training administrator, and a technical writer.

What Was Done

1. A plan was developed and objectives set to try to stabilize the current PC environment. It included setting up processes, support procedures, and training. The first thing on the list was switching all existing PCs and LANs to Windows and Novell Netware.

2. A standard desktop was developed and tested and a rollout schedule was put together. The rollout started, and all existing LANs and PCs were converted over the course of four months. At the same time, the trainers developed courses for the standard desktop and how to use the LAN. They were just learning PCs themselves. After the first LAN rollout (to an IS area), a survey was sent out to determine the quality of the work (not great). Procedures were updated for next time based on survey results.

    As all of this was going on, a new mainframe electronic mail package, which the team had inherited by reorganization, was being rolled out. One trainer and two administrators were kept busy training, providing support, and answering questions. The package was not popular, and users complained bitterly about its lack of functionality.

There were many struggles with PC/LAN technology, volume of support, and volume of requests for PC purchase and installation. The feeling at the time was that manufacturers and developers purposely designed their products in such a way as to prevent them from interfacing cleanly with any other product. As some LANs were being converted, new ones were being installed. Customers were still not happy. PC staff were picking up calls for PC support, but no logging or tracking was taking place.

3. A Help Desk phone number and user ID were selected and publicized. The Help Desk number was prefaced with a phone menu so that users could select hardware, software, mainframe, or electronic mail support. Some options contained commonly asked questions about electronic mail so that people could get their own answers.

   A list of services was developed.

   Pamphlets were sent out explaining services of the group and how to use the phone menu. Inventory stickers were printed up with the support number.

   Trainers took the PC software calls and PC support staff took the hardware calls. Customers still weren't happy with support. Problem resolution took too long.

4. Standards and ordering procedures were put together and published for hardware and software. Convincing customers that standards were vital to a supportable environment was not easy. Everyone had a favorite spreadsheet or word processor and just couldn't live without it. Fortunately, within six months, standards were adhered to almost 100 percent. They were sold on the basis that not having standards cost too much in support and in incompatibility. Many users using nonstandard software had experienced that incompatibility, and everyone could relate to the cost issue.

5. A Help Desk package was purchased (Quetzal). The PC staff reorganized so that someone was almost always available for PC help, and began to log calls.

6. A hardware maintenance agreement was set up with a hardware supplier. One very welcome on-site technician provided hardware maintenance support and helped with the setup of new PCs, which were still coming in at an unmanageable rate. Relationships were formed with various suppliers to make ordering processes easier.

The administrative work involved in ordering PCs and in maintaining software licensing was horrendous.

7. An Open House was held (about five months after the group was formed) to market the standard software, the services of the group, and the capability of the technology, and to explain the concept of PCs and local area networks. The event had demonstrations, seminars, an open server on display, and tours through the computer room. It was extremely successful.

8. Standard software was upgraded to new versions. Trainers gave upgrade seminars. Customers and trainers had a hard time accepting the rate at which PC software changed.

9. A year after the original team was formed, the PC support staff were split off into a separate team. The support function required a full-time person to look after it, and one of the staff was promoted to manager. Two staff were added. A separate support desk area was set up and staff took turns on the Help Desk—one person full-time, a second when things got busy. Most requests were logged. LAN monitoring software was purchased and installed.

The Result

- After one year, PC support had its own dedicated team and manager. Processes and procedures were in place, standards were in place, and a standardized environment was in place. Customers knew what the PC Help Desk did and how to get service.

- The PC environment had grown in one year from 200 PCs to almost 600, with eight local area networks (three remote), all able to communicate with the mainframe.

Challenges

- Growth. In the first year, the Help Desk never really got control of the support load or the growth. The business was very demanding, and there were a lot of emergencies.

- Staff. Some staff found it difficult to accept the fast pace of change in the PC environment. These people sometimes hindered progress.
- Lack of knowledge and experience. So many people were learning at the same time that it was very difficult to do things right. It took awhile before quality of work was reliable.
- Administrative tasks, such as PC ordering and invoicing and software licensing. They just took too much time.

Observations

- Make every effort to get the staff you need, not the staff you're given.
- Planning is all-important, even when there is no time.
- Market—make time to go out and talk to your customers.
- Outsource whatever business you don't want to be in.

The following is the original proposal for PC support.

PC Support Proposal

Two plans for support are required: short term (6–12 months) to deal with immediate issues and concerns, and long term to deal with ultimate direction and strategy. The long-term PC support plan should be integrated with business plans, and with plans for other technologies. It must address questions such as: What will the technology requirements for our strategic applications be in the future? How will we be building future applications?

Short-Term Plan for PC Support

Objectives:

1. Stabilize our current PC environment: get the PCs and LANs working.

2. Increase PC expertise, in both IS and the client areas.

3. Get control of the processes involved in PC support, including the following:

   - Request, approval, ordering, delivery, and installation of PCs.
   - Maintenance of an inventory of PC technology.
   - Support/problem logging.
   - Training.

- Maintenance/upgrading.
- Security.

4. Provide PC support and consulting to IS and the client areas.

What We Have to Do

1. Develop, with the clients, an interim PC policy that covers:

   - Suggested standard hardware and software configurations.
   - Nonstandard configurations: if IS cannot provide support, we must find out who can. We must make sure that all configurations are supportable.
   - Number and location of LANs to be installed over the short term (6–12 months).
   - Printing.
   - Software upgrades.
   - Host access.
   - Remote access.
   - Hardware maintenance.
   - Security.

2. Solve the outstanding major problems (e.g., LAN system hang-up, LAN printing).

3. Off-load work from Technical Support as much as possible. Appoint and train LAN administrators and persons who can perform LAN maintenance. If possible, hire a consultant for approximately 6 months for skills exchange.

4. Put processes or people in place for:

   - Request for PC hardware/software.
   - Approval—for example, ensure client sign-off at appropriate level.
   - Ordering.
   - Receiving.
   - Inventory control.
   - Delivery and installation.
   - Billing and payment.

   A coordinator should be appointed to monitor PC orders, from request to installation. This person (with the help of a PC inventory package) would schedule installations with the clients and the installers, to ensure that all necessary equipment was received and would be installed at a mutually convenient time. This person would also ensure that the client received a quick PC lesson immediately after the installation so that the client could make immediate use of the system.

5. Develop an education/publicity strategy to propagate PC knowledge as quickly as possible throughout IS and the client areas. As well as formal courses, this might include lunchtime demonstrations by clients or IS. We would be empha-sizing self-learning.

6. Assign IS staff to visit client PC users regularly to see if there are any problems, and to make sure clients have everything they need from us.

7. Set up a PC phone hotline. Staff a support desk. Log problems. There are PC packages available to keep track of problems, and to display possible problems and their solutions.

8. Appoint IS staff to handle PC consulting.

9. Leverage client PC expertise wherever possible—can clients take their turn on the hotline? In consulting? In R&D?

Note: Regarding PC application development: we need to learn more about this, and to stabilize our PC base before we embark on major work in this area. PC application development should be treated as any other project—it must be part of our strategy, and must be prioritized accordingly.

Proposal/Action Plan

1. Work with the clients to determine the real PC requirements for the next year. Based on these, work out an interim (6–12 months) PC strategy. We need to understand the problems and priorities.

2. Put together a dedicated (i.e., not matrix) PC support team. In order to ensure proper support for this very specialized technology, all PC functions should be covered by this group—everything from LAN setup and maintenance to admini-stration of the request, purchase, and delivery cycle for PCs. The team could be composed of:

   • A coordinator for PC processes (as in step 4 above).

   • Two PC LAN/operating system/communications experts.

   • Three or four PC support persons. These people would do client support, consulting, and some training. IS staff could rotate in and out of some of these positions to ensure cross training.

- The team should be headed by a manager, who would work with the clients to develop the interim strategies, and who would be involved in setting longer-term direction.

3. Stabilize our current environment—define, prioritize, and address the problems, and ensure that all required tools (e.g., for LAN management) are in place.

4. Define and set up a management system for the PC processes (as in step 4 above). Communicate these processes to all IS and client areas.

5. Design and start a hotline Help Desk function.

6. Plan, communicate, and implement informal education sessions, self-help sessions, visits by support staff to clients, and so on.

Time Frame

From startup through team selection and education, environment stabilization, process setup and Help Desk education, implementation would be roughly four months.

CHAPTER TWELVE

Help Desk Case #2: Starting into Automation

The second Help Desk story deals with a company that is improving its Help Desk through the use of automation.

The Technological Environment

- There are 5,000 users, but half of these only access the Help Desk for wide area network issues. Approximately 1,000 users access the mainframe via PC and local area network, the rest via terminals.
- Remote access exists to both local area networks and PCs via wide area network.
- Wide area network includes satellite communication and runs across the country.

The Help Desk

- Provides support for mainframe and communication issues.
- The Help Desk is part of an internal organization that provides computing, communications, and all related support to the major divisions of the business it serves. The organization is located within

its own computing facility. Functions at the facility include computer operations, technical support, communications support, wide area network support, and the Help Desk. The Help Desk reports to the manager of Operations.

- PC and local area network support are provided by another Help Desk within the same organization, but at a different location.

History

The company recently consolidated two major data centers into the shared facility. All data center functions were moved to the new facility and combined. A number of staff were taken from each data center to staff them, and the rest were either placed somewhere else in the company or let go. The consolidation was smooth from a technological point of view but not quite as smooth from an employee point of view. Resentment lingered, and there were cultural adjustments to make between the two groups.

Before consolidation, the Help Desk had been part of Console Operations in each data center. After consolidation, the Help Desk function was split out on its own, in recognition of the importance of customer support to the success of the data center. Just after consolidation, the Help Desk consisted of two people. When the call load remained steadily low, one person left to help out with another area in the very busy environment. Consolidation had necessitated a significant amount of work, and everyone was almost frantically busy. An initiative to automate the consolidated data center was also in progress.

The environment was constantly changing, as the call traffic to the Help Desk started to reflect. The Help Desk, which was now staffed by only one person, was getting calls almost nonstop. Calls came in on any one of seven lines, which overflowed to the console area of Operations. All lines were constantly busy. Nothing was logged, customers were constantly getting busy signals, and the Help Desk person was unable to handle the load. An automation project was going on in the data center at the time, and the automation consultants were called in to help. Two more staff were assigned to the Help Desk and a Help Desk improvement project was created. Project management responsibility was given to a service/quality champion.

The Challenges

- Consolidation had damaged relations between the two divisions; people were having trouble working together.
- There were no Help Desk procedures, and no procedures for dealing with second-level support groups.
- customers still had a hard time getting through to the Help Desk; the lines were always busy, especially when there was any kind of system problem.
- The Help Desk staff were located in an isolated area away from the other support groups. They were out of the informal communication loop and out of sight of the manager.
- Help Desk staff were having trouble changing attitudes and processes. The "us versus the customers" mentality was firmly ingrained.
- Help Desk staff were spending too much time on each call. In an effort to please customers, they were spending an excessive amount of time talking to the customers and not enough focusing on the task at hand.

What Was Done

1. In order to get an idea of what kind of support the Help Desk was dealing with, an ACD unit was installed so that call volumes, wait times, and calls abandoned could be gathered. Calls were not logged, but calls were manually counted, by type, as they came in. Two phone lines were on the ACD in May.

2. A mission and set of objectives were developed for the Help Desk:

   Mission:

   - To provide all customers with a single point of contact for mainframe and network support.
   - To provide timely service and solutions to customers.
   - To be a pleasure to deal with.

Initial Objectives:

- Make phones the number 1 priority of the Help Desk.
- Calls handled or resolved within two minutes.
- Calls picked up before three rings.
- 50 percent of calls handled by a voice response unit, 45 percent of calls handled by Help Desk, and 5 percent of calls handled by console operators (off-hours).
- Abandoned call rate less than 4 percent.
- Calls and incidents tracked in problem management system (INFOMAN).
- Educate customers to help themselves.

3. A plan for improvement was created.
   This plan included automation, problem management, Help Desk procedures, and training for Help Desk staff.

4. A Help Desk procedures manual was started.
   Priorities and some of the most common processes, such as terminal and printer resets, were documented by a part-time student.

5. The Help Desk was relocated.
   The Help Desk was moved to a central, bright area. The area is near the console room, near the technical support group, and near the Operations manager. Communication with all groups improved immediately. The manager could now see what was happening in the group, and was easily accessible for any questions or emergencies.

6. Started working on customizing a problem logging and management system (INFOMAN).
   At this point (August), the number of calls per month, which had been averaging about 6,000, dropped to 4,000 (see Figure 12.1). The change was attributed to better call handling and a more stable environment. Customers were getting through on the first call, were getting more resolutions on the first call, and were not having to call back.

7. Implemented a voice response unit (VRU) to automate the most frequent requests. The VRU was set up with six lines.

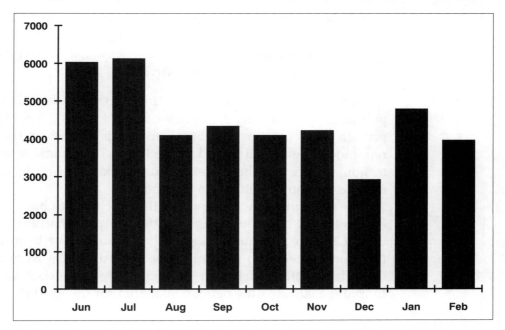

Figure 12.1   The number of Help Desk calls dropped in August.

The cost of the VRU, the communications lines, and a development system (to allow new functions to be developed and tested parallel to the production VRU) came in at about $100,000. The cost was justified on the basis of:

- Being able to free Help Desk staff time for more analytical functions, such as identifying and eliminating recurring errors, identifying processes for automation, and resolving more problems at first call.

- Being able to provide faster service to customers. Customers could resolve problems themselves quickly and would have less down time, more time to spend on the business.

- Future application. As the network grows, technology becomes more complex, and the number of users expand, the need for automated processes will also grow. As these and other process are identified for automation, they can be added to the VRU.

- Being part of the data center automation project. Concurrent to the Help Desk improvement project, a project to automate data center processes was under way. The VRU was part of the whole automation initiative.

The most frequent Help Desk functions were identified as store polling (approximately 25 percent), user ID resets (23 percent), and printer resets (30 percent). Store polling is a function that allows retail locations to call in and request sales data transfer from store to home office via the wide area network. The first to be implemented was store polling, in December.

The first function to be put on the VRU was to have been user ID resets, but because of the way the company had implemented user IDs (three unique letters), what should have been a simple function turned into a painful one. The user IDs were not long enough to define each user uniquely using a telephone keypad. Employee IDs are now being considered for this purpose.

Result

- The Help Desk is staffed by two people (the third has been reassigned), providing staggered coverage from 7 A.M. to 6 P.M. One of the staff is on contract. After hours and on weekends, calls are routed to the console, and the appropriate person is paged. Staff are not required full-time to answer calls and are able to spend time on analysis for further improvement.

- Of the 4,000 monthly calls, 18 percent are being handled by the VRU. Two percent of store polling are special cases and cannot currently be handled by the VRU. Five percent of calls are abandoned. (Call reports from the ACD and the VRU are not fine enough to show where the calls are being abandoned.)

- The store polling process has become simpler and faster for retail outlets. A process that used to be manual and time-consuming has become something that the customers can do quickly for themselves. Customer acceptance has been high.

Still to Come

- Further automation, via the VRU. Get all customers requesting store polling to use the automated function and add printer resets to bring the total calls handled by the VRU to more than 50 percent.
- Better call statistics to investigate the 5 percent abandon rate to find out who is hanging up and why.
- Normalization and documentation of procedures within the Help Desk and with other support areas.
- Technical and customer service training, so that more problems can be resolved by the front line.
- Logging of all calls: want to modify INFOMAN to provide automated entry and tie inventory in.
- Becoming closer to the PC Help Desk. Need more communication between Help Desks, especially since users who have PCs access the mainframe through the local area network. It is important for each group to keep the other up to date on what is happening in each environment.
- The organizational unit that the Help Desk belongs to is undergoing a major reorganization. More change is ahead for the Help Desk.

Observations from the Improvement Project

- The Help Desk would benefit from having someone completely responsible for support (Help Desk manager or supervisor) rather than having to share part of an Operations manager.
- Having people with the right attitude (focused on the customer and on the business) on the Help Desk is essential. Changing old mindsets is sometimes impossible and cannot be trained away. Don't settle for this—get the right people in.
- Automate where possible. Automated functions work; manual ones cause problems.

CHAPTER THIRTEEN

Help Desk Case #3: Working Well

In this example, an established Help Desk that is functioning very successfully is examined.

Technological Environment

- Approximately 500 retail outlets, most run by their own AS/400 hooked to a front-end cash register system and back-end data storage system.
- Stores are hooked to a satellite network for access to the head office mainframe for electronic mail and various other retail applications.

Help Desk

- Supports a live retail environment.
- Works out of the head office location.
- Consists of ten people. Two are outsourced staff who support older systems that are gradually being phased out.
- Staff work in shifts to keep the Help Desk staffed from 7 A.M. to midnight (to handle the different time zones), seven days a week.
- Call load is approximately 2,400 calls per month.

Background

This group is part of a larger IS department that supports the retail locations directly. The whole department is partially funded by store owners, so costs are watched very carefully. The Help Desk has been in existence for many years, and has matured into a very effective and successful function. Its customers, a tough group at best, are very pleased with Help Desk service.

Call Handling

All calls go directly into a VRU. The caller is asked to enter store number, a system code, a priority code, and a voice message describing the problem. By the time the caller hangs up, the VRU has sent all the information to the AS/400, which has logged the call. Help Desk staff pick the call up from the AS/400 and look after it in order of priority. All calls are resolved in less than five hours. There is no such thing as an outstanding call.

Reasons for Success

- Very focused:
  There are no questions about whom the Help Desk serves, or what services it provides. Everything is written down and understood by both sides. A service-level agreement was recently put into place. Some services other than those specified in the agreement are provided, but at extra cost.

- Priorities are clear:
  Priorities are well established: 1—System failure, 2—Critical programs, 3—Noncritical programs, 4—Hardware, 5—General questions. They are printed on fluorescent paper, laminated, and sent to each customer. Two sets of priorities are printed for two different systems. Customers keep these lists by the phone for easy access, and abide by them. They have to give a priority when calling into the Help Desk. The priority list also contains symptoms to look for,

so that identification is easier. For example, "You cannot create or process customer work orders" or "Isolated hardware such as the printer or screen is not working."

- Staff understand the business:
  All staff on the Help Desk have spent time as employees in the retail outlets. They understand the business and understand customer concerns and problems. When there is a problem, they know which other store functions or systems might be affected, and can get all aspects of the problem resolved quickly. Customers really appreciate the knowledge that the Help Desk staff have.

- Help Desk is accountable to its customers:
  Help Desk customers pay for Help Desk service, and they are very demanding about getting value for their money. This forces the Help Desk to maintain a high level of efficiency. This isn't always a positive. Getting funding for improvements is sometimes difficult.

- Flexible staffing:
  The Help Desk has ten staff, two of whom are contract staff working on older systems that are being phased out. Each of the remaining eight staff take turns working off-hours from home. When it is a person's week to work at home, that person works from 8:30 A.M. to midnight, with two hours off in the middle of the day. One disadvantage of having staff work at home for a week is that they are out of the communication loop. A lot happens on a Help Desk in a week.

Measures of Success

- Whether the customers want to pay the Help Desk.
- Meeting the service-level agreement. The agreement contains the following:

  - Method of operation, describing responsibilities of each party, hours of service, after-hours service, priorities, and response times.
  - Support and services, describing what systems are supported, what third parties are involved, who supports what, and what

the procedures are for interacting with each of the parties involved in support.

- Fees, detailing out regular support fees and additional services and their related charges.

Challenges

Stores are growing and expanding and will require extra support. Unfortunately, there is to be no increase in head count. Outsourcing is being investigated, but there is a major drawback: the Help Desk requires very specialized knowledge (as well as two languages) not generally available. Help Desk contract positions have been advertised at stores, but store staff generally like where they live and don't want to move close to the head office. An option being investigated is to set up contract staff with remote support capabilities so that they can work for the Help Desk from home without moving.

References and Further Reading

Adams, E. J. 1993. "Beating Dependency on Help Desks," *MacWEEK* 7:39 (October 4), 12.

Appleton, E. L. 1993. "Bonding with Customers through Better Service," *Datamation*, 39:21 (November 1), 69.

Archell, D. 1994. "Keeping Your Clients Content," *LAN Magazine* 9:1 (January), 30.

Arnold, B. 1993. "Expert System Tools Optimizing Help Desks; Customer Service Moves Center Stage; Compaq Builds Smart in Response," *Software Magazine* 13: 1 (January), 56.

Asbrand, D. 1993. "In Search of a Few Help Desk Heroes," *Corporate Computing* 2:2 (February), 28.

Asbrand, D. 1993. "User Satisfaction Is Essential to Successful Projects; Bringing End-Users into the Development Loop Can Forstall Potential Problems Later," *InfoWorld* 15:7 (February 15), 50.

Bader, R. 1993. "The Shape of Integrated Computing and Telephony," *P.C. Letter* 9:9 (May 3), 7.

Blaisdell, M. 1992. "Marketing the Benefits of an Internal Help Desk," *InfoWorld* 14:35 (August 31), 49.

Bodin, M. 1993. "ACDs: A Part of the Main," *CALL CENTER Magazine* 6:5 (May), 54.

Bodin, M. 1994. "Putting It All Together," *CALL CENTER Magazine* 7:2 (February), 26.

Brousell, D. R. 1993. "The Elusive IT Payback," *Datamation* 39: 3 (February 1), 100.

Buchok, J. 1993. "Systemhouse, Canada Post Sign 'Mega' Outsourcing Deal," *Computing Canada* 19: 9 (April 26), 1.

Campbell, G. 1992. "The Price of PC Support," *Computing Canada* 18: 14 (July 6), 21.

Castaldi, A. and D. Daniel. 1993. "My IT's Better than Yours...or Is It?" *Computing Canada* 19: 4 (February 15), 35.

Chamberlin, B. 1993. "Knowing When It's Time to Outsource," *LAN Times* 10: 24 (December 6), 80.

Cohen, G. 1993. "Voice Response Systems Tackling UI Queries," *Computing Canada* 19: 6 (March 15), 37.

Computer Conference Analysis Newsletter. 1993. "Outsourcing," *The Computer Conference Analysis Newsletter* 320 (May 25), 12.

Corporate Computing. 1993. "Selling the Idea to Your People: Be Honest, Be Positive, and Create Ownership among Staff Who Will Be Affected. Keep Them Informed," *Corporate Computing* 2: 2 (February), 112.

Crevier, D. 1993. *AI: The Tumultous History of the Search for Artificial Intelligence.* New York: Basic Books.

Cummings, S. 1993. "The Changing of the Help Desk," *LAN Times* 10: 7 (April 5), 65.

Currid, C. 1993. "IS Has to Protect Users from the Gooky Stuff inside Their PCs," *InfoWorld* 15: 20 (May 17), 66.

Currid, C. 1993. "Sticking to ABCs of Management Helps Make IS the Good Guy," *InfoWorld* 15: 25 (June 21), 72.

Dolan, T. and S. Smith. 1993. "Getting Support," *LAN Magazine* 8: 11 (October), 77.

EDGE: Work-Group Computing Report. 1993. "Software Support: Software Publishing Outsources Support for Selected Products," *EDGE: Work-Group Computing Report* 4: 177 (October 11), 3.

Eliot, L. 1993. "As Users Demand More, New Help-Desk Trends Emerge," *LAN Times* 10: 7 (April 5), 65.

Ellison, C. 1993. "Tech-Support Hold Blues," *Computer Shopper* 13: 2 (February), 836.

Ferranti, M. 1993. "Help Desk Package Taps Neural-Nets," *PC Week* 10: 39 (October 4), 33.

Francis, B. 1993. "Automate Your Asset Management!" *Datamation* 39: 11 (June 1), 47.

Gianforte, G. 1993. "Good Software Tools Are the Key to Effective LAN Support," *LAN Times* 10: 3 (February 8), 59.

Georgianis, M. V. 1993. "Reseller to Offer 24-Hour Support; Corporate Software Taps Fast-Growing Market," *Computer Reseller News* 511 (February 1), 180.

Graziano, C. 1993. "User Organization Tackles PC Asset-Management Issues," *LAN Times* 10: 14 (July 26), 13.

Greenfield, D., and F. Derfler. 1993. "Not Just Network Management, Integrated Network Management," *PC Magazine* 12: 19 (November 9), NE53.

Harding, E. U. 1993. "Help Desk Practices Change; Firms Must Automate, Add Technical Expertise," *Software Magazine* 13: 1 (January), 25.

Harding, E. U. 1993. "IS Explores Multisourcing: Trend toward Selective Use of Third Parties," *Software Magazine* 13: 9 (June), 28.

Hare, C. C. 1992. "Downsizing Changes Role of Help Desk; Network Managers Face New Expectations of Quality Support, Service," *LAN Times* 9: 16 (August 24), 55.

Help Desk Institute. 1993. *Help Desk Practices: A Survey of Help Desk Institute Members.* Colorado Springs, CO: Help Desk Institute.

Hinners, B. 1993. "Problem Busters," *LAN Magazine* 8: 11 (October), 101.

Horwitt, E. 1993. "Outsourcing Hits Human Snag: Contractual Pitfalls," *Computerworld* 27: 6 (February 8), 15.

Korzeniowski, P. 1993. "Help Desk Suppliers Vie for PC/LAN Users," *Software Magazine* 13: 4 (March), 97.

Korzeniowski, P. 1993. "LAN Auditing Easing Management Chores," *Software Magazine* 13: 13 (September), 85.

LaPlante, A. 1992. "Reigning in Corporate Systems," *InfoWorld* 14: 35 (August 31), 46.

LaPlante, A. 1992. "Help Desk Consolidation Simplifies User Access, Reduces Costs," *InfoWorld* 14: 37 (September 14), 66.

Leaf, D. 1993. "How Much Automation Do You Really Need?" *LAN Times* 10: 24 (December 6), 82.

Levine, R. 1993. "Managing a Material World," *MIDRANGE Systems* 6: 18 (September 28), 51.

Major, M. J. 1993. "Who's Minding the Store?" *MIDRANGE Systems* 6: 4 (February 23), 23.

Manion, R. 1993. "Why It Makes Sense to Break the I.S. Shackles," *I. T. Magazine* 25: 3 (March), 14.

Middleton, T. 1993. "It's Time to Duel for Dollars; Rethinking Outsourcing," *Corporate Computing* 2: 6 (June), 27.

Moad, J. 1993. "Inside an Outsourcing Deal," *Datamation* 39: 4 (February 15), 20.

Mohan, S. 1993. "Lotus Notes Users Get Phone Access to Database," *LAN Times* 10: 12 (June 28), 55.

Morrissey, J. 1993. "Novell Taps Outsourcing; Seeks to Broaden Third-Party Strategies for NetWare Support," *PC Week* 10: 17 (May 3), 109.

Muns, R. 1993. *The Help Desk Handbook: The Help Desk Institute Guide to Help Desk Operations and Problem Management*. Colorado Springs, CO: Help Desk Institute.

Newton, H. 1993. "A Summary of Erector Set Telecom," *Teleconnect* 11: 5 (May), 10.

Newton, H. 1994. "Headsets All Around: Computer Telephony Moves onto LANs," *PC Magazine* 13: 3 (February 8), NE1.

OSINetter Newsletter 1993. "Unifi Communications Offers Telecom Software for Windows," *The OSINetter Newsletter* 8: 11 (November), 27.

Patch, K. and M. J. Turner. 1993. "A Fresh Outlook on Outsourcing: Users Find Farming Out of the Network Operations Pie Has Its Benefits," *Network World* 10: 8 (February 22), 34.

Pepper, J. 1993. "From Help Desks to Help Windows," *CALL CENTER Magazine* 6: 11 (November), 32.

Polilli, S. 1993. "Is Outsourcing a Bargain?" *Software Magazine* 13: 4 (March), 36.

Quindlen, T. H. 1993. "Agency Help Desks Add a Personal Touch; Automated Systems Track Computer Problems but They Cannot Replace Human Interaction," *Government Computer News* 12: 10 (May 10), 64.

Quinn, B., and G. Low. 1993. "ACD Issues: Things to Keep in Mind When You Shop," *Teleconnect* 11: 4 (April), 98.

Radding, A. 1993. "Now You Can Outsource Remote LANs," *Datamation* 39: 14 (July 15), 36.

Robichaud, M. 1993. "Balancing Control with Partnership," *Computing Canada* 19: 4 (February 15), 38.

Safer, A. 1993. "Outsourcing: Gentle Wave Sweeps Maritimes," *Computing Canada* 19: 8 (April 12), 16.

Semich, J. W. 1994. "Here's How to Quantify IT Investment Benefits," *Datamation* 40: 1 (January 7), 45.

Sewell, K. E. 1992. "No Rest for Help Desks," *Computerworld* 27: 1 (December 28), 14.

Seymour, J. 1993. "Where Do You Put Information System Resources?" *PC Week* 10: 8 (March 1), 73.

Stevens, L. 1993. "Support Services Balancing New Demands, Less Resources," *MacWEEK* 7: 7 (February 15), 16.

Stevens, L. 1993. "Choosing Hardware Support Means Weighing Trade-offs," *MacWEEK* 7: 13 (March 29), 12.

Ubois, J. 1992. "Help Desks Save Time, Resources: In-house Support Staff Can Answer Questions," *MacWEEK* 6: 41 (November 16), 16.

Van Kirk, D. 1993. "IS Managers Called on to Justify IS Investments: Quantifying the Benefits of Client/Server Systems Proves to Be an Elusive Task at Best," *InfoWorld* 15: 6 (February 8), 39.

Wallace, P. 1993. "Setting Corporate Computing Standards: IS Managers Assume a Leadership Role in the Definition of Core Business Requirements," *InfoWorld* 15: 11 (March 15), 60.

Wallace, P. 1994. "Help Desk Consolidation Speeds Tech Support," *InfoWorld* 16: 4 (January 24), 55.

Waltz, M. 1993. "BBS Products Provide Link to Outside World," *MacWEEK* 7: 14 (April 5), 57.

Willett, S. 1993. "Vendors, Users Turning to Outside Help for Technical Support," *InfoWorld* 15: 18 (May 3), 12.

Willett, S. 1993. "Galaxy Automatically Tracks Network Resources and Updates a Database," *InfoWorld* 15: 39 (September 27), 45.

Withington, F. G. 1993. "Outsourcing: Flower or Weed?" *Datamation* 39: 21 (November 1), 124.

Wylie, M. 1993. "Preventing Worker Burnout While Supporting the Users," *MacWEEK* 7: 39 (October 4), 12.

Index